A MAZE IN THAILAND

THE FORTUNES
AND FIASCOES
OF A FREE SPIRIT

MARK THUMANN

The events and conversations in this book have been set down to the best of the author's ability, although some names and details have been changed to protect the privacy of individuals.

ISBN: 978-1-957723-81-5 (Hard Cover)
     978-1-957723-82-2 (Soft Cover)

Thumann. Mark.
A Maze in Thailand

Edited by: Karli Jackson

Published by Warren Publishing
Charlotte, NC
www.warrenpublishing.net
Printed in the United States

This book is dedicated to Kevin Patrick Messina and Kimberly Benton Haas. Well, I can see you two have become acquainted "over there." That was a fine trick: the two of you showing up together unannounced at that dive bar on Rawai Beach. (The Cure soundtrack was a nice touch, Kim). Thanks, guys, for giving me the ... motivation? No. The justification for seeing this project through. I miss you both! But please understand if I "tarry" a bit longer before coming to visit you. And yes, Kevin, I'll be sure to bring along some of those Monsoon Mushrooms from Phuket!

Along the road of life are many
pleasure resorts, but think not that
by tarrying in them, you will take
more days to the journey. The day
of your arrival is already recorded.

—AMBROSE BIERCE, *A CYNIC LOOKS AT LIFE*

PROLOGUE

SHAKEDOWN STREET

Yet man is born unto trouble,
as the sparks fly upward.

−Job 5:7 (King James Version)

Ploy couldn't look. She had her head down, exposing the subtle shaking of her shoulders. She made a heartrending sound, a hybrid of a moan and sigh. I held her hand, but my gaze was focused straight ahead through the droplets of mist swelling and streaking down the windshield.

I couldn't look away.

About ten yards in front of the cab, our driver was kneeling in the middle of the road. His back was to us, and he had his head down with his hands pressed together in front of his forehead, as if he were praying. But he was not praying. He was pleading. Two young Thai men, dressed in jeans and T-shirts, stooped menacingly over the cringing cab driver. All three seemed to be mere half-shadows in the scarce light of a dying streetlamp.

The shorter one, sporting a buzz cut and a fat, self-satisfied face, asked a question. The taller cop had long black curls, which obscured the features of his face but did not impede his aim. He spit as he swung a wide slap upside the head of his groveling target. Next, it was Buzz Cut's turn to inflict abuse, delivering another palm-swat to the face of the prostrate prisoner. The two sadists switched job assignments after each question/head slap. It was the classic "bad cop/bad cop" routine.

This continued for a couple of minutes, until Long Hair gave up while shaking his head in disgust. He then stormed directly toward me, yanked open the car door, and demanded, "Okay, where is it?"

"I don't know what you're talking about," I replied.

"Don't play games, white boy," he said, in almost perfect American English.

I looked him in the eye and said, "I already told you: I didn't buy anything, and I don't have anything—and you've already patted me down twice, for God's sake!"

"Then why does that old man keep saying you bought something?"

"Maybe because you're slapping the shit out of him."

"No, you lie," he muttered, "Let's go—both of you."

He called for his partner, and they put us in their undercover vehicle: a gray and rusting Honda. We pulled away, leaving the dismissed driver kneeling in shame in the soft rain. I rode shotgun and drank from the bottle of white wine I had picked up somewhere along the route of my evening rampage. Before the wine, I had picked up Ploy. She was an exceptionally sweet college girl from Khon Kaen, visiting Bangkok during summer break. Earlier that night, she and her girlfriends were crowded around one of the larger tables near the dance floor of the infamous Spicy Club. I was by myself, kind of. I strolled over and placed my wingman, Tyrannosaurus Rex, on the opposite end of the table. I hit the switch. His batteries fired up, and the miniature menace of the Cretaceous period charged through the forest of beer bottles, across the open plain of tabletop, and onto Ploy's lap. She hadn't left my side since.

Her friends wanted to go to another late-night joint, and Ploy was determined to bring me along. Just after exiting Spicy Club, Ploy whispered to me: "My friends all 'play ecstasy.' I never do before—but want to try."

Time for some bad decision-making. The girl wanted party favors. One a.m. was not an ideal time for that sort of thing. But I was buzzed, and it was Bangkok. I made inquiries with our taxi driver as we pulled out onto Sukhumvit Road. We drove around for a while, until he found his guy on a darkened side street. The cabbie took my 1,000 baht, got out, and walked behind a small shop. Five minutes later, he was back in the car and handing me a small crumpled ball of foil. I stashed it in the small inseam pocket of my cargo shorts. Just seconds later, 21 Jump Street sprang out of the darkness. But the intrepid duo was not as good at pat-downs as it was at beat downs.

The M&M-sized wad of aluminum wrapping was still in my cargo shorts, and I was still (potentially) in a whole lot of trouble.

"Where are we going?" I asked.

"The police station. But first, we're going to your hotel for your passport. Where you stay?"

"Wattana Mansion, Ratchada Soi 17."

***

As the Honda streaked down the barren four-lane thoroughfare, I admired the beauty of early morning Bangkok—a cityscape bathed in bright neon and segmented by side streets that flashed past like the elusive images of a fleeting dream. I was deep into some serious thinking: *If I failed to ditch it before the police station, I was screwed. Perhaps I was screwed anyway. They could always produce something later, after I made my "confession." No doubt, the Royal Thai Police had even more options for enhanced interrogation in the privacy of a police sub-station.*

No. I could not let the situation unravel so that the sweet soul by my side was implicated in anything illegal. She was not the spoiled college kid of wealthy Bangkok elites. Those entitled brats always walked away unscathed in Thailand's two-tiered system of justice. Yet a country girl from Isan, lacking social status, would most likely see her promising future wrecked. But not on my watch.

I had just met the young lady, but I knew in my heart that Ploy was an angel: trusting, compassionate, generous, and kind. She had an unadulterated goodness, a purity of soul too unique to escape attack in this unjust world. I was going to have to do something drastic to salvage this situation. Hell, she might be the last innocent girl in the Kingdom!

As we pulled into the parking garage of the hotel, I said, "Hey, dude, my bottle of wine is cashed. Are you going to let me grab my vodka out of the room when I get my passport?"

"No. You're done."

Well, that left no doubt. I made my decision. The four of us walked across the bright, polished lobby, as the nasty coven of receptionists cast wicked glares our way. No matter: I had long before acquired immunity from the inevitable dagger-stares coming from that gang of prudes.

After a socially uncomfortable ride in the elevator, we were in room 1108. I walked over to my travel bag and began to rummage through it, intentionally taking a little extra time. I grabbed the bank envelope that was underneath my passport, pulled it out, and withdrew all ten $100 bills. I walked over to Long Hair, handed him the cash, and said, "Hey, dude, I can't find my passport. Will this do for identification?"

He smiled while quick-counting, then looked askance at his partner.

"This is just fine. You can look for your passport later. Actually, it's getting late. You don't have to go down to the station after all. Have a good night."

The vice-squad superstars quickly vanished. Almost as quickly, I hustled Ploy out to a taxi and sent her back to her friends. It hurt two days later when I had to pull the "it's not you, it's me" routine with Ploy. But it just wasn't okay for someone so sweet to be anywhere near a scoundrel like myself.

This—my most expensive first date ever—occurred in the summer of 2008, and I did not see those dirty cops again … until 5:30 in the afternoon on the eighteenth of June 2020, when, shaking from surprise, I stood surrounded in the broiling heat of a Phuket Town side street. Handcuffed, I was in the process of being pawed, patted down, heckled, and interrogated by eight plain-clothed cops. Despite being overwhelmed by the shock of the situation, two images flashed on the movie screen of my mind: me in my hotel room, handing Long Hair a grand in cash, and that cab driver, kneeling in total submission on a rain-slicked street, while those two sociopaths slapped him silly.

Just then, a forty-something female cop emerged from the ranks and seemed to take command. The rest of the gang deferred to this matriarch of the vice squad. It is a scientific fact that all Thai women are born with the acting gene, and this lady performed wonderfully: she expertly transitioned into the role of "good cop" in this twisted version of a daytime drama.

Reaching up to pat my shoulder and soothing me with motherly tones, she explained that this was "no big deal." It was "nit noi" (just something little). I was "a nice man who just made a small mistake." She offered the assurance that "everything would be okay" and tossed out other life rings of hope. Now that we had ostensibly become allies, she eased into a light interrogation.

"Where are you staying in Phuket Town?"

My mind jumped into high gear. *Shit! I can't let them know that I stay at Lek's house. Jesus, she could be screwed for life! As careless as she is? And on the one day that her family is visiting from Isan! And how happy and proud she had been last night, showing her mom how well she was doing for herself ... and now to have her place ransacked, and hauled off to jail in front of them?* I flipped the switch to bullshit mode.

"I don't stay in Phuket Town. I just came here for the day, from Kamala Beach."

"What? You don't stay here in Phuket Town?"

"No. I stayed here during the lockdown, but I already moved to Kamala Beach. I only come here today to shop and see some friends."

"When you stay here before, for lockdown, where you stay?"

"Oh, I stayed at the Wide Condominium—"

"Really?"

"Yes, first I stayed at the Wide Condominium. Then I went to Kamala Beach to stay with my friend."

"No!" erupted the closest cop. "You stay in Phuket Town! Don't lie!"

"I'm not lying! I do not stay in Phuket Town. Everything I have is at Kamala Beach with my friend. I've came here only for today!"

The lady cop wrapped her arm around one of the guys, and they both walked off, speaking in subdued whispers. As soon as her back was turned, the other goons quickly shuffled me over to a gray sedan with windows wrapped in black tint (surely, this was the preferred pool car for date night). They then squished me into the middle of the back seat. My wrists were wrenched behind me, screaming the pain of flesh on fire as the steel cuffs burrowed into bone. One cop sat on my left side, and another squeezed in on my right. And then two more cops sat down in the front seat—all humanity hidden behind four pairs of dark shades. This wasn't going to be good. Not at all.

PART 1

ACCIDENTS AND AMBUSHES

If trouble comes when you least
expect it, then maybe the thing to
do is to always expect it.

—CORMAC MCCARTHY

CHAPTER 1

SWIMMING IN SINGAPORE (MARCH 2020)

Indeed, none but the Deity can tell
what is good luck and what is bad
before the returns are all in.

—MARK TWAIN

When it was announced that our aircraft was beginning its descent into Singapore, flight attendants and fellow passengers began preparations for landing, and I began preparing my passport for the scrutiny of immigration officials. To say that my only form of photo identification had been neglected to the point of deterioration would understate the case. Downtown Portland, Oregon, in the aftermath of the George Floyd riots later that year, would be in better physical shape than the condition of that battered blue book on March 17, 2020. After almost a decade of hazardous service, the passport was due to expire in exactly four months ... if the tatters of its tattooed pages did not disintegrate first. It had taken all of my personal positivity and charm to convince Singapore Airlines officials to even allow me to board this plane. Now it was going to take steady hands and super glue to perform the cosmetic surgery necessary to gain even reluctant approval from Singaporean (and Thai) officials. Free in-flight cocktails assured the steadiness of my hands, and extensive experience with the miracle adhesive provided the skill set necessary to doctor the documentation to an almost acceptable state.

I realize normal travelers would assume that someone flying to the other side of the globe in such a state of disarray must be either a rookie or a screwball. This certainly was not my first overseas excursion; therefore, I must plead guilty to the second charge—although I prefer the term "free-spirited." I was once again flying by the seat of my pants, but I had long ago ceased to be concerned with such chaos. Even on the rare occasions when I embarked with a solid plan, those Crazy Fates almost always felt it necessary to inject last-minute mayhem into my itinerary. And I refused to give those interlopers the satisfaction of seeing me upset.

In fact, I had even acquired a certain rebelliousness. In this case, I had booked the ticket at the outbreak of the COVID-19 crisis and was traveling *toward* the birthplace of the virus. This decision was based, first, on the absurdly low cost of the airfare. Secondly, I had been temporarily residing in Seattle as I recovered from minor surgery, and I foresaw the Jet City becoming the first major metropolitan casualty of the pandemic. In fact, the city shut down the day after my departure, and just weeks later, its neighborhoods exploded into such mindless violence that the debacle would become a bona fide case of civic suicide.

I had rationalized that it would be far less expensive and far more comfortable to convalesce on the beach in Thailand. And thanks to the fast-drying properties of glue, I managed to make it through Singaporean security with the only repercussions being a few dirty looks. (In contrast, my admission into Thailand would have to be secured through the purchase of a duty-free bottle of Johnnie Walker Red, which I gave as a "present" to the immigration officer in charge.)

I had over twenty-four hours until the departure of my flight to Bangkok, and this made finding a hotel room a top priority. Due to the onslaught of COVID-19, transfer passengers were restricted to the airport, and this hindrance made my first order of business to check for vacancies at the three hotels located within the airport terminal. Dodging the masses of masked strangers, I explored the vast entertainment complex—which also serves as an airport—while searching for accommodations. All three hotels were at full occupancy; however, the classiest hotel had a rooftop pool, which was open to non-guests. *Perfect!* A lounge chair, food service, and a swimming pool under the night sky seemed like fantastic amenities for a second sleeping arrangement. But first, I needed to locate two more items: swimming trunks and vodka. I found the Smirnoff in seconds, but I got lost during the swimsuit search.

As I wandered the first and second floors (confused by the conflicting directions of various vendors) I inadvertently strolled into a more immediately important location: the airport smoking section. Like everything else at the Singapore airport (free movie theater, superb shuttle system, etc.), the smoking section was top-notch. It was an outdoor courtyard with cushioned seats scattered about the greenery of small gardens, and it had a bar/convenience store. I found the place so pleasant that, after mixing a soda with my vodka, I forgot about swimming and sleeping at the hotel pool. There was entertainment to be had right here.

Over the years, I have come to learn that airport smoking lounges are wonderful spots to shoot the shit with strangers, strike out when trying to hit on single women, and haphazardly pester the world's introverts with unwanted conversation. Within twenty minutes, I had engaged in all three of these activities.

As I replenished my drink, I noticed a blond guy in his mid-thirties sitting across the way, staring at my booze bottle with a hint of envy. As my attitude was well into the tipsy-friendly zone, I waved the man over and poured him a drink.

"Thank you," he said, in a more-than-slight European accent, as he looked around with eyes that were simultaneously aloof and curious.

His demeanor and darting eyes made me think of a guy at a party checking out the ladies—while his girlfriend is in the bathroom. It also occurred to me that this character had a singularly familiar face.

"I'm Mark," I said, as we shook hands with absentminded disrespect for pandemic protocol.

"I'm Gilbert. Where are you from?" he inquired politely.

"I'm from Alaska in the USA. And what about you?"

After a brief pause, he replied in a low tone, "The Netherlands," and he flashed a shy smile that lit up the dimmer sections of my memory bank. I recognized that the reason the man looked so familiar was because of his remarkable resemblance to the actor Nicolas Cage (in his younger days). We spoke for a while, and while he was not conceited, he almost seemed so, on account of his reticent style of communication.

When a middle-aged Asian man sat down on the opposite side of the courtyard, Gilbert leaned in and said, "There's a cop."

The gentleman was dressed in a dark blue suit and had a full head of graying hair, but I saw no obvious signs indicating that he was a member of law enforcement.

"How do you know?" I wondered aloud.

"A lot of practice. It's a good thing to practice recognizing the police—if you want to stay out of jail," Gilbert answered.

Out of respect for my new friend's cool self-possession, I let the cryptic comment slide by without a reply.

"So where are you going?" I asked at length.

"To see my Thai girlfriend."

"Oh, cool! I'm going to Bangkok also. What flight are you on?"

"I'm not going to Bangkok. She's meeting me in Laos."

"That seems like an inconvenient place to meet up."

"It's convenient, if you are not permitted into Thailand."

Hmm …. Now my curiosity grew stronger than my respect for privacy, and with just a few carefully chosen questions, I had a stranger relating his incredibly bizarre and riveting account of a dramatic predicament he had experienced in Thailand. Apparently, there had been some difficulty with a gang of "ladyboys" over on Koh Samui. This trouble had consisted of police involvement, false accusations, planted evidence, character assassination, and revenge. Ultimately, this Dutch renegade had bolted the island, then absconded from Thailand by heading north to a life of anonymity on the Laotian side of the Mekong River. It was a harrowing story of adventure and cunning survival. I listened intently. I was both curious and envious.

"I'm not sure why I told you that story," Gilbert said, as he polished off his drink. "I don't talk to many people in general, and most of my family and friends do not even know that story."

"Well … I have ways of making people talk," I admitted.

"Look, I've got to make my flight," he said. "What's your full name? I'll send you a friend request on Facebook. You may want to visit Vientiane sometime."

So we traded information, he rushed off to his gate, and just like that, an interesting conversation became just another faint airport memory. However, his adventure story had me thinking. Several months earlier, I had made a half-hearted effort at documenting some of the more outrageous events of my life, but the fire of inspiration flamed out when I physically lost the first four stories. Discouraged and disgusted, I shelved the project and blocked my mind from even thinking about it ... until I met Gilbert that day at the Singapore smoking patio.

His plight was so fantastic that, at first, I thought maybe karma had caught up with me, and a stranger had fooled me into believing an outlandishly untrue tale. This could be payback for the way that I used to concoct ridiculous stories about my life in America, in order to have some fun at the expense of gullible Europeans. But because of the way the younger man had comported himself with a certain indifference toward my opinion of the veracity of his claims, I began to believe that he had spoken the complete truth. His ordeal was so wild that I knew I had no *individual* stories as suspenseful as his. But *collectively*?

Bereft of company, I abandoned the patio, found those elusive swimming trunks, and made my way to the hotel. The evening sky was set with the white-gold sliver of the moon, and this provided an exotic ceiling above the swimming pool, which I used as my bed, lying on my back and floating with my face turned toward the few flickers of visible stars that survived the city's lights. I pondered where to start over. Many of my Thailand adventures were distant in time, but I would soon be right in the bullseye of the "space."

***

I considered the challenges of writing a book about my escapades in the Land of Smiles, stories that ranged from the bizarre to the ridiculous, and from the risky to the truly dangerous. Because my trip was scheduled for just a month, the constraints of time were my first concern. But this potential problem was flipped on its head when COVID-19 exploded to pandemic proportions, and geographical lockdowns became the worldwide response. I would enjoy an incredible streak of luck and stay one day ahead of every pandemic lockdown on my inbound journey. And the day after my arrival on Phuket, air, land, and sea travel were shut down in all directions. I would have several months to focus on writing.

My second consideration was the possibility that I might not have enough material for an entire book. However, in an ironic twist so perverse that it was obviously the work of those Crazy Fates, this concern proved to be completely unfounded. This was because the longest, most enigmatic, and potentially life-altering story was neither in my notebooks nor in my memory, but was waiting for me down there on the island of Phuket. I use the word "waiting" because those Crazy Fates had arranged everything already: they had constructed a labyrinth so complex and so confusing, that if I did not choose my path with the utmost caution, my very freedom could be confiscated indefinitely. When that drama began to unfold, I was simultaneously constructing the tales of my past, and it became evident that there was plenty of material for a book. However, it remained unclear if I would be in a physical position to finish the product.

As I floated trance-like upon the pool's dim water—a solitary soul under the gloom of the Singaporean sky—I pondered the most daunting aspect of this project: how was I going to weave a cohesive theme through such an eclectic collection of life experiences in that forever puzzling country? My mind wandered through the imagery of past adventures in other countries as well, until I recognized an incident on my last trip to Central America that had many fundamental similarities with most of my misadventures in Thailand. I began to consider that a brief account of that episode might prove to be an effective template for highlighting the commonality of my exploits in that country often (and accurately) advertised as "Amazing Thailand."

CHAPTER 2

TROUBLE AHEAD, TROUBLE BEHIND (2016)

There are a great many opinions in
the world, and a good half of
them are professed by people who
have never been in trouble.

—ANTON CHEKHOV

I did not want to be walking on that particular street at that particular hour: 1:30 a.m. is a risky time to be alone and on foot in El Barrio Amon. Like much of San Jose, this section of the Costa Rican capital is harmless during daylight hours, yet potentially perilous from dusk until dawn. However, for more than ten hours that day, the city had suffered a constant and torrential rain that formed flumes in the abandoned streets. The flood had rendered me a prisoner without provisions; I had been stranded in the Tennessee Williams suite of the guesthouse. When the storm finally ceased, I was left with two choices: stay safe and starving, or take a chance and chow down.

Huge cockroaches scampered across the broken pavement, dodging the pitter-patter of dripping rain. The storm's residue gathered and then plunged in fat drops from storefront awnings, blocking the sparse light of scattered streetlamps. The need to watch for potholes in the heavy gloom hindered proper visual surveillance, but the brooding stillness of the empty streets allowed for a heightened sense of hearing. Halfway between the Hemingway

Inn and the all-night soda, I heard the slaps of shoes on the sidewalk behind me—two pairs of feet. The smacking sounds soon quickened, and my neck hairs whipped upright, but I kept my pace. My legs were becoming alert with adrenaline, forcing me to focus on maintaining an unhurried stride. I soon spied a shadow passing on my left, its footfalls thumping a weird rhythm. The hooded shape walked with a pronounced limp. The gimpy figure cut back onto the sidewalk in front of me, while the other stranger matched my strides, just slightly trailing in my wake. A lead ball formed in my belly, and an electric current buzzed lightness into my limbs. I saw trouble ahead, and I felt trouble behind. Here it comes—

Hop-walking in front of me, the stranger suddenly and drastically reduced speed, while simultaneously his trailing accomplice shifted into high gear. Arms wrapped around my waist, and I was jerked from behind while the gimp lunged at my pockets. My right hand was free, and I jammed it into the front pocket of my jeans, groping for the black canister. It was in my panicked grip, yet—for a helpless second—the small cylinder snagged sideways. I pulled it free while twisting my torso and shaking loose of the arm-hold. I spun a full circle and stretched out my arm with the mace upright and aimed. Suddenly spooked, my assailants jumped back in a panic. The tandem turned and fled. I followed. One attacker proved to be fleet of foot and escaped into the drizzle of the dark calle. But the bandito with the bum leg? He wasn't faking, and he wasn't fast. I caught up with him a half-block away where he learned a hard lesson under the streetlamps of an all-night cigarette kiosk, in front of which I used to spend long nights in passionate conversation with the lone soul inside.

***

I do not begin with this story in order to gloat over a vanquished bandito, or because of this story's particular setting. I relate this encounter because of its metaphorical significance. Much like this episode, the tales in this collection are descriptions of the personal trouble and fear that can result from the continual clashes between an individual's freewill and the powers of Fate. The stories depict the combustible situations and the unpredictable outcomes these factors create and continually influence. Ultimately, the following accounts detail the twisted mess that results when these components operate actively and simultaneously in a person's life. The situation most resembles a labyrinth: a seemingly insolvable maze of options, false corridors, obscene coincidences, trapdoors, and the possibility of no exit route. It is the maze of human experience where an individual must be in sync with his instinct. In the confusion of a complex life, the reliability of one's instinct is vitally important. Although it is a vague compass, a person's intuition can mean the difference between the path to salvation or the road to perdition.

I will be the first to admit that personal choice results in 90 percent of the trouble recounted in these true tales from my time in the Kingdom of Thailand. But if one backs up far enough, he can trace every trouble of his life back to the choice of walking out the front door. Furthermore, the farther one wanders from that front door, more choices become available … at least in the beginning. But when he goes too far into the maze, his options dwindle until he has no hope of retracing his way back to the point where it all went wrong. Instead, he must fight the fear and soldier on through this bleak territory where good choices may help in the short-term, but are potentially ineffectual in the long run: there may be no exit in this section of the maze. This is the point when those Crazy Fates have the most power and enjoy the greatest portion of their sadistic entertainment. And to compound the individual's problems, these situations of limited choice are magnets for trouble and fear, which grow inexorably, like a sickness of the soul.

The previous story is a prime example of the labyrinth-like situations that I have gotten lost in and struggled to escape, while finding trouble so pervasive that I was sure the Fates were at work. I chose to enter a dangerous barrio after dark, just as I chose not to stockpile food in the hotel room or purchase an umbrella. But these are just small choices in a corner of the maze. The big mistakes (falling for the wrong woman and ignoring my instinct) were made a year, six months, and even six weeks before I ended up alone, broken-hearted, and despondent in San Jose. This minor drama was just an eventuality to be played out, but not taken seriously: those Crazy Fates had already made it clear that they were controlling the game.

I find it strange how most people fail to consider or reflect upon the idea that much of their present life and their future existence is determined by the constant interplay between their own freewill and the arbitrary nature of Fate. Consider that every choice one makes, no matter how carefully deliberated, will always have some degree of random chance associated with the eventual result. Of course, we can increase the odds of our desired outcome, but we are never in full control, and we never know how a future outcome will influence our next set of options. It may limit or expand the next set of choices, or in the event of a tragedy, it could be the end of the road. So we are not only half-blindly groping through this maze of life, but also challenged by the fact that the pattern of the maze is ever-changing. This concept is in many of the following stories, and a few of the tales epitomize the very extremes of this model. I did not intentionally set out to demonstrate this concept; however, I did find the recipe for the most chaotic illustrations.

But first, some explanatory notes: I should state that many of these stories involve situations where the prime motivation was to have a good time, for which I am unable to apologize. Bering Sea fisherman do not apologize for having fun for fun's sake, and the reason for this is twofold. First, the extreme risk of the profession allows—no, demands—that one live in the moment. Life can be so easily and capriciously extinguished on the Bering Sea that one learns to enjoy each day to its fullest. If the Fates can allow for arbitrary death, they should be forced to confront frivolous fun. That is how we pay them back. Secondly, the tasks of the daily grind on a boat are essentially meaningless, except for the meaning we force out of that repetitive labor. A fellow fisherman, the legendary Joseph Sean DeCrick, may have said it best: "Thu, if you can't get out of it, then you better get into it!" One can imagine that this attitude inevitably carries over to vacation time, and it explains how someone like myself can feel obligated to inject some action into a languid afternoon on a tropical beach.

And I still believe this is an acceptable attitude, so long as one is willing to accept the potential consequences of good-natured hell-raising. Likewise, one must also take responsibility for the trouble acquired through carelessness and accept that his disorientation in the maze is due to his own improvidence. And he should also realize that there is always the potential for the final (and most dangerous) type of trouble: the random kind that finds us despite our good behavior and careful precautions.

One final note before we enter this profoundly enigmatic maze known as the Kingdom of Thailand: for logistical and artistic reasons, these stories are arranged according to the nature of the trouble found in each one. This means that the tales are not assembled in perfect chronological order. This may make your path through the labyrinth more challenging. Stay close behind and holler if you lose sight of me. Take my word for it: you do not want to get lost in here all alone.

CHAPTER 3

SHANGHAIED IN BANGKOK (2003)

Down, down, down. Would the
fall *never* come to an end?

−Lewis Carroll,
Alice's Adventures in Wonderland

Beads of sweat dripped from my forehead. The salty drops seeped into my squinting eyes. My pupils swam as they also struggled with the shocking transition from the darkness of the karaoke den to the morbidly bright Bangkok daybreak. Sweat soaked my shirt. The smell of stale beer stifled my breathing and my attention span. Gasping for air, I glanced about the café's street-side patio. My mind was still reeling from the bizarre scene that had just unfolded, and I managed just two thoughts: "Where is that waiter with my water?" and "Do they sell liquor in this town at 7 a.m.?"

Across from me sat the two gray-haired Thai men in tailored suits who had just invited me to join them. Seeing my desperate condition, they had waved me over to their table and offered me the rattan chair, which was the last open seat during the busy breakfast rush. We attempted communication via hand signals, eye contact, and shy smiles. After these polite preliminaries, they resumed what appeared to be an early morning strategy session.

Just then, I was startled by a hard clap to my right shoulder. Assuming my ice water had arrived, I looked up. My brain jolted with the electric shock of recognition, and my heart did a roller coaster plunge to the pit of my stomach. It was Tiger.

The agitated young Thai lifted his shirt, revealing a pistol in his waistband, and then pointing to a (possibly phony) police badge dangling from his neck, he growled, "Get the fuck up! Let's go!"

There I sat, stunned and searching the anonymous and oblivious faces of a crowded café for a sign of hope or rescue. But the two suits sitting with me both put their heads down, avoiding eye contact with an apparent pariah of polite society. Tiger had not spoken one word of English all night, but he now showed a mastery of the language in command form. And he was backed up by at least eight fellow miscreants from the previous night's karaoke party. The wretched-looking gang of societal misfits milled about like feral street curs on the sidewalk out front. I really had no other option than to follow him—Tiger could be an actual cop, with bogus charges and backup from corrupt commanders. How could I possibly know?

So this was Thailand? I did not remember existential dread as a selling point in the brochures. Earlier in the year, I had listened to tantalizing stories of beautiful beaches and exotic women. These descriptions had been recounted by several shipmates in the commercial fishing industry, and I had made it my mission to make 2003 a year of solo discovery. Just a month before, on the Bering Sea of Alaska, I was working alongside a character named Vui Wu on the fishing vessel US *Intrepid*, when the Scorpions' poignant love song "Still Loving You," with its lonesome guitar riffs and haunting vocals, inspired an enthusiastic sing-along from my mischievous thin-whiskered Vietnamese friend. Seeing my puzzled glance, he flashed his secretive grin and explained, "All Asian love the Scorpions!"

So when I stepped out of my hotel at 1 a.m. (thirty minutes into my first overseas trip), it seemed like destiny to hear that same heartrending song wafting into the Bangkok air and naturally combining with, and accentuating, the enigmatic odors (food stalls, garbage, condensed humanity), the peculiar sights, the surreal neon glow, and the profound dream-like sensation unique to the streets of that city. As I was planning on flying to Koh Samui in the morning, on my way to Koh Phangan's infamous Full Moon Party, my only intention that first night was a quick convenience store beer run. But upon hearing that talismanic music, I followed it to its source: an open-air restaurant fronting the street. Ordering a pitcher of beer, I scanned my surroundings and noticed just two other customers, a cute young Thai couple. Eager to make new friends, I sent them a pitcher of beer, and they soon joined me at my table. We awkwardly made our acquaintance through the use of facial expressions and rudimentary English vocabulary. Before long, friendship seemed to bloom, and my new pals, Tiger and Noi, invited me to accompany them to a karaoke joint still (illegally) open at that hour. With just six weeks to explore this mysterious country, I quickly accepted their invitation to experience the after-hours scene of Bangkok.

I followed them up three flights of stairs and through a secret bathroom entrance shielded by a shower curtain. Once inside the "club," I found myself seated with a group of Thais, drinking beer and eating fried peanuts. Eventually, I examined my surroundings more closely, and I was reminded of the cantina scene from the original Star Wars movie. Strange characters of every type appeared in the dim light: tattooed mafioso, ladyboys, aggressive prostitutes, and even an "Alice the Goon" from a Popeye cartoon. Pretty soon the whole crowd gathered around my table, and things started getting weird. I was shocked when Tiger informed me that in exchange for a sum of money, I could have a "date" with his girlfriend, Noi. Soon, other ladies (both biological and the surgically transformed) were offering their "services" as they all angled for a trip to my hotel room. Tears were trickling down Noi's frightened and ashamed face. To this day, I am convinced that she was crying for my impending doom, and not on account of Tiger callously treating her like chattel. I had a fleeting image of a Thanksgiving feast—with myself as the turkey upon the table.

With my inner alarm bells ringing, I attempted to pay the bill and bolt from the scene. But settling the check became a complicated process; I had only a wad of twenty-dollar bills, no clue about the exchange rate, and zero knowledge of the Thai language. I was soon besieged by the whole tribe vociferously arguing in Thai. The participants pretended as though the disagreement stemmed from the bill of fare, but as time dragged on, I became convinced that they were actually arguing over who had first rights to my person. After what felt like two more hours of patient endurance, I had had enough. I had been warned that saving face was the highest social value in this culture, and I had done my best to be polite and tolerant. However, when I began to feel trapped to the point where panic began to set in, I realized that I was in true physical danger. I shouted a warning and then got physical, pushing and muscling my way back down the stairs until I reached the exit. I then speed-walked several blocks up the street to the outdoor café.

And there I was, overwhelmed with the shocked incredulity one experiences just a handful of times in life. This is a moment so surreal, so precipitous, and so unexpected that one is completely uprooted from his reality—a reality now exposed as illusory. This is an experience so traumatically unreal that the mind refuses to acknowledge a personal connection: you watch yourself as if you watch a character in a movie, or as you watch yourself in a dream, knowing in your soul that this event could not, in fact, be real. You are sure that at any moment you will be snapped back into real life. You even feel like you failed to prepare, that you should have read the script in order to execute your lines in the confident and smooth style of a polished actor. But this moment is short-lived, and the next moment you feel nothing under your feet in the way of gravity. There is no support. You are on your own. And the most disturbing aspect is that you have no reference point on how to behave, or how to decide upon a course of action that will allow you to survive. You are abandoned and in a free-fall. This is the moment where previous rules no longer exist. This is the moment you make everything happen according to your instinct to live—and your fear of not living.

The abject gang of Bangkok bottom-feeders surrounded me once I stepped out of the patio gate, and I was marched up the street like a POW. The heat became even more oppressive and paralyzing. There was the pounding of my heart, the pounding of my head—and the pounding deep inside my gut was the sheer terror of one particular fact: I had not told a single soul that I was leaving the USA, or where I was going, or when I would be back. I was in no man's land. And that is the territory where you find your instinct and survive. Or you do not, and perish.

Every thug in that motley gang had at least one cell phone glued to his or her ear while spouting bursts of spouting burts of Thai that sounded like gibberish to me as a non-speaker. But I did not need a translator to realize they were calling in transportation of some sort and nefariously arranging a secret destination for their new prisoner. At the next corner, a taxi cab was waiting, and when we reached it, Tiger opened up the back door and ordered, "Get the fuck in!"

Unfortunately for him, another voice had just boomed inside my head.

"Don't get in that car, Mark!" bellowed the mysterious voice of natural truth, the voice of instinct.

I obeyed the order. I stepped forward, slammed my right fist roundhouse fashion into Tiger's jaw, pivoted, spun around the open cab door, and began a furious sprint. My running style was part Walter Payton in the intentional collisions with human obstacles, and part Forrest Gump for directionless desire. I bounced off of concrete pillars, panhandlers, and confused commuters, but always digging my feet into the pavement and refusing to look behind. I cut through tight alleyways in a slum-themed neighborhood, and I jumped over canals of stagnant scum water. Ducking underneath clotheslines and leaping above crumbling fences, I finally reached a large open-air public building. I stormed inside, then sprinted through its hallways and classrooms. It was an all-girls school! It must have been first period—the astonished plaid-uniformed young ladies gasped and pointed at the wild white man making a mad dash through their daily routine. Finally, I made it out the back fire exit, and after sprinting several more blocks, I felt safe enough to hail a cab. Sliding in, I thrust my room key in front of the man's surprised face and shouted, "Go! Go! Go to this hotel now!"

I laid flat in the back seat with my head just high enough to peek out the window. Sure enough, a few blocks farther, I spotted that criminal crew speed walking and searching along the far sidewalk. But we cruised by them undetected, and I was soon back at the hotel, shaking and shell-shocked.

I charged the reception desk and thundered orders as if I were a marine drill sergeant: "Tell the bellboy to get my fucking bags! Now! Not 'in a little bit,' not 'soon'—NOW! And I want an airport shuttle right now also!"

The staff was not at all inclined to argue with a lunatic, and I was soon back inside the airport terminal facing a crucial life decision: Would I fly back to America and chalk this event up to an "I tried it but it's not for me" experience? Or would I man up and undertake this challenge of surviving solo in an unfamiliar and potentially treacherous world—the same way that I faced the daily dangers of fishing on Alaska's Bering Sea in the harshest physical environment imaginable?

I was so panic-stricken and traumatized that I certainly needed outside counsel. Luckily, at that moment of crisis, I had the good fortune to reconnect with a famous former pirate. These days, this retired buccaneer often holds court in the cocktail lounges of airports and advises those in need. After two or three "doubles," the bearded swashbuckler grinning on the label of the dark rum bottle soon convinced me that it was both my right and my duty to get on that plane to southern Thailand in order to finish the adventure that I had promised myself. I committed to finishing the journey, and now seventeen years later, I can say, The Captain was absolutely right!

CHAPTER 4

OUTLAWS OF KRABI (2003)

Paranoia is just a heightened
sense of awareness.

−JOHN LENNON

The instances in my life when I have woken up unaware of my physical location are too numerous to count. The occasions when I have woken up on a boat number in the thousands. However, one particular morning was the first and only occasion when both circumstances overlapped. The soft slapping of water was the sound that startled my consciousness, and underneath me, the light shifting of my "bed" of wooden planks confirmed that I was definitely on a watercraft of some kind. Opening my eyes, I recognized that I was in the galley of a decrepit wood-constructed vessel, which had apparently been converted into a sort of houseboat. I began an immediate search of my short-term memory in an anxious effort to ascertain where I was, and how I got there. Fat, green horseflies buzzed obnoxiously overhead, but it was the itchy evidence left by overnight mosquitoes that affirmed I was still in Thailand. And then arrived the slow recollection that I was in Krabi Town, on the country's west coast. Two days earlier, I had crossed over from the east coast after a short stint on Koh Phagna ....

Koh Phagna ... for a moment, I lay there, indulging in the fondest memory of this adventure so far: After a dangerously close call in Bangkok, I had managed to navigate my way to that island in time for the much-heralded Full

Moon Party. However, I was sleep-deprived, disoriented, and emotionally drained. Being unfamiliar with both Thailand and guidebooks, I had booked a bungalow on the beach farthest from the party's location, but because of my condition, I didn't really care anymore about attending the internationally renowned beach rave. And looking to have some private thoughts free from distraction, I took a tall bottled beer down to the beach to stare upon a grim, overcast sundown mirrored by the drab gray of the sea. I sat on the sand and wondered just what the hell I was doing so far away from my native land. I had attempted to communicate the wild events of Bangkok to fellow travelers, but they had all seemed disinterested; most were far more concerned with the ongoing Rugby World Cup than the welfare of some wayward American. My self-assurance was wounded, and I was exhausted. I had felt just as isolated in that crowded boat of tourists as I did now, sitting alone at the edge of an unfamiliar sea.

Just when I thought a full depression might descend upon my soul, and while staring at the desolation down shore, I spied an incomplete image sauntering across the sand and through the encroaching gloom. A strange thrill engulfed me as I considered that another presence was also far away from the lunar free-for-all. Could this be a sign? The figure approached, framed by a cloud of beach bugs, which hovered about its sharpening form. I soon realized this was a *female* form! As she drew nearer, it became clear that this was indeed a young lady, in a light sundress with long, dark hair and a bright smile that illuminated the shadowy dusk. I thought: *Could this be another real event disguised as a dream sequence?*

Before long, the gorgeous apparition was standing in front of me, flaunting a smile that seemed to indicate an invitation. After we exchanged awkward greetings, I learned that the phantom's name was Nat. She was Thai, and despite the language barrier, it became clear that this meeting was designed by those Crazy Fates—she was also a refugee from the full moon extravaganza, and she was as delighted as I was at the prospect of a dinner for two. This chance encounter lead to a week-long, joyful introduction to the heavenly feminine hospitality that is so widespread in the Kingdom ....

***

"*Who* the fuck are you?"

Snapped out of my reverie, I raised myself up and was confronted with the sight of a monstrous, muscle-bound mariner, an English Sinbad replete with shaved head and gold earring.

"Well, I'm Mark—but I was going to ask you, '*Where* the fuck am I?'" I countered.

"You're on my goddamn boat, is where you are!" he barked.

The man seemed pissed off, but nonetheless I hoped he could also be reasonable.

"Hey, I'm sorry. I didn't mean to trespass. I'm just not sure how I got here," I stammered.

"American?"

"Yeah, I'm from Alaska."

"All right … wait a minute. Did you come over here with that mental case? The Kiwi?"

Thunderbolt. Oh yeah, I had been with a New Zealander named James. I was riding on the back of his motorbike when the tire blew out, and we wiped out. That explained the swelling bulge on the back of my head and the apparent amnesia of the morning.

"Yeah, I think so … I hit my head pretty good last night when he wrecked the motorbike."

"Ah, well, my name is John. You're all right here, but I can call for a long-tail boat that can get you back to town."

"That would be great. I appreciate it, John."

So, luckily, the big guy turned out to be a big and decent guy, and while waiting for my boat taxi, I questioned him about his set-up here on the water—ostensibly, the boat needed major repairs, and he was stuck indefinitely. I detected that he also had other long-term business, but it seemed to be confidential information, certainly off-limits to an unknown vagabond.

Instead, he gave me some advice: "Listen, Mark. This Thai chap that's coming to pick you up? His name is Long. Give him 200 baht for the ride, and then be done with him. He's bad news. He's got a bad rep among the expats here. I don't trust him as far as I can throw him."

I remember thinking that this Long character must be huge. Giant John looked like he could toss the average Thai at least twenty yards.

Soon the chopping grind of an outboard motor cut through our conversation, and we were then boarded by a shirtless, bald, middle-aged Thai who flashed a big smile at our introduction and immediately affected an attitude of fawning helpfulness. Once we were underway, the long-tail boat skimming across the placid, mud-choked estuary, I dropped my guard and forgot the warnings of Big John. At first, Long seemed to be just a magnanimous and guileless native of southern Thailand. My generally trusting nature seemed to have survived the Bangkok drama, and I soon found myself at ease with this eager-to-please, moon-faced pilot. By the time Long nudged the boat's bow alongside the tall wooden dock at Krabi Town, we had already made plans for that evening.

***

My new friend was eager to showcase his city, and to accept the responsibilities and benefits of playing tour guide. However, after just two days, I realized that Long was not motivated so much by hometown pride and an eagerness to please, but that he was capitalizing on an opportunity to eat, drink, and sleep for free. This did not particularly bother me: I was throwing money around like a drunken sailor (which I was). But I also got the sense that Long had other motivations. He insisted on knowing where I was, what I was doing, and where I was going. I began to feel the same sense of claustrophobia that I suffered from cloying girlfriends of years past. He inspired a vague uneasiness in my soul, which soon evolved into a desire to escape his company.

There was something abnormal about his eyes. They were never calm, but darted from side to side with constant wariness. They were the eyes of an escaped convict or someone tortured by a guilty conscience. But his eyes were also clever, sly, and perceptive. Although Long spoke very little English, I felt he had insights into my thoughts, and this added to the creepy vibe I felt in his presence. I began to regret our association and scolded myself for giving away the location of my hotel to this complete stranger. It would be impossible to shake loose of his company so long as I remained in Krabi Town.

My conscience clawed at me, and I began to doubt my perceptions. Could this just be residual paranoia from that crazy first night in Bangkok? Was I making an unfair judgment of character? But then I thought of Tiger: he had displayed the same overly accommodating and sycophantic behavior that I now recognized in Long. I had been taken by complete surprise when Tiger had turned out to be a cutthroat. My instinct was telling me that Long was a similar threat—and perhaps even more dangerous.

During the time I spent with him, Long had explained his personal history. He had grown up in a very strict Muslim household, and he had apparently been the black sheep of the family. He was currently estranged from his parents, and he seemed both ashamed and resentful of this situation. He could not follow all the dictates of his religious instruction, and I sensed a self-loathing because of it. Long scorned scandalous Western culture, but he lusted after Western women. He had been expected to live a sober lifestyle, but sold drugs for side money. I sensed I was dealing with someone with a very unhealthy psychology, and this reinforced my desire to get away. Also, Long had been pushing me to purchase a large quantity of marijuana. It was an amount that would never be considered appropriate for just personal use. This also made me highly suspicious of Long's motives. Was he trying to set me up? I did not want to hang around to find out.

I decided to purchase a sample amount of the ganja just to get Long cleared out of my room for the night. After his departure, my instincts took control by letting my mind know that we were moving out. Long's opportunism reeked of that creepy karaoke club in Bangkok, and one shakedown/kidnapping attempt was enough for this vacation. I studied the trusty guidebook and determined to move to the beach town of Ao Nang. At first light, I departed my hotel after (foolishly) getting a recommendation from the clerk, who directed me to accommodations about thirty minutes north of Krabi Town.

***

Through the taxi's back window, I watched the mangrove swamps disappear into the morning haze, while up ahead the fronds of palm trees fluttering in the breeze cheered my soul with the promise of an open coast. I was soon feeling free and easy in the comfort of a private air-conditioned bungalow. I rigged an extra blanket over the front window to create a cave-like setting, and then I dozed off in the dark. Sometime later, I awoke to pounding on the front door. Half-asleep and half-annoyed, I yanked the door open and was shocked at the sight of Long's inquiring gaze. *How the heck did he track me here?*

A resigned dread crept upon me as I hurriedly pieced together an alibi for my obvious abandonment. I lied that an American friend had called just last night to arrange a meeting here in Ao Nang. Long either bought it, or he just played along for form's sake. I only half-cared. The bottom line was, thanks to a carelessly indiscreet hotel clerk, I once again found myself trapped by Long's suffocating presence. This annoyance did, though, give birth to an indispensable new travel rule: never tell the people you are *leaving* the location of where you are *actually going.*

***

The reader is probably wondering: why would I so readily resign myself to this intrusion? Because I understood intuitively that I was at the very beginning of what has become a lengthy and humbling educational process. My personalized textbook is titled: *Thailand for Really Big Dummies* (it runs over 900 pages and retails for somewhere between $50,000 to $123,000). My instincts told me that I needed to be extremely cautious about the real motivations and the actual capabilities of everyone I encountered in this bewildering Land of Smiles. This wariness was a direct result of the shockingly duplicitous behavior of Tiger back in Bangkok. I still did not know if that youngster was an actual police officer. If so, he was a corrupt cop working with scam artists to entrap and rob unsuspecting tourists. He was most probably impersonating a cop, but I would never know. I only knew that he could have damaged me without the use of physical force. The danger in Thailand is rarely from an obvious enemy. The real peril cloaks itself in the form of those who ingratiate themselves into your friendship. And you never know if someone is a cop or a crook. He is frequently both.

My gut told me that I needed to handle Long with the same caution that I should have used with Tiger. I understood the importance of quickly breaking off the relationship—diplomatically (if possible) and with finality (an absolute necessity). Again, it was not physical intimidation that inspired this decision. The need for action was driven by the nebulous sensation of deep anxiety that Long's nearness provoked. This must have been how poor Frodo and Sam felt when Gollum signed up for their excursion to Mordor.

But for now, I needed to just go with the flow. He had already made plans for that evening, inviting four of his gang to my place with the promise of a night out on the town. First, we were going out for a seafood dinner (financed by me, of course), and afterward we were to go see the Muay Thai fights. When I agreed to this plan, I had no idea we would be taking motorbikes off-road through the dense jungle under a black sky to a square concrete stadium in no man's land. Although I was excited to see the martial art in its authentic form (as opposed to the diluted version tailored for tourists), I was also filled with an ambiguous—yet profound—feeling of dread: that vague torment of the soul, which the great Hunter S. Thompson, throughout his body of work, frequently referred to as, simply, "the Fear."

The Fear increased as we careened through swampy bogs underneath the massive canopy of encroaching jungle. As my fingers clenched the handle-hold of the back seat of a bike that bounced bronco style over the muddy ruts, frightening ideas formed in the dark side of my imagination. No doubt this gang of semi-civilized crooks were drug-runners, petty thieves, and societal outcasts. I pondered the fact that Long's friends shared the same home village and same fundamentalist upbringing as their leader. Perhaps they also shared his same self-disgust resulting from the conflict between the dictates of their strict Muslim upbringing and their own rebellious desires for earthly pleasures. Did they feel hatred for the Western culture that intruded upon their homeland and tempted them with its casual attitudes toward sins of the flesh? Could their shame be strong enough to foment a desire to lash out at a symbol of the culture they despised—me?

In that particular situation, I was at their mercy; we were thick in the middle of a moral and literal wilderness. I could be kidnapped—easily too (this was not Bangkok)—and held for ransom. I had read of this tactic being practiced by radical Islamists in the southern Philippines, and here in the south of Thailand, a similar insurgency had recently grown in both size and violence. Actually, those bloodthirsty fanatics in the Philippines had lately been skipping the ransom stage and proceeding directly to the beheading of unlucky Western backpackers. And this barbarism was committed merely in an effort to kill off tourism. Who knew the possibilities? The Twin Towers had been toppled, the US had invaded Iraq, and the world was boiling in hatred, much of it for people who looked just like me.

But that evening, I did my best to ignore the Fear by distracting myself with a combination of strong local brew and an over-compensation of interest in the Muay Thai fights. This spectacle consisted of several bouts between youngsters of varying age levels (from eight up to sixteen years of age). And although I had arrived under an anxious strain, my worries faded away as the evening unfolded. I appreciated the rustic pageantry and authenticity of the experience: an austere concrete shell of a structure with stadium seating, traditional Sarama music played live by two old-timers on drums, another clanging a cymbal, and a village grandmother operating an oboe-like wind instrument. The haunting combination of sounds produced by this ensemble made an ideal soundtrack for both the brutality of the boxing and for my own sketchy circumstances.

I bought Long and his hoodlum entourage tickets for the nosebleed section, but I was going all-in for first-class seating, which was a dedicated leather sofa ringside and unlimited beers for the 1,000-baht ticket. I was the only person in first class, and I was also the only foreigner in the entire venue. No doubt I was as conspicuous as a patchouli oil-scented sociology major in the Philippine jungle, yet I felt no threat from the crowd—except for the bandits who had brought me here.

The vast majority of those in attendance were gambling. In fact, considering the frenzied activity in the placing of bets, one might think that the very purpose of Muay Thai was to provide an avenue for that particular vice. The most fervent bettors were swarmed around three sides of the ring: the first-class side had been roped off to keep my view unobstructed. These raucous fanatics, chewing Kratom leaves, shouting out the odds, exchanging wads of cash, and screaming encouragement to the fighters, were getting an intense workout themselves. Sweat dripped from their bodies, and spittle flew from their mouths. All the while, the frenetic musical score mimicked both the pace of the pugilists and the briskness of the betting.

The climax of the experience occurred during the contest between the two twelve-year-old fighters. The kid in the blue trunks was getting whipped pretty good. His energy and effort drained as the round continued ... until the bell rang, and he appeared bereft of all vitality. After the boxers returned to their corners, one of the ringside rabble-rousers suddenly leaped over the ropes and executed a double face slap to blue trunks, while screaming saliva drenched epithets at the poor kid. I was stunned and left wondering: *Is that his old man? His trainer? His manager? No!* It soon became clear that the taskmaster was just one of the wagering wild men. He had been infuriated by a perceived lack of effort (and potential loss of personal funds, no doubt). Although this was clearly a merciless motivational technique, it proved effective. Blue trunks turned up the heat in the next round, pummeled his opponent, and won the fight.

"Amazing Thailand!"

Ironically, this tourist slogan was the truest statement to be found in the Kingdom.

Because of the front-row sofa seating, free beer delivery, and the wild novelty of the whole scene, I was able to forget my ongoing troubles, and the Fear did not make another appearance that evening. We just rumbled back through the wilderness and into town, where Long first invited himself to crash at my bungalow and then divulged "our" plans for the next night. Our agenda for that next evening consisted of Long and me taking a long-tail boat to the half-moon party on Railay Beach: a stunning shoreline enclosed by sheer limestone cliffs that deny inland access. Long announced that he was counting on me to be the smooth talker at the party so that "we" could hook up with some Western ladies (never mind his wife and two kids back at the village). He arrived early that evening, quickly locked the door, and secured the windows. He had brought something special (and quite illegal) for the party: yaba pills.

On several previous occasions, Long had given me a sales pitch on the little red pills. I had never heard of these narcotics before, but from his explanations, I understood that they were a type of amphetamine. While Long was in the bathroom, I made a quick assessment of the legal and ethical issues, and then I impetuously swallowed two pills. I reasoned that if I were going to be up all night with a possible sociopath, I might as well be on high alert. Besides, if I were going to engage in some cultural experiences specific to Thailand, then I was certainly going to choose the subtle buzz of the native narcotics over such culinary delights as deep-fried crickets. But when Long came out of the bathroom and realized that I had already washed down two of the pills with a can of Leo beer, he freaked out. He explained that yaba pills were for smoking, not swallowing, and they definitely were not supposed to be gobbled up two at a time. Despite my rightful distrust of the shady opportunist, on this occasion he spoke the truth, of which I was fully convinced three days later, when I finally fell asleep.

***

The night started off with some promise when two young cuties from Denmark were our only companions in the long-tail boat, which made quick work of the calm sea on a smooth trip to Railay. Unfortunately, Long also made quick work of making an unfavorable impression upon our skittish shipmates. What was is it with the sinister vibe that emanated from Long? Christine and Jennifer both looked at me with fearful eyes, which were also incredulous: *What was this nice American doing with a local gangster?* Oh well, Long's off-putting lecherous glares were amateur hour compared to the fumbling, bombastic American jackass persona I planned to affect at the party. It was time to implement the most expedient of all relationship break-up tricks: be such an ass that the unwanted party (Long) *volunteers* to go away.

I had already suspected that this half-moon party would be a tame affair, and as the boat glided past the massive limestone slabs draped in dark green jungle, I could see by the beach's sporadic campfires that the celebration would be about the size of a typical Midwest American family reunion. If I played this right, I could offend everyone, then go through the line-up a second time and still be back to Ao Nang by 3 a.m. I got off to a smashing start.

***

Just one beer into the evening, I was chatting up an English lass while Long hovered around us, as he struggled mightily but helplessly to follow the conversation. Perfect! Now all I needed to do was give a generous helping of offense to the freckle-faced, sandy-haired cutie. If I knew English women (and I believed I did), I just needed to lure her into a political discussion. (I'll take "USA Saves England Twice in the 20th Century" for $200, Alex!)

Because it was the autumn of 2003, this was an easy task. I baited my hook with a chunk of Iraq War and cast my line. Bam! Fish on! Within minutes I had Sandy Hair struggling against her inner rage ("Oh, that Bloody George Bush! The Bush family only wants oil!"). I merely struggled with concealing my self-satisfied grin. As I conversed, I kept an eye on Long, who looked on with intense concern as his supposed "ringer" of a wingman threw the game. Then I went straight for the kill shot with a quick summary of the Enlightenment, the Founding Fathers, and a slam against George the Third in particular, and the English Monarchy in general.

Game over! Sandy Hair burst into a violent sobbing fit, stood up, and stormed off, unable to articulate her outrage. The shell-shock on Long's moon-face was a priceless mental image that I treasure to this day. The disappointed disbelief was so genuine in my bandit friend's countenance that I would have extended instant sympathy—if I had not known the man had a wife and kids back home.

At that moment, I was beyond confident that Long would voluntarily end our association. In fact, I believed that he would be sprinting away from me before the break of dawn. My confidence soon became cockiness. Batting second and third in the order were two stumble-drunk Irish man-haters, whom I was able to dispatch within seconds of opening my mouth. This encounter caused Long's face to express a desperate and depraved self-pity. I quickly attempted to console him with my heartfelt regret and to beg his forgiveness, while wondering if I should receive an Oscar nomination on account of my acting range in a dual role.

But then the clean-up hitter stepped to the plate. Batting fourth and playing center field was Allison, twenty-two years old, a blond bombshell from London, batting .420 on the season. Alli sat down next to me on the driftwood bench, passed me a lit joint, and introduced herself. Maybe it was overconfidence or perhaps poor judgment from the ganja, but I threw her a waist-high fastball straight down the middle: I boasted of sending the lead-off hitter away in tears. Alli stood up smiling and said, "Well, you'll never make this lady cry!" while she emptied her bottle of mineral water onto my lap, and then stood up pointing and laughing at my crotch.

I had to laugh along with her, even as I protested, "Now look! I've got to walk around the rest of the night looking like I pissed myself!"

"No, you don't!" she countered coquettishly.

"How's that?" I asked.

"American ass! Just take off your shirt and jump in the ocean! Then it will look like you just went swimming."

"Very good strategy—pretty smart for a crazy English girl!"

I followed that plan as my dumbfounded wingman kept watch over my belongings. After diving underwater, I stood up in the chest-high surf only to see Alli running toward me as she stripped down to just her bra and panties. *No way!* my mind revolted in disbelief, but before I could make a sound, she had disappeared underwater. And a second later, I was flipped over as her arms wrapped around my knees and she pushed up. When I recovered and stood back up, her arms were already wrapped around my neck, and a spontaneous make-out session was underway. My plan had backfired! But on the bright side, it had unraveled in such a way that put me into a state of euphoric amusement—particularly when I witnessed Long's facial expression. It was frozen in a permanent state of total confusion, a look that must be the expression of the hopelessly insane. I would not see anything close to this look until several years (and a few chapters) later ....

But for the time being, I had to face the fact that Long looked upon me as a semi deity because of my sorcerer's skill in bending the will of Western women. This belief was reinforced when we motored back to Ao Nang in the company of the same two Danish backpackers who insisted on sitting to either side of me in the stern of the long-tail boat. Long was oblivious to the fact that they clung to me not out of infatuation, but out of fear of him. Both ladies were so unsettled by Long's presence that they implored me—and *only* me—to escort them back to their hostel. I assured the ladies that I would see them to safety, but for the meantime, I needed them to just play along as though they would be meeting us later that night. I also advised them to depart Ao Nang discreetly, and I would meet them on Koh Phi Phi. Long was appeased when I (disingenuously) informed him that I had concocted a double date for us later that evening, and he left for the Krabi docks where he had a morning booking, piloting his boat for other tourists.

I returned to my bungalow in a state of hyper-agitation. Both Christine and Jennifer were in outright fear of Long. My instinct must be correct: there was something sinister lurking inside that gangster's heart. But how could I escape to Koh Phi Phi without him knowing? He worked at the damn Krabi pier! Either Long or one of his gang would see me buying a ticket or boarding the ferry, and they might follow. What did he want? I thought about it until I realized the obvious answer: money. Of course, it had to be money! I had worked seven out of the past eight months on the Bering Sea making great money, and not spending any of it. And here I was throwing it around. For God's sake, after two weeks in Thailand, I still didn't even know the exchange rate! I just handed over whatever was asked and picked up the tab for anyone in the general vicinity. Long and his crew must have thought I was loaded—and they were just trying to figure out how to score. Not smart, Mark. Pretty damn stupid, actually.

These worries were compounded by the effects of the yaba, which were subtle yet constant. I was wide awake and jumpy. Even sipping whiskey did little to soothe my nerves. I paced about the bungalow as my mind raced. That morning would be a rare opportunity to break free, but the bald bastard blocked my escape route. Just then, inspiration struck. I grabbed up the guide book and studied, and then developed a plan: take the bus *three hours* in the *opposite* direction, around Pgna Na Bay, all the way to Phuket Town. I would spend the night, and then take the ferry from Phuket to Phi Phi tomorrow morning. Long and his crew would be scouring Ao Nang and Krabi Town, searching for a phantom who was already long gone. A perfect plan!

I immediately packed and left the bungalow without notifying management. I was not going to make that same mistake again. After flagging down a motorcycle taxi, I was soon situated on a bus making the eight a.m. Krabi to Phuket run. Feeling proud of my evasive tactics and quick thinking, I enjoyed the easy relief of escape until mid-journey. That was when I noticed a shady Thai character two rows behind me wearing aviator sunglasses and a baseball cap. He was talking furtively and almost continually on his mobile phone. Every time I stole a glance back over my shoulder, a haughty, sinister smile creased his face. Was this yaba-inspired paranoia? Could this be another member of Long's gang?

Goddamn it! I was being trailed! I was sure of it. Yaba trip influenced or not, the Fear had returned in full force. The Fear was real. I could see it in the reflection of those mirrored shades. When you sweat while sitting still directly under the blowing air conditioning, it means the Fear is hard at work. And I was drenched with sweat as I listened to my tail's muffled communications. Once in a while, I caught the word "farang" in a tone of angry resentment, and I was sure the spy was relaying the play-by-play back to headquarters. Or, wait, was this just the yaba? Or was I going crazy? I took another slug of Sang-Som. Why did whiskey fail me now in my time of need?

I decided to assume the worst. When the bus rolled into the Phuket bus station, I had already chosen an upscale hotel from the guide book; I needed a place with security, bell boys, English-speakers, and room service! I was going to hole-up like an informant in a mob flick. I elbowed my way first off the bus (not a time for manners), and jumped on the first motorcycle taxi while yelling, "Go! Go! Just go!"

We fired out of the station, and after a few blocks, I pushed the scrap of notepaper in front of the driver's face: Pearl Hotel. After paying quadruple for my driver's silence, I burst into the hotel lobby, shirtless, soaked in sweat, and reeking of whiskey and fear. The astonished reception staff was exceptionally kind in their forbearance as I went all-in for a luxury suite on the tenth floor, then threw down an extra 500 baht to ensure confidentiality. I doubled the sum with the incredulous bellhop. I bet he tells that story still; the 1,000 baht tip was no doubt a record in his personal history. Room service also saw a record day in tips, as I ordered liberally from the drink menu … although I could summon neither sleep nor peace of mind.

By 9 p.m. I could no longer tolerate the isolation and claustrophobia. I had worked up just enough liquid courage to explore Phuket Town in order to accomplish some reconnaissance. If danger still lurked, I wanted to know a little about its nature and direction. Walking out of the hotel and seeing no apparent threat, I paused to choose right or left on Montri Street. I fortunately chose right. Much later in my Thailand career, I would learn all too well that taking a left onto Montri Street would have led me to the bleakest of dead-ends: the Phuket Provincial Prison.

I hustled down the avenue toward a billboard-sized, neon-pink sign: The Pink Lady. I easily convinced myself that the sight and possible company of lovely local ladies just might drive away the Fear. I pushed open the double doors and, noting the lack of a doorman or security I proceeded down the carpeted steps to a subterranean reception area and bar. This was a gentlemen's club that catered to an elderly Asian demographic. There wasn't another Westerner in sight. Actually, there wasn't another person in sight, other than the vixen behind the bar. Evidently, the clientele and hostesses were all involved in private parties in back rooms.

Oh well. Nina behind the bar was exceptionally gorgeous, and it appeared I would be her only customer. So, I bellied up to the bar and killed time with B-52s and clumsy conversation. After a while, I realized that my tobacco supply was empty, and I walked over to the cigarette machine tucked away in an alcove. I bought another pack, and when I returned to my spot, I realized there were now two other customers at the far end of the brass-railed bar. *No way. No. Fucking. Way.* I sat down and struggled with my breath. I lit a smoke from the pack. *No. Fucking. Way.* I knew the faces of both men sitting twenty feet away. One was the secret agent from that morning's bus ride. The second was Long himself! He was unmistakable in the same tan beanie covering his chrome dome. I stared at myself in the mirrored wall behind the bar. The seriousness of the situation hit me full-on. Long had had me tailed, and then he'd followed me here himself—*three hours* from his home and place of employment. He certainly did not come this far to return the toothbrush I had left on the bathroom sink.

I had been too obviously careless with my money, and it must have convinced Long that I was a very rich Westerner. He must have been planning all along to rob or defraud me somehow. And how could he have found me in a bar that I had just spontaneously chosen at random out of the dozens of clubs in Phuket Town? They had been following me—that was an absolute certainty. And now I was trapped. These were the statements of fact that my brain conveyed to the reflection of my physical self.

The other two gave no sign of acknowledgment, not even a single look in my direction. I wondered why they did not at least steal a glance. What if I tried to sneak off? Wasn't it possible that I might be able to get just enough of a head start to escape? But then it occurred to me: *Long's not worried about that because he has part of his crew outside watching the door—the only door and the only way out. The streets were just about empty when you arrived, and now it's much later. There will be no one to see you get grabbed up.*

Nina returned and took my order, but she did not understand from the winks of my eyes, and other obvious nonverbal hints, that I was trying to indicate to her the trouble surrounding me. After another hour, she did not understand a word of my whispered plea for her to call the police: *I'm in trouble! Please call the cops* …. She just smiled and giggled.

***

It was 1 a.m. and a half hour till closing time; still, my eyes just stared at their counterparts in the mirror. I pondered writing a note. But to whom to give it? Even if one of them could read English, the backroom crowd had already departed. I could cause a scene, just start destroying things and force Nina to call the authorities. No, I thought. I was forcing myself to remain calm amidst a potential panic attack when I realized I needed to empty my bladder before it burst. I asked Nina for directions to the toilet, and she pointed me to the sign on the far side of the empty dance floor directly behind me.

I felt eyes on my back as I crossed the room to the sign with the arrow pointing up; the restroom was up a flight of stairs back to street level. I was shaking as I relieved myself, but I thought to glance about the bathroom. There was a window, a waist-high window. I finished pissing, crossed the room, and tried to slide it open. The frame was welded shut. *Shit.* I looked over to the sink and spotted a stainless steel cigarette-urn. I acted without thought. I grabbed the cylinder with both hands and swung it like a battering ram. Glass spread outward, and I hastily trimmed off any shards still clinging to the frame. And then I hurtled myself through the opening and out into the alley. And I ran. Fast.

I stuck to the alleys for several blocks until I reached another large hotel, which I circled, before coming back and scampering through the front lobby. Thankfully, someone on the night shift spoke English, and he arranged a taxi, which I slithered into before being delivered back to the Pearl Hotel. After that insanity, I took no more chances. I stayed at the Pearl an additional day and night, drinking from room service in the dark and still unable to sleep. As I replayed the events over in my mind, I became fully convinced that this had not been some attack of paranoia. For my interpretation to have been false, the situation would have needed an impossible number of coincidences to have taken place in far too short of a time frame. Over the years, I have remained so sure of the threat posed by Long and his fellow outlaws that I have never once even considered returning to Krabi Town ... although there would soon be very little desire for me to go anywhere else in Thailand other than the magical island upon which I landed that very next day: Koh Phi Phi.

CHAPTER 5

ABOUT AN ISLAND (2020, 2003–2012)

But not so. How arrives it joy lies slain
And why unblooms the best hope ever sown?
—Crass Casualty obstructs the sun and rain,
And dicing Time for gladness casts a moan ....
These Purblind Doomsters had as readily strewn.
Blisses about my pilgrimage as pain.

—Thomas Hardy, "Hap"

Five hours cramped inside a decrepit minibus among a dozen strangers is an unbearable amount of time to be stifled by a "face mask," that intrusive accessory that in the year 2020 had become the essential requirement of social interaction. But because Thailand's mask mandate was backed by a 20,000 baht fine for non-compliance, I had faithfully followed the rules since arriving in Bangkok eight days earlier. And now, after leisurely making my way south, I checked into a Phuket Town hotel room, shed the mask, and enjoyed a few moments of unobstructed breathing.

My relaxation was short-lived. I had forgotten to buy cigarettes and needed to make one more shopping trip. This was not a major hardship because, in this country, if a person trips while walking out the front door, nine times out of ten he will land within spitting distance of a 7-Eleven store. Another quirky aspect of this mysterious Kingdom is that as soon as I step off the airplane, I am overwhelmed by a world of unpredictability and strange coincidences, an existence dominated by Fate. My freewill always seemed to be in a defensive position, as I was constantly forced to react to unexpected events. Therefore, I was startled, but not shocked, when Lek pulled up on a beige motorbike just as the "Biiiiing bing" of the 7-Eleven doorbell announced my exit from that oasis of convenience.

The black-haired wisp of a girl, dwarfed by the oversized motorbike, gasped while I pointed and smiled in mutual recognition. This was a highly improbable encounter: eight years had passed since I had last seen Lek, although I remember that final encounter clearly. I was flat on my back and still struggling with the aftershocks of anesthesia as I watched tears stream from the sincerity of her downcast eyes, which left glistening streaks upon the passionate concern of her face. My own face, mummy-wrapped and numb, was the source of her sorrow, and the focal point of discussion among the eclectic, gift-bearing group that was gathered about my bedside: Lek and Sak (her man, and my "fixer"/friend), Dom and P-Kwoy (the two brawny, tattoo-covered cooks from the kitchen of the Sunflower Beach Bar on Koh Phi Phi), and Brigid (the sweet absent-minded American lady) with her fearless son David (who, being just twenty years old, still exuded the idealism and vast potential of youth). These two American free spirits had been staying at the same guesthouse as myself, and for the past week we had bonded over our shared enthusiasm for sport-fishing on the Andaman Sea.

I was in Phuket's Vachira Hospital with this unusual mix of caretakers on an oppressively humid tropical afternoon, but just yesterday Sak and Lek had been fifty kilometers to the north, while the rest of us were ensconced at the far end of Loh Dalum Bay in one of the last pockets of semi-isolation remaining on the gorgeous but tourist-besieged island of Koh Phi Phi, located forty-five kilometers southeast of Phuket. Accessible only by sea, there were just three choices of transportation between the two popular islands. Option one being a two and a half hour crossing on one of the regular ferry boats. Option two would be an hour and a half trip on a chartered speedboat. Option number three was a forty-five-minute jaunt on a speedboat hauling ass over an open sea at 3 a.m. on an unscheduled medical emergency run. We had been compelled to make option number three our selection, because of a desperate situation brought about by an episode of unexpected violence that occurred just a few hours earlier.

While it was certainly an unforeseen assault that had necessitated our sudden dead-of-night crossing, this personally traumatic event was really the climax to a story that had originated years earlier. If I had paid closer attention and pondered the actual dynamics of my situation, I may have foreseen—and possibly avoided—the humiliation and disfigurement that were the results of a ruthless yet senseless ambush. At least, this was the interpretation that I formulated later that night, while Lek snoozed peacefully beside me, and I relived, re-analyzed, and reevaluated the episodes and conditions of that epoch of my life's history.

As I reorganized my memories and attempted to construct an accurate timeline, I reflected that when this chaotic event occurred in October 2012, I was already intimately familiar with Koh Phi Phi. I had spent sixteen months of vacation time on the island over the previous nine years. During my first attempt to reconstruct this story, I realized that in order for it to be accurately presented, the narrative needed to be framed by its distinctive setting: the dream-like beauty of the Andaman Sea surrounding a sublime tropical landscape inhabited by a fluctuating population of local Thais, condescending expats, and a multinational congregation of tourists. It is a self-contained world with a vibe as mercurial as the monsoons, and a history of intrigue, mystery, and overwhelming tragedy. This uniqueness of the setting is an important factor in this story, but just as important is my relationship with this special place. In order to fully appreciate this tale, the reader should be aware of a simple fact: I loved Koh Phi Phi. I loved that island under the same conditions as a romantic loves a beguiling mistress: with intense joy, calm forbearance, and—regrettably—the same blindness.

***

My initial visit was in late September 2003, and the love affair began some time during that first week. I became enamored with the island's diverse natural beauty, the brick-paved streets devoid of motorized traffic, and the small-town ambiance, which often facilitated speedily forged friendships among strangers. This laid-back "beer and a hammock" atmosphere allowed a lifestyle I embraced like a long-lost friend. My immediate infatuation was certainly influenced by the contrast between my instinct's confident assessment: this island was authentic in its promise of hospitality and safety, and the reality of my recent experiences at previous stopping points on my holiday itinerary.

Those earlier experiences had given me a crash course on the dark side of Thailand. I had lost my trusting nature after a panicked footrace, escaping an attempted kidnapping six hours after first arriving in Bangkok. And my newfound wariness had become more like cynical paranoia after another narrow getaway, when I slipped away from a shady gang of drug-runners led by a character of overbearing creepiness. That escape was not completely assured until the crew of the ferry boat threw lines as we departed Rassada pier in Phuket. The anxiety of my shocked soul was not eased until the sky became a familiar dome of open blue as I straddled the railing on the bow of the boat. But my spirit truly soared when my astonished eyes first beheld the sight of sheer facades of limestone karsts dressed in vivid green vegetation rioting out of the choppy sea, just before the boat glided into the dreamy turquoise expanse of Tonsai Bay.

While the island immediately impressed itself upon my subconscious as an impregnable sanctuary simply because of the inherent protection provided by its geographical isolation, I was also overwhelmed with relief at the sight of a familiar face. An old friend and Bering Sea brother, Don, had been awaiting my arrival since we had made the accidental online discovery of our simultaneous Thailand expeditions. Over the years I have come to appreciate a particular truth: when besieged by trouble in a foreign land, the face of a fellow Bering Sea fisherman is a most hope-inspiring sight. They may laugh at you, but they won't judge you (after all, it could very well be them in the same scrape!). And after battling the tribulations of the Alaskan fishing industry together, there was no doubt about our allegiance in the event of misfortune in a strange land. The rendezvous with Don not only reinvigorated my spirit of adventure, but it also proved to be one of those "phenomena of Fate," a seemingly trivial event, circumstance, or choice that sparks a complete alteration of personal Fate. In this instance, the life-changing choice was precipitated by a stubborn resolve on a change of accommodations. This experience having occurred long before his present domestication, Don was still infused with a passion for discovery, and he insisted on us leaving the drab guest house in Ton Sai village in search of beachfront real estate.

And it was while wandering down an obscure back trail that followed the twists of a swampy tidal stream that we were hailed by a shaggy-haired shirtless apparition, his bronze wiry muscles glistening with sweat as he waved the six-foot carcass of a recently expired serpent about the air in a primitive display of victory. This was how I came to meet the most intriguingly unique and soul-inspiring individual of my many travels. Perhaps because we did not resemble typical tourists, Ben took an immediate interest and liking to the both of us, and he shepherded us to his family's beachfront guest house on the easternmost corner of Loh Dalum Bay.

We were afforded the prime end unit of the two-story structure. It was the only unit with a balcony, an intricately constructed viewpoint concealed by a vine-wrapped railing and perched directly above Ben's modest Sunset Bar. It possessed an unrivaled view of the vast sky-blue bay, which was wrapped in the horseshoe created by the brilliant white beach and the jagged ridges of jungle-green mountains. This special spot became my sanctuary from the troubles of travel, my refuge from the rat race of modern life, and my retreat from the insane grind of my "other life" as a Bering Sea fisherman. It was landing in this spot, its healing influence on the equanimity of my soul, and most importantly, the profound affection that I acquired for Ben and his family that forever altered not just physical aspects of my life, but changed my emotional and spiritual life as well.

If not for that chance meeting on an obscure trail, I doubt that I would have made even one return trip to Koh Phi Phi, and I most certainly would not have come to regard the island as my home away from home, nor would it have become the focal point of the many daydreams I conjured in the great battle against boredom and monotony in the factories of fishing vessels. And God only knows the different decade of life I would have experienced had I just stayed put in that guest house in town. But I followed that twist in the road, and in less than a week, my future would be grounded to and guided by my desire for this refuge. From that moment, I became like a planet orbiting a sun, its movements controlled by the irresistible force of gravity. Although I ranged so far out, I was always pulled back to this place.

***

And the following year, the force of this attraction grew exponentially as I spent four months of joyful contemplation on that same balcony. My bond with Ben and his family strengthened to the extent that I was now referred to as "Uncle Mark." This title was bestowed upon me by Millie, the elder of Ben's two daughters. The exceptionally bright three-year-old had become my co-conspirator in the late afternoons, when we ambushed unsuspecting tourists with water balloons dropped from the confines of my camouflaged balcony. Precocious and endearingly demanding, Millie inherited the aristocratic accent of her English mother and the stubborn will and mysterious eyes of her Thai father. She made for a good partner in my Happy Hour bombing campaign, her cuteness deflecting any outrage from offended farang. She also functioned as an unwanted alarm clock, with her piercing, plaintive voice breaking through the boozy haze of midmorning dreams: "Uncle Maaark! Uncle Maaaark! I need another ballooooooon!" Her need to replace a busted water balloon obviously outweighing my need for sleep, I dutifully awoke to fulfill my obligations.

Most afternoons I spent reading, writing, and daydreaming out on the balcony. Down below, Ben amazed me with his unique style of craftsmanship as he continued improvements on his palm-shaded, sand-floored bar. Often, he would take a break for an "attitude adjustment." Shimmying cat-like up the adjacent tree, he would flip himself onto the balcony, and we would share a joint of the local herb. Sitting in the shade, and soothed by the soft breeze, Ben shared his family's history, specialized knowledge of the island's natural characteristics, and his always interesting perspectives on the topics of philosophy, spirituality, and politics. With his long, disheveled hair, crooked smile, Rasputin eyes, and unique insights, he appeared to me as some village shaman or even island prophet. Although I am a year older, I always regarded him as the wise teacher and myself as the inspired student.

Those carefree days in the fall of 2004 were filled with the delight of newborn friendships with both locals and fellow travelers. I seldom walked through the village without an exuberant attitude and a contagious feeling of goodwill that was impervious to inconsiderate tourists and other minor nuisances. I also took up new hobbies: flipping fake snakes in the path of intoxicated Irish lasses pub-crawling through town, playing Huck Finn after a torrential rain by sailing an inflatable raft down the town's flooded streets, goading fellow tourists into drinking trips characterized by halfhearted attempts at fishing, and taking midnight cruises off the coast of Hippies Bar while lighting up the sky with fireworks shot from the sterns of long-tailed boats. I also passed the time sharing bottles of vodka and other party favors with my new Thai friends, locals who manned the tattoo parlors and massage shops, bar-tended and bounced at the pubs and beach bars, and piloted the long-tail boats. Those single-engine scows were the island's primary form of transportation—except during low tide, when they would be beached like stranded seals upon the sand and surrounded by exposed fragments of limestone.

***

After sunset, while the younger backpacker crowd staggered through the streets, booze sloshing out of the plastic buckets that they so often shared by slurping from the same straws, I could usually be found on the beach at Hippies Bar. Making fast friends with the laid-back staff, I acquired my own "spot," a gazebo-sheltered hammock where I lounged about and amused myself by conjuring tall tales in order to impress unsuspecting Europeans. My exploits included Super Bowl victories (playing wide receiver for the Dallas Cowboys) and daring sex trafficking stings, which I executed as a special agent for Interpol. On a lucky night, there would be an uptight English gal or two in the ever-changing crowd sitting about "my office." In these situations, I would carefully educate the British ladies on the particulars of Phi Phi Island politics, gradually building up to the revelation that, having been elected in a landslide the preceding October, I was in the second year of my two-year term as Mayor of Koh Phi Phi. I can still vividly recall that feeling of mischievous joy in witnessing a grown woman tearfully burst into hysterical protestations: "That is absolute rubbish! I literally *hate*—Literally! Hate!—America! You Americans think you should rule over everybody and everything in the whole world!"

As an explanation for this apparent cruelty, I should remind the reader that these were the Bush years, a time when the world's brainwashed youth believed America responsible for all the earth's problems. It was also a time when Americans in Thailand were as numerous as liberals at a Trump rally. Always outnumbered, humor had become my sole weapon for defending the honor of my homeland without hurt feelings or bloodshed.

***

The experiences of that autumn had cemented my love—for life on the island, for the second family I had found in Ben and his clan, for the new friends I had made, and even for myself, or that part of myself that seemed to exist only in that world. I remember reflecting on all of this in mid-December when the ferry boat pulled away from the pier, the towering cliffs and curve of coast fading from sight like a lost dream. I recall thinking I had been recharged, and that I was now ready for the battle of another back-breaking A-Season fishing through the bitter Alaskan winter. I was confident that after fighting through those brutal months, the reward would be a return to my island refuge.

These expectations of mine seemed realistic in that they were based on the assumption that my life would continue to follow a previously established pattern. This pattern was more or less controlled by my own decision-making and by my own competence in the implementation of those decisions. But that was a long time ago, a time when I had stubbornly maintained a resolute attitude of personal empowerment and still held a belief that justice was assured by a righteous Creator. I had yet to learn the bitter lessons of disillusionment, and I had not yet learned to fully employ reason in order to question my blind faith in a naive philosophy riddled with contradictions and results that did not square with reality. Little did I know what a silly faith and what a ridiculous approach to life it was that I had embraced. I was unaware that the innocence of my illusions and the idyllic charm of that island were fated to be washed away just nine days after my parting look at the island's deep green coastline.

The trouble resulting from foolish behavior and careless decision-making is usually uncomfortable, and frequently painful, but always bearable. The disconcerting consequences resulting from bad behavior are always tolerable because one knows that he deserves the painful repercussions. He earned them fair and square. But when one is knocked flat on his ass while essentially minding his own business? That kind of pain is overwhelming because it is tainted with the sting of injustice. The misery becomes unbearable when one realizes the cold indifference of Nature, or God, the Fates, or whoever is supposed to be in charge of cosmic justice. Whichever one of these entities you choose to believe to be "in charge" is of no importance: the fact remains that tragedy will strike randomly and indiscriminately, destroying the virtuous alongside the wicked, and meting out torture to the moral, the immoral, and the amoral in equal measure. Despite the fairy tales and myths the human race has fabricated in defense of its collective sanity, suffering is spread like fertilizer in a field. And when one is a witness to or a recipient of undeserved calamity, the pain is compounded to the tenth degree when the *unfairness* and *indifference* of the Universe is revealed in a cruel epiphany.

And that is what transpired on December 26th of 2004, when the universe demonstrated its detachment by unleashing a catastrophe upon the coastal communities of the Indian Ocean. The Sumatran-Andaman earthquake erupted with such violence that devastating tsunamis were launched in every direction, delivering death to over a quarter million people, physically injuring just as many, while administering psychological damage to countless more.

On Koh Phi Phi, a little after 10 a.m. that day, the water in Loh Dalum Bay drastically receded, leaving a vast plain of sand and small tidal pools of fish. This novelty enticed many curious individuals out onto the beach. And then, as if Nature had designed a cruel booby trap, the first of a series of tsunamis stormed into the bay, ambushing the unprepared population, and crashing a hell into a heaven. Substituting malice for indifference, Nature doubled the attack as a tsunami also slammed into Tonsai Bay on the opposite side of the low-lying isthmus. The collision of the dual waves effectively pancaked the most densely settled area of the island, engulfed it in water, destroyed the majority of structures, swept life and property out to sea, and left shell-shocked survivors adrift in a literal wasteland. It is estimated that as many as four thousand souls perished on Koh Phi Phi as a result of this disaster (over a hundred children lost one or both parents), many more suffered both physical and psychological injuries, and most of the buildings and infrastructure of the island were destroyed.

It was still Christmas Day in Arizona when I was thunderstruck by news of the catastrophe. As my family gathered for the holiday feast, I sat alone in stunned silence, watching the surreal nightmare unfold on television and clinging to the desperate hope that my friends were okay. As the months passed by, I lost my faith in a benevolent Creator. I felt an angry helplessness and guilt as I was unable to return to the island to help, or to get any solid information about the Fate of my friends. In fact, it was not until two years later that I finally—and fearfully—approached the location of my former residence on Loh Dalum Bay. I found a work-in-progress at the site, along with Ben, whom I embraced with joyful relief, until he looked at me with swollen, vacant eyes and said, "Uncle Mark. Everybody dead."

Along with several members of his extended family, he had lost his wife, daughter Millie, and Millie's three-month-old sister, Tia. I spent several days with Ben. I listened to his story as he recounted how the implacable force of the sea had ripped Millie from his arms and washed him halfway up the nearest hill, where he awoke with a broken leg and a shattered heart, surrounded by the fragments of his former life. Even now, I am amazed at his strength and courage in managing a months-long search of the island for the bodies of his loved ones, while also fighting through unimaginable emotional torture to begin the rebuilding process. He collected driftwood, sections of busted boats, and other debris that had washed back to shore. With these broken pieces of history, Ben constructed a restaurant, bar, and guesthouse in honor of his family, and in defiance of the perverse powers of an unjust heaven.

Today, in the same place where I once idled away afternoons, the Millie and Tia Sunflower Beach Bar and Restaurant is a place of refuge from the loud chaos of the island's party scene. It is a unique place where, unlike the rest of Phi Phi, the tragedy of the tsunami is still remembered. The tables are made of broken long-tail boats, each one a memorial to a departed member of Ben's family. His family is now enriched with new members, as my friend has encountered new relationships; among them is a beautiful, compassionate, and intelligent third daughter who is the future heir and current caretaker of the sacred ground.

I did not begin this tale with the intention of writing about the tsunami; however, it would be impossible to write an authentic story that takes place on Koh Phi Phi without some description of that overwhelming tragedy and the profound transformation of the island and the people in its aftermath. Because I was not present for the nightmare itself, I am limited in my ability to completely understand and describe the calamity; however, having numerous intimate friends and loved ones among the victims, having listened and learned from my friends who survived, and having lived for extended periods of time on the island, I can speak with understanding and insight on the altered complexion of life on Phi Phi.

After the massive effort of the initial cleanup, reconstruction was then delayed by disagreements between landowners and other community members regarding the development plan. This complication was compounded by the atmosphere of uncertainty generated by the ambiguous schemes and capricious enforcement of building restrictions by the Thai government. But once these obstacles were either overcome or ignored, the material regeneration of Koh Phi Phi exploded, and it soon accelerated at an unprecedented rate. This boom was a blessing in the beginning because in order to repair the lives of a broken people, it was essential to jump start the economic engine of the community: the tourist industry. Once the train of progress left the station, though, it became impossible to slow down. In fact, development only increased as collective greed became the prime motivator, while consideration for the common good and long-range planning were disregarded.

That the aesthetic character and infrastructure of the island were deteriorating annually was obvious every time I returned and strolled through town. What was not immediately evident was the growing threat that lurked underneath the surface: the soul of the community was being corrupted by the selfishness of landowners and investors, the careless ignorance of most visitors, and the increasingly cynical attitudes of many local citizens. Attempting to identify the root cause for this contamination of the population's spirit is an exercise in frustration similar to deciding whether it was the chicken or the egg that came first. Had the tsunami triggered this transformation of the community's spirit of love and respect to an ethos of cynical greed, which was now being manifested by the over-development of the island, the growing Thai intolerance of inconsiderate farang, the self-absorbed ignorance of those same foreigners, and a lazy disrespect for the environment by all? Or was the fundamental cause of this demoralizing situation already at work, and the tsunami just a random event that had only delayed the inevitable?

Whatever the root cause, the island community was caught in a self-destructive cycle of negativity, cynicism, and apathy. As the overcrowding and over-building accelerated, so increased the dishonesty, the stereotyping of strangers, the larceny of local bandits, the scams of hustlers, the dissipated stupidity and insensitivity of the young party crowd, and the angry violence this cycle inevitably generates.

Although this regrettable change in the collective attitude and its pernicious effect on the Phi Phi experience was drastic, it was also gradual. For the first few years, I was able to ignore the warnings of my intuition— just as a lover disregards the subtle signs of a partner's growing disinterest.

In fact, I made an extra effort to carry on as before, with a happy heart, a jocular attitude, and plenty of pranks whenever I left "headquarters" on the bow of the large wooden "boat" that was the Sunflower Beach Bar's primary structure. It housed Ben and his tribe on the second floor and myself in the adjacent "VIP" room. With her piercing wail, Ben's new baby girl showed promise as a hell-raiser; at the time, however, she lacked the proper arm strength to assist in a successful water balloon campaign.

**

I kept my antics tame at "home." But on the "road," it was business as usual, with the massage ladies often jumping in surprised terror when I tossed a very real-looking fake snake (or frog or lizard) in front of a gang of those gossipers singing their sales pitches from the shop's front porch.

"Thai massage?"

"Where you go?"

"You want Thai massage?"

My ears eventually echoed with the teasing question, "Hey, snake man, where's your snake?" followed by a chorus of giggles.

The early evening, when the village walkways teamed with tourists, was the best time for "fishing," the game where a chagrined traveler looks around with confusion, amusement, or annoyance for the $10 bill that he had been bending down to grab ... only to see it flutter away, super-glued to the length of dental floss which I manipulated from my seat inside a tattoo shop. (A change purse or a full beer works well as bait too, but never use Thai currency!)

These pranks were never performed maliciously, but with the intent of spreading laughter and goodwill, and they were accompanied by many acts of kindness such as guiding home impaired revelers lost late at night, assisting the injured to the medical clinic, providing recommendations and warnings concerning island activities, or advice on where to score weed. The local Thai population had an amused affection for me that could be attributed to a mindful generosity, which I demonstrated by, say, arriving on Christmas Day wearing a Santa hat and carrying two big garbage bags of gift-wrapped toys that I'd randomly distribute to the island's children on my return ramble through town. Also, aided by lucrative fishing seasons on the Bering Sea, I was able to spread as much wealth as possible, several times assisting my Thai friends who were in need of loans during tough times and always providing extra income through generous tips and purposely poor negotiation tactics when making all sorts of purchases.

Unfortunately, each year brought a younger, less-informed, more self-absorbed crowd. This unappealing demographic, I believe, was the result of rapacious business leaders encouraging a free-for-all party environment. This permissiveness gave rise to late-night raves on the beach, where immature partygoers endeavored to give us drinkers a bad reputation by swilling themselves stupid, screwing openly on the beach (or worse, flagrantly shagging upon Sunflower's memorial tables), talking smack to Thai bar employees, and littering the beach with trash every night. Faced nightly with such blatant disrespect, many locals—simmering with resentment—would extract revenge by stealing from the clueless, booze-addled tourists, or in a gang of six to eight aggressors, administer a beat-down of some fool whom they believed guilty of offensive behavior. Eventually, helping female tourists—often drunk and hysterical—search for a "lost" purse or cell phone, brokering the peace between warring factions, and assisting injured victims to the clinic had become full-time work, as the deterioration of the island's laid-back culture became increasingly obvious.

This was the state of affairs in October 2012, when a romantic relationship sparked up again between myself and Joy, a Thai lady who had been my companion the preceding year. But the relationship now had the extra dynamic of the "third wheel." Joy's friend, Jeab, often accompanied us to various drinking venues, and I happily picked up the collective tab. This was the routine until the evening when Jeab, wasted and belligerent, caused an embarrassing scene, demanding that I buy her another drink. As she continued her outrageous tirade, I stepped out of the bar and strolled down the beach. I had decided that I could no longer associate with such an ill-mannered and inconsiderate person without endangering my positive attitude. During the ensuing weeks, I ignored Jeab any time our paths crossed (which happened daily on that little island). Unfortunately, this reasonable solution to a problem caused by an unreasonable person was not acceptable to the other party. I discovered this fact late one night, while once again escorting an inebriated and geographically challenged tourist back to his lodgings.

I was hanging out with my old buddy, Bob, at his tattoo shop listening to his latest exploits of gathering magic mushrooms on Phuket, which he would then smuggle to Phi Phi for sale at a huge profit. Just then, an inebriated shaggy-haired backpacker stumbled upon the scene, pleading for help in finding his hotel. I hated to leave mid-story (Bob's goofy ideas and their absurd consequences usually had me in tears of laughter), but I volunteered to help the distressed drunk. Although Bob (being uncharacteristically sensible) tried to dissuade me, I felt obligated to help the lost soul.

After directing the boozed-up youngster to the lobby of his hotel, he decided on a change of plan. Because he was drunk (and perhaps because he was Italian), my charge insisted on a slice from the pizza stand which faced the 7-Eleven where Jeab happened to be scouting victims (her usual scam was to spot a drunken male farang, make herself available for a hookup, and then rob the target blind after he inevitably passed out). I pleaded for him to just go to his room, but the kid was too stubborn, and I became too tired to argue. At this point, I should have left him and gone the other way. My instinct screamed at me to do just that—the Fates had set their trap, and I had the option to escape; however, another side of me felt duty-bound to make sure my drunken charge did not fall into Jeab's clutches. So I agreed … under the condition that he not say one word to the woman outside the convenience store. But because he was drunk (and perhaps because he was Italian), the unthinking ass shouted some rude comments out to Jeab, who only needed that spark to ignite her resentful anger. As I tried in vain to quiet him, I noticed the scorned woman pull out her mobile, dial, and then bark instructions into the receiver.

Before you can say "speedboat," two Thai henchmen came flying in on bicycles and, ignoring the Italian imbecile, bolted straight for me—throwing punches, elbows, and kicks. I fended them off, until one of the attackers produced a broken Chang beer bottle, which he swung downward across my face. The slashing blow carved a deep slice from just below my left eye, down the cheek, through both lips, and all the way to the tip of my chin. In the next moment, all three perpetrators had vanished, and I was on my knees watching a pothole fill with my blood and listening to the unscathed Italian violently sobbing and apologizing.

From the assailants' perspective, the ambush was ideally located at the inside corner of an L-shaped turn in the main thoroughfare—the perfect blind spot at 2 a.m. There were no other witnesses, nor was there anyone to render immediate assistance. I got back on my feet, told the Italian to fuck off, and holding my face in my hands I proceeded down the long stretch of the L. There I was spotted by Koy, who had just finished her shift at the Irish bar. Extremely kind, and gorgeous in a cowboy hat, Koy was an old friend who immediately burst into sobs and questions before rushing off to fetch ice wrapped in a cloth towel. After applying it to the flaps of skin that used to be my left cheek, she escorted me back to the Sunflower compound, where I shouted for my good friend, Fai, to awaken. After convincing him that this was not a late-night social call, Fai emerged from his room, descried the bloody disaster of my face, and immediately sounded the alarm, shouting out Thai phrases interspersed with a few "Uncle Marks." Soon, the entire family and staff had mobilized, with Ben in command and furiously issuing orders as he punched numbers into his mobile phone.

Within minutes, the running lights of a speedboat ranged into sight as it entered Loh Dalum Bay, cut its engines, and eased close into shore. Under Ben's instructions, my assigned bodyguards, P-kwoy and Dom, had already packed necessities. And after wading through the shallows and jumping aboard, we were soon skipping across the slight chop of the sea, while overhead the white blurs of stars traced across the deep, black sky. The skipper shifted to full-throttle, and as the boat's bow slammed and bounced from crest to crest, I timed the next leap to chance a swill from a fresh bottle of Chang (weapon of choice of Thai hitmen!), but the beer never touched my throat, and my shirt was soon soaked.

I thought, *I timed that jump perfectly! Why did that beer not reach its intended destination?*

Feeling for my face, I realized that my lips had been rendered useless, a fact confirmed when I made an unsuccessful attempt to light a cigarette. My lips could not form an airtight seal on the filter. This was the moment I discovered a new travel rule: if you cannot physically drink a beer, or light a smoke, then you are truly fucked up.

Fortunately, I could still speak. It was also a lucky circumstance that my one friend in Phuket Town was also the one guy certain to be wide awake at 3:30 a.m.

Sak picked up the phone on the first ring.

"Hey, buddy," I managed into the phone.

"Hello—where are you?"

"On a speedboat coming to Phuket right now. Can you pick me up at the pier? Right now?"

"Okay, okay, okay …."

Despite the traumatic circumstances, I was overwhelmed by a feeling of intense pride and joy at how selflessly and immediately my friends had rallied to my side. I was also filled with astonished gratitude the next afternoon, when upon regaining consciousness post-surgery, I found myself surrounded by the same group of caring souls. They crowded about my hospital bed, and each expressed their love and concern in their own way. My two American fishing buddies had jumped on the first ferry boat to Phuket that morning. Brigid had canceled her scheduled flight home and was grilling the doctors about my pain medication. Her son, "Danger Dave," outlined his plan of *swimming* back to Phi Phi to seek retribution. Sak and Lek had brought flowers and a stash of snacks, while Dom and P-kwoy were all smiles as they stood a silent watch.

However, despite these examples of kindness, there was no remedy for the disillusionment and sorrow assailing my soul. The reality had become impossible to ignore: my sanctuary from the madness and brutality of the Bering Sea, and my refuge from a selfish, dissolute, and intellectually vapid culture, was rapidly degenerating into a state of self-centered corruption and violent cynicism indistinguishable from the ugly world that I had hoped to escape.

This interpretation was only reinforced three days later when I returned to the island in order to file a police report. The Koh Phi Phi Police displayed a callous disregard. Essentially, they laughed in my face and treated the matter as a joke. These "authorities" (whose livelihoods depend on the tourist economy) stalled and stonewalled, and three weeks later I still did not have a police report for the assault! But I did see Jeab. She was laughing and carrying on with the police force as they busied themselves playing beach-soccer in the late afternoon sun, until final darkness arrived well after 8:00 p.m. on the night of my final attempt to file the report. My appointment had been for 7:00 p.m. sharp. Quite obviously, Jeab was making carnal payments to ensure her freedom.

(Here we pause for a good hearty laugh and a public service announcement: anyone traveling to the Kingdom of Thailand is hereby warned that the pervasive corruption of the Royal Thai Police is rivaled only by its utter incompetence. They can be relied upon to serve justice only when pressured by political power, or when motivated to do so by financial or sexual incentive.)

Intent on revenge, my Thai friends on the island searched after the culprits, but it became clear to everyone that the assailants were outsiders from the mainland, cowards who were now long gone. I was left with the consolation of the many tearful apologies and outpouring of love from countless friends on the island. I felt extra sorrow at their shame, and I tried to play it off as no big deal.

***

I have returned to Thailand several times since that event, but only twice to Koh Phi Phi, which was enough to ascertain that the community spirit had continued to decay, and that the same economic, governmental, and cultural problems had only expanded. And now from a condo in Phuket Town in the year 2020, while finally addressing this epoch of my life and this island's profound impact on it, I received the most demoralizing news to date.

While searching online for updated information on Phi Phi's COVID-19 lockdown, I stumbled upon this headline from an Argentinian publication: "La Isla de Tailandia Que Se Olvidó Del Tsunami." For the Spanish-impaired, this translates to: "The Island in Thailand That Has Forgotten About the Tsunami." The article relates that the only memorial to the tsunami victims on Koh Phi Phi, the Tsunami Memorial Garden, had been removed three years ago and replaced with … another hotel. A "memorial to oblivion" was the sardonic phrase used by the article's author. The spoken sound of those words stung me into sad embarrassment. After reading that line, I could not help myself from thinking that the soul of Koh Phi Phi had also sunk into oblivion. The tsunami was a random, uncontrollable tragedy, but what has transpired on the island afterward is almost as tragic. Because honoring and respectfully remembering those who perished *is* controllable by human action. And so is behaving with respect and kindness to one another and the natural environment.

But I am not a defeatist, and hope for a turnaround survived in my heart. I knew one island family that still behaved with love and respect, and once that foolish lockdown ended, I would make another pilgrimage to see my old friends once again.

PART 2

COURTING CALAMITY

If you could kick the person in the pants responsible for most of your trouble, you wouldn't sit for a month.

—Theodore Roosevelt

CHAPTER 6

ROOD AND THE RAPSCALLION (2007)

If you're going to kick authority
in the teeth, you might as
well use both feet.

—KEITH RICHARDS

I f a traveler is likely to wreak a bit of havoc in a foreign land, it is highly
advantageous to acquire and cultivate the friendship of a well-respected
local citizen. Ideally, this person possesses the connections and talents
of a "fixer," a person who is coolheaded, charismatic, and inured to the
foolishness of foreigners, and in fact, takes an amused spectator's delight in
the outsider's impudent and irresponsible behavior. More importantly, a fixer
should be intimately familiar with each of the two most distinct segments
in any society: the lawbreakers and the law enforcers. More specifically, this
special agent is comfortable circulating in the company of either of the above
populations while navigating the nuances of the murky territory where those
worlds intersect.

Being an unruly mischief-maker, I have fortunately been blessed to enjoy
the friendship of just such a character. This friendship has been tested and
strengthened over the course of almost two decades' worth of trips to southern
Thailand. Since our first 2003 encounter in Phuket's Kamala Beach, a hard-
bitten but gregarious Thai fellow with an impish grin and the name of Rood
has been my good pal, trusted advisor, and watchful guardian. Actually, the

term "fixer" understates the case. Rood has, on countless occasions, proven to be my salvation by rescuing me from crazy criminals, offended authorities, devious local ladies, logistical disasters, and personal financial crises. Despite the overwhelming challenges inherent in the task of keeping a reckless vagabond's holiday free from (major) injury, (extended) jail time, (exuberant) fines/shakedown fees, and (most importantly) death, Rood always preserves his cool composure with lighthearted laughter and a bemused grin, which betray the fact that he is actually enthralled with my entertaining antics. And only on a handful of occasions has he ever aimed his notorious scowl in my direction, saving that steely glare for the intimidation of his adversaries or the instruction of his children. The following tale recounts just one of my many misadventures in which this good friend played his part to perfection.

***

After enduring a frustratingly long post-tsunami hiatus from the Land of Smiles, I finally returned on a much-anticipated morning in September 2007. On a sultry night shortly thereafter, while carousing carelessly somewhere in the Sukhumvit Road subsection of Bangkok's temptations, I inadvertently acquired a new girlfriend. These things happen. Poor planning, my natural nonchalance regarding capricious Fate, and five months of Bering Sea-imposed celibacy made me easy prey … and my Mickey quickly capitalized on the opportunity. Mickey was a lovely, doe-eyed, young Thai lady whose sweet demeanor masked an iron will. Almost immediately after our first meeting had turned into an overnight affair, that iron will began to focus on corralling my unsuspecting heart and changing my name to "Boyfriend." Of course, I was blissfully unaware of this new dynamic, until a few days later when I informed her that I was flying to Phuket. She responded by jumping exultantly onto my lap, enveloping me in an eager hug, and exclaiming, "Oh, good! I never have holiday at beach before! What time we go? Now we must go straightaway to apartment for my clothes!"

Being a huge fan of conflict avoidance, I was soon making the necessary travel arrangements for a party of two. My final call was to my advance man in Phuket. He assured me that his personal vehicle would be curbside outside baggage claim when I arrived. Satisfied, I ended the call having sheepishly avoided informing Rood about the sudden "we" development to the itinerary.

I figured that the explanation could wait until our airport reunion. Waiting might just give me the time to devise a credible story.

Even after priming myself with doubles at the airport bar and smuggled whiskey and soda on the flight, my mind was still in a state of perplexed reflection. I glanced searchingly at the enigmatic countenance of my napping companion, but I was still unable to determine just how it came to be that I was "taking sand to the beach" in flagrant violation of my personal travel rules. After descending through the bulging rain-pregnant clouds, the plane was cruising over swaths of vivid green vegetation when I had an epiphany: a reason in the *past* was simply irrelevant to my *now*! So what if I had a young woman attached to my upcoming joyride? I had not (consciously) invited her; therefore, I was morally free from blame if she proved incapable of holding on when the inevitable jolts, shocks, and free-falls materialized up around the bend. Besides, I was now eager to witness the reaction of my old friend and teammate to my first curve-ball of the season.

With luggage collected and anticipation mounting, I played lead blocker as Mickey—perfecting the slow-motion saunter of Thai womanhood— trailed complacently behind. I nudged and stealth-elbowed my way through the mass of humanity and overstuffed backpacks choking the exits of Phuket International Airport. Squeezing our way out into the sweltering humidity, the cause of such intense congestion was soon apparent: taxi-stand bottlenecks. The disoriented mob of tourists (consisting mostly of clueless Phuket greenhorns) was being driven herd-like into file behind the outrageous lines that had already formed.

It was quite obvious to my Thai-skeptical eyes that what appeared to be an attempt at social order was really just a clumsy endeavor to fix prices and attain market control. Freelance taxis could circle about the airport exits, but the syndicate had total control of the official taxi stands and employed henchmen who patrolled the baggage claim areas mendaciously convincing the timid and the unaware that the taxi stands were the only sanctioned transportation providers.

Oh, this is perfect! I exclaimed inwardly, while feeling a surge of conceited pride.

I had purposely withheld from Mickey the fact that we had a prearranged ride so that I could play the part of the suave street-smart traveler, but this was a real opportunity to show off! Actually, I detest ostentation and its choke hold on American culture; however, after a life of mishaps and lost causes, any opportunity to be "The Man" must be seized. And when circumstances are so queerly arranged that both righteous arrogance and contempt for authority are possible? Damn the torpedoes—full speed ahead!

Having also sized up the situation (and being the child of a conformist society), Mickey began to pull on my hand in an attempt to coax me to the nearest cattle chute. But gently tugging my new love toward open sidewalk and glancing back with a smile, I said, "Not happening. Let's go."

With my head held high and a pompously disdainful glare, I strutted forward with my eyes concentrated on the heavily-tinted windows of a certain black Honda sports car idling curbside twenty yards beyond our designated taxi stand. Immediately, the shrieks of whistles and nerve-rattling shouts pierced the heavy air, and the nearest fraud of a security officer made a brash yet poorly executed attempted to arrest our forward progress by grabbing at my right shoulder. My reflexive action was to slap his hand away and shout, "Fuck off!"

Stunned, he began to shout out in high-speed Thai a call for reinforcements. This was an unnecessary plea because several fellow foot-soldiers were already rushing the scene. As I slipped Mickey's sweaty grip and prepared for battle, a cold, commanding voice thundered from behind me, and then the voice became a storm of threats and insults as its infuriated owner closed in on the scene. My attackers halted their charge in shocked obedience.

Turning around, I saw a powerfully built man dressed in all black, his rage-contorted face behind black Terminator sunglasses and his right arm pointing additional commands. Seeing my familiar, relieved grin, Rood—The Man—transformed from pissed-off drill sergeant to amused accomplice, and with a deep laugh he signaled for us to come along, but not before directing one final scowl at the lame gang of lackeys sulking in defeat.

Mickey, having deferred to friendship and custom, was a confused spectator from the backseat as Rood and I laughingly rehashed the event, with my comrade intermittently shaking his head in disbelief and incredulously repeating a terse but on-target question utilizing just one English word: "Already? ... Already? ... Already?"

Of course, he was also taking the occasional sly glance at the rear-view mirror, and then looking askance at me with a sarcastic grin escaping his lame excuse of a poker face. And because his English was several notches more advanced than that of the gal sitting in the back (who was staring at me with looks alternating between grudging admiration and prudish displeasure), I was able to quickly relate the events leading up to my current domestic situation without fear of an offended lady and, consequently, a frigid "honeymoon bed." Instead of annoyance at us boys having a third-party distraction, though, Rood seemed genuinely thrilled, and I quickly guessed the reason: he believed (mistakenly) that my rabble-rousing would be harnessed by female company, which would make for a hassle-free experience for my kind but foolishly naive host.

Now satisfied and focused on driving, it was Rood's turn to show off. The focus this time was his new stereo system. He inserted a CD well known from previous trips, and soon the fast-paced guitar work of Mark Knopfler came blasting from the high-fidelity speakers as Dire Straits launched into "Sultans of Swing." While I rapturously looked out upon the flashing scenes of vibrant tropical flora and austere rural architecture, the song rose to its chorus with Rood boisterously singing along. Just then, I arrived at a certain conclusion: you know you are with the coolest dude in the Kingdom when he can scare off a gang of taxi-mafia and also belt out the lyrics to a cult classic rock song unheard of by the rest of his countrymen.

Winding into Kamala Beach from the north, the ocean road straddles the sheer cliffs that stand as sentinels over a long, shallow, crescent-shaped bay of fantastic blue lined with serrated white streaks of froth from the sluggish breakers easing into shore. Although at times the waves can create just enough violence to entertain the casual surfer, the bay's usual aspect is a languid tranquility, which is also reflected in the personality of the town itself, where a friendly mild-mannered tribe of locals leisurely entertain an older, calmer sort of holiday-maker with just enough booze joints and single ladies patrolling pool tables to prevent the mellow from taking the tragic step to the mundane. If this were a typical scene out of suburbia, Kamala is the quiet responsible neighbor with the tidy lawn and sedentary lifestyle, while Patong to the south is the booze-swilling, hell-raising trailer trash down the street known for keg parties, fist fights, public nudity, and guest appearances on the television show *Cops*—if that neighbor could keep it up for 365 days a year.

Kamala may seem dull in comparison, but in truth, Patong's seedy depravity is so widespread and predictable that it proves even hedonism becomes tedious with repetition. Patong's reputation draws a tourist crowd of ignorant, stumble-drunk, and ill-mannered farang who foster animosity and disdain among the increasingly cynical locals; this is one big reason why I have come to shun that soulless beach town. Another reason is that there are several ruthless outlaws crawling about Patong's underbelly who believe themselves wronged, slighted, or short-changed by a middle-aged man who, coincidentally, happens to look exactly like me. And I would hate to have my ticket punched and shown the exit door from this Earth solely because of a case of mistaken identity. Also, I think that Rood has come to doubt my claim of an identical twin, as I sometimes do when I wander too far into the darkling caves of distant memory and encounter hazy images of native narcotics, brouhahas, and narrow escapes facilitated by desperate late-night calls to my own personal 911 line in Kamala.

I have always felt sympathetic to Kamala's lack of excitement, and being an altruistic soul, I believed it my Christian duty to assist in creating a more ebullient ambiance in that listless outpost of progress. So a couple of days after settling into our ocean-view room, having the required "Boys' Night Out" (playing pool and coaxing Rood to throw back enough shots to ensure a healthy hangover and a proper scolding from his wife), and lazing about the beach with my new love, the first hints of boredom encroached upon my spirit. During dinner on that third evening, Mickey and Rood were jabbering along in machine gun blasts of rapid-fire Thai, while I stared complacently out at the last rays of light fading under the growing gloom. I groped for some spark of inspiration to rescue me from potential malaise. If I had a better grasp of the Thai language, conversation with good friends may have sufficed, but after thirty minutes of half-heartedly listening, I was able to snag and translate just a few of the words that zipped across the table: *ba* (crazy), *mow* (drunk), *kee-mow* (really drunk), *ting-tong* (foolish), *baba-bobo* (half-witted), and of course, *farang* (foreigner). It did not take a genius or a detective to deduce the identity of the particular farang my good friends were referencing. Many other variations of this same conversation were littered about my history—memories of friends and circumstances of bygone holidays scattered across the Kingdom. I had heard it all before.

Finally, there was a ceasefire when Mickey strolled off for the ladies' room, and I took the opportunity to discreetly ask, "Hey, Rood, where can I buy some fireworks here?"

"Cannot! Kamala not have fireworks shop."

"Yes, I know there is not a fireworks shop here, buddy, but that was not my question."

Observing the gleam in my eye, my pal quickly understood, his grin faded, and his eyes sought shelter among his shoelaces.

"Now, I know that *you* know someone, and money always talks!"

"But it's not a holi—"

"Stop, Rood. I know it's not a holiday. But I need something to do. I'm getting bored, brother!"

Maybe it was the "brother" that won him over—or knowing the futility of resistance—but eventually my man caved, pulled out his mobile, and commenced brokering a deal. By the time my unsuspecting sweetheart returned, it had been decided that the next day at 1 p.m., Rood would pick me up at the Benjamin Hotel (my usual headquarters in Kamala) for a hastily planned fishing trip—at least, that was the cover story prepared for Mickey. I didn't want to worry the poor girl, as she was already suspecting that her intended was a little rough around the edges.

Although she would be on her own, Mickey was an understanding woman, and she became downright enthusiastic after I slipped her a thousand baht of fun money on my way out the door that following afternoon. In stark contrast was my reluctant driver who, with a frustrated grimace and a shake of his head, managed just enough forbearance to accelerate out of town and navigate the tight curves and steep slopes of the unmarked country road meandering into the gloom of shaded mountain jungle.

My friend had yet to inform me of our destination or give any details regarding the upcoming transaction, and as we pushed farther into the wilderness, I began to get a spooky vibe of disorientation. It was a sensation that conjured up the memory of being taken in the night, deep into the no-man's land of impenetrable jungle outside Krabi Town by Long and his gang of low-level criminals. They had insisted that I witness authentic Muay Thai matches arranged far from tourists or authorities, and the situation made for an atmosphere of creepy isolation. But that event was characterized by authentic danger ... or at least the potential for it.

Presently, there was no real danger. For although Rood's gruff silence was uncomfortable, any apprehension for my safety would have been absurd. This reality was driven home when he commenced to sing along with the Cyndi Lauper song already torturing my eardrums. Certainly, my sidekick had several skeletons stuffed in Memory's closet. I was aware of an underlying unease, even a palpable fear, emanating at times from certain locals whenever Rood approached them. I was familiar with the bar-room gossip, which held that in his wild youth my friend had run with a rough crowd. Actually, Rood did not just run *with* a rough crowd; in reality, my man had *run* the crowd (as in, he "ran a crew" in mob-speak). But whatever illicit actions had occurred in my friend's life-history, they were just that: history! The man that I had come to know was a man of integrity who was compassionate, generous, and full of love. And despite the sheer quantity of aggravation my irresponsibility and improvidence had caused him, I knew that I could trust Rood with my life. I could even count on him to (eventually and reluctantly) facilitate the fun and excitement of my travel experience.

With these reassuring thoughts playing in my mind, I spotted a rusted sedan ahead idling on the shoulder of the forest road. As we pulled over, a shirtless, tattooed bruiser exited from the driver-side door, gave Rood a nod, gave me a sneer, and then popped open the trunk of his car. From behind, I could see a staggering stockpile of multicolored and wildly designed packages jutting out of the trunk, and I chuckled to myself, "Now this is how it's done!"

Growing up on the fireworks-forbidden northern side of the Ohio River, I knew this sort of clandestine commerce was the only way authentic incendiaries and rockets could be obtained by Cincinnati adolescents. My brother and I would pester a favorite uncle until he relented and chauffeured us over the Mason-Dixon line and into the backwoods of the Kentucky foothills, where enterprising hillbillies peddled pyrotechnics from the flatbeds of pickups and the trunks of bulky Monte Carlos.

So, while Rood and the mysterious bootlegger exchange preliminaries, I (wide-eyed and salivating) pawed the merchandise and examined the esoteric Chinese product descriptions. Being a stranger to Chinese linguistics and realizing this would necessarily be a trial-and-error endeavor, I hailed the sales agent and cut to the chase:

Me: "How much?"

Rood (translating) to Agent: "How much?"

Agent to Rood: "How much for which product?"

Rood to me: "For which ones, Mark?"

Me to Rood: "For everything."

Rood (shaking head in disgust): "How much for everything in the trunk?"

Agent to Rood: "Is this farang fucking crazy?"
Rood to Agent: "Completely crazy. Also, stupid!"
Agent (eyes shining with lust): "12,000 baht."
Me (pulling out money roll): "Cool, I'll take it."
Agent (joyously looking skyward): "Thank you, Buddha!"

Thus, without ever beginning, the negotiations were finalized, the exchange was made, and after enthusiastic handshakes and well wishes, Rood and I retraced our route back to that undefended beach settlement presently enjoying its customary—but suddenly endangered—tranquility.

***

With three contraband-stuffed garbage bags slung over my shoulder, I struggled up the hotel's worn wooden staircase, cringing at the raucous creaks provoked by my misplaced steps, and scolding myself for failing to recollect the proper foot placement necessary for a stealthy ascent. Assuming that the obnoxiously loud groans of the neglected planks had alerted my increasingly vigilant sweetheart of my impending arrival, I lost any hope of secretly smuggling my explosives out to my office on the shore-exposed balcony. Acknowledging the futility of such an attempt, I resigned to immediately admit my guilt and manfully accept the consequences. Mickey was sprawled out on the bed and entranced by the sappy banality of a Thai soap opera when I pushed open the door and said, "Hey there, Mickey!"

"Hello, daaarling! Ooh! You catch too much fish!"

"Uummm … no. We don't catch *any* fish! But coming back, we stopped at the market."

"Really? What you buy for me?" she exclaimed, bolting upright.

"Something really cool! You'll love it!" I answered, grinning sardonically and offering her a package of what I call Sky-Screamer Double-Loaded Rockets.

That was my first (of many) encounters with Mickey's infamous "hatchet-faced glare." This look was always accompanied by a contemptuous "humph!" and a sullen turning away, followed by an indeterminate (depending on the infraction) time period of the "cold-shoulder treatment." But considering there were no punches thrown, nor missiles launched in my direction, I was content with her reaction and excused myself.

Once outside, I carefully weather-proofed and stowed my arsenal, fired up the CD player, mixed up a whiskey and cola, and stretched out for some

late-afternoon tanning. I reassured myself with the thought, "She'll be fine
…. I just have to wait her out!" but it was a mere twenty minutes later that
the financial punishment for my crime was handed down.

"Maaark," she called from inside. "Mark! I must have 1,000 baht to go
buy food!"

"But I already gave you 1,000 baht, and why do you need so much food?"
I pleaded.

"Five hundred baht for food—and 500 baht for *tip!*" she proclaimed.

The thinly-disguised menace of her tone left no room for negotiation, so
I peeled off another 1,000 baht note, paid my fine, and went back to work in
earnest on the amber bottle of spirits resting at my feet. By the time Mickey
returned, carrying two armloads of papaya, durian, and other mysterious
tropical fruit, I had replayed several times in my mind Rood's parting words
earlier that afternoon: "Mark, you must wait to shoot fireworks! Cannot shoot
fireworks here in Kamala!"

Try as I might, I was unable to find loopholes in his instructions, so I did
my best to ignore the ammunition cache that waited within arm's reach of
my lounge chair. Now and then, I stole a reconnaissance glance at the sliding
glass door, only to see that Mickey was still fully absorbed with her fruit
and mesmerized by the absurd plot-lines and maudlin histrionics of Thai
television. Obviously, I had yet to be pardoned.

***

Sometime later, the sun relaxed its oppressive grip on the afternoon and began
to ease itself downward in the hazy sky, a movement mirrored by the descent
of whiskey remaining in my bottle. As the searing white disc gradually slipped
closer to its appointment with the steely blue border of the sea, its progression
was accompanied by the slow transformation of Kamala Beach as she shed
daytime's drab outfit and began to dress in her more intriguing and seductive
evening gown.

This transition is first heralded by the exuberant shouts and wild laughter of
emancipated schoolchildren just released from the bonds of tedious authority
and obsolete teaching techniques of the K–12 public school that anchors the
southern stretch of beach road. Dressed sharply in the same pressed khaki
uniforms, and complacently wandering in clusters of frivolity, they flaunt their
liberty with the accidental harmony of unguarded laughter, as they meander

about the food carts and vendors camped on the sandy shoulder of twisting pavement. In response, those elderly guardians of subsistence commerce patiently chastise the mob of youth in subdued undertones, even as they slip treats (on the sly) to the favored ones. This lively soundtrack is soon joined by the whoops and forceful commands of high-strung shirtless teenagers, as they coordinate the removal of parasailing gear, gaudy speedboats, and flashy jet skis, pushing them onto the trailers of tricked-out pickup trucks that struggle with straining engines as they yank their cargo up the steep, brick boat ramp. Next, one can hear the sweet giggles and crass cackles of bar girls who tease and gossip, while fine-tuning their makeup under the nascent glow of neon lights adorning the porches of expat-owned bars. These one-pool-table dives blast the heavy bass and lively rhythms of Eminem and the Red Hot Chili Peppers upon the sea's freshening evening breeze. The slight gusts of salt-tinged air ease inland cooling off the early dinner crowd of tourists who babble to each other in their native tongues, while Nepalese tailors beckon them with smooth sales pitches.

Next, nature makes her contribution as a colony of frogs croaks forth from the stagnant brackish water of the beach's canals, while the crickets provide constant, piercing back-up vocals. Underneath it all, as soft and subtle as the rustling of dry leaves, the never-ending rhythm of the surf stokes the latent loneliness of untethered hearts. From the balcony, this soundtrack of sundown rises up from below and creates the ideal backdrop for the surreal visuals settling upon the scene, as second by second the dwindling daylight fades, rallies, and then fades again. The sun's last rays cast a fantastic, other-worldly glow about the common earth and paint the landscape with pastel, dream-like hues. Looking west over the water, one watches the last orange-smeared cloud wisps dissipate into the blue-black mystery of the Andaman horizon, while overhead the first pure pinpoints of stars pierce the overwhelming solitude of night sky with the intensity of lost lovers—a sight that unsettles the forever-wandering soul of a terrestrial nomad.

And when the spirit of this particular drifter is upset, it inevitably searches for a distraction ... and a fifth of Sang Som whiskey, a bit of rolled-up local herb, Van Halen's greatest hits, and $400-worth of Chinese pyrotechnics can make for one hell of a distraction!

So, disregarding the warnings of my friends, I began to unpack, examine, and inventory my arsenal, while plotting the logistics of a minor aerial assault.

As luck would have it, the balcony contained several potted plants: excellent launch pads if I desired to engage the heavy artillery. Of course, I had a few empty soda cans and liquor bottles for the small-arms fire. But from the start, my intent was just to launch a few bottle rockets and shoot off a couple of Roman candles—just a taste, a little something to drive away the forlorn feeling presently assailing my state of mind. It would be just a minor test launch. Afterward, I would spoil Mickey with a fine dinner out, relax with a nightcap, and then settle in for an early night. I wanted to be well rested for the planned boat ride to Koh Phi Phi the following morning.

Using the still-burning roach, I began to fire small rockets from a hand-held bottle, finessing a soft arc over the palm trees that buffered the beach from human development. As I admired the first few rounds, the glass door slid open, and I was slapped out of my revelry by the unmistakable, grating tone of northeast Thailand matriarchy.

"Mark! Mark! What you do? You play firework? Your friend tell you 'no,' but now you do! You must stop now!"

"Oh, hi, honey! What did you say? I can't hear you," I replied as I touched the roach's cherry to the twisted wicks of three whistling bottle rockets and then aimed the shot toward the breaking surf.

"Mark! You must not play firework!"

"Five minutes, Mickey, and then I stop, and we go eat."

"Humph!" she grunted, and began her hatchet face routine for the second time that day. "I go shower. When I finish, we go out!" she demanded and stormed back inside.

Just as the door closed, there arrived a completely unexpected development: at the far end of the beach, on the opposing curve of the bay's ellipse, I saw a streak of light and heard a piercing whistle and the "crack!" of an explosion.

"What the …?" I muttered incredulously. "I'll be damned if that isn't return fire!"

I quickly assembled and launched a return volley of upgraded weaponry, which boasted larger payloads and greater range, deciding to demonstrate early dominance over the western skies of Phuket. However, my unseen adversary was undaunted, and he returned the favor with an equal barrage from the north.

"So that's the way he wants it? Well, he gets it!" I announced, while assembling an even more powerful response.

And what began as a minor skirmish quickly escalated into a battle royale. Thunderous booms echoed over Kamala Bay, and spectacular blooms of sparks showered down in umbrellas of gold, red, and green.

The battle was still raging when I was interrupted by angry shouts from just below the balcony. From a tin-roofed hut, there emerged a sinewy, wild-eyed Thai man. He was gesticulating furiously with one arm while holding a baby in the other.

As he assaulted me verbally from below, Mickey stepped outside to interpret: "That man have family, and baby sleeping! Now you must stop firework!"

"Okay, honey. I come inside now," I muttered in resignation.

Chagrined, I shouted an apology down to that tattooed, amphetamine-addled wraith and then stepped inside to soothe my agitated Isan princess. But I would have to wait for her to finish her fourth shower of the day (showering, eating, and sleeping accounted for 95 percent of that lady's daily routine).

While biding my time within the confines of the hotel room, I was shocked by another salvo of mortars launched from the bay's northern expanse of beach.

"Son of a bitch!" I cried. "The son of a bitch can't abide by a ceasefire? All right ... well—!"

I bit my tongue and attempted to ignore my impudent adversary, until another round burst over the bay.

"Fuck this!" I railed, and with my gal still luxuriating in the shower, I bolted outside and went straight for the good stuff.

Determined to see an all-out victory, I furiously began to ignite the biggest pieces of ordnance: professional-grade fireworks designed for large-scale holiday displays. Directing fire to the northwest, I soon witnessed the night sky illuminated in blazing light as multiple explosions tore open the salty air and shocked the senses with the power of a blitzkrieg. And this time there was no retort: my enemy had been vanquished. And all was quiet on the northern front.

Yes, I had secured a hard-fought victory, but I had also unintentionally gained a new and far more dangerous enemy. The scrawny wild man had resurfaced below, and he was now having an absolute shit-fit. He was swearing and shouting threats at the same decibel level as the just concluded battle royale. There was no mistaking the intensity of rage pulsing through the veins of this indignant native.

Concluding that any attempt at diplomacy would be an exercise in futility, I couldn't resist remarking, "Wow, that dude's got a real short fuse!" as I shuffled back inside to find that the air conditioner was no longer needed.

The frozen gaze that greeted my entry signaled the coronation of my previously permissive lover. Mickey had become the Ice Queen. I knew she meant business when she declined dinner out, barely condescending to grace me with just a scrap of explanation. She now preferred to stay in, but she would be very supportive if I left on my own. Since my stock of whiskey was just as depleted as Mickey's store of patience, I bounced down those irksome steps, whacked my head on the same low-hanging lobby ceiling for the twenty-seventh time that decade, and slipped into the Lemon Tree Bar next door.

There I happened upon another Mickey: the bar manager, who was a former fling from a Phuket holiday two years prior. Now, this Mickey (for clarity's sake, I'll call her Mickey #1) was the classic "cool chick"—an unflappable, witty, and pragmatic businesswoman. We had enjoyed lively times together, and we might still have been linked romantically, if not for the unbearably discordant pitch of her voice. Unpleasant under the best of circumstances, when she became excited, the sound of her speech (in Thai or English) was downright intolerable. But we had remained friends, and as she poured me a generous shot of whiskey, she embarked on a frank—yet subtly sarcastic—interrogation concerning my new relationship.

As I danced around the barbs of her hooked questions, we were suddenly interrupted by uncivilized sounds of chaos coming from the street. Sensing trouble, Mickey #1 bolted from behind the bar and threaded her way through the crowd in an effort to resolve the unknown crisis before it could have a negative effect on her tip jar. Having had my share of drama for the night, I remained seated and happily Mickey-less for the moment. But it was a short moment, because Mickey #2 (my Ice Queen) suddenly arrived on the scene. She was shaking, scared, and shedding guileless tears.

"Hey—hey, Mickey. What's the matter?"

"Oh, Maaark! That crazy man! Outside now—say he want to kill you dead!"

"What? You mean skeletor?"

"Not funny, Mark! You must come back to room! Now!"

"I wish you would make up your mind about having me around, Mickey. Besides, if he's outside, I should probably just stay here."

Just then, Mickey #1 returned to the scene looking upset, but she was composed enough to calmly declare: "Mark, there is a bad mafia man outside. He have gun and say he going to shoot stupid farang dead!"

"He can't settle for just shooting me wounded?"

"Not funny! I know this man. Really bad mafia man. Really crazy! Come on Mark! I take you out the back way. Then you go stay your room."

"Screw that! Mafia or not, he can't just go shooting tourists. Give me your phone."

Mickey #1 handed over her phone, and I hurriedly punched 1155 for the tourist police. Unable to connect with an English-speaking dispatcher, I had to pass the phone to Mickey #2, who explained the situation. After a terse (for Thais) verbal exchange, the tourist police were on their way to assist me—or so I thought! If I substitute the word *arrest* for the word *assist* in the previous sentence, the description of the event is factually correct. For when they promptly (for Thais) arrived on the scene, the gun-toting speed freak shouted out his version of events, while my pleas were ignored. The cops' assessment of the situation was soon made clear: I was handcuffed, then tossed into the back of a police car and carted off to confinement.

***

It is absurdities such as this botched effort that have spawned the sarcasm often attached to the catchphrase, "Amazing Thailand." To state the case plainly, here was a dude undoubtedly sporting a criminal history, obviously in the throes of a dangerous drug addiction, brandishing a loaded firearm in public, and endangering innocent lives. Yet I was the party assumed guilty and hauled off to the hoosegow. The situation was as absurd as it was unnecessary, but it also proved to be a useful experience in that it prepared me for several future interactions with various ranks of the Royal Thai Police. These future encounters would leave me not just unimpressed, but downright cynical regarding Thai law enforcement. However, this story concludes with a resounding endorsement of the Thai police entrusted with the protection of that placid community, an endorsement only made possible by the crafty political maneuvers and unfailing friendship of my holiday guardian.

The Kamala Beach jail is not a facility bustling with activity. Just as the town's personality exudes mellow, the criminal element is just as unassuming, if not downright nonexistent. In fact, I had the entire cavernous holding cell all to myself, except for a dozen or so huge mutant cockroaches. I have had worse cellmates, but I really did want company just then. Due to the generosity of the night guard, I was provided with a 16-once bottle of water (which I utilized as a missile defense), and I was able to engage in another battle. While boisterously singing the unofficial Thai national anthem (the Eagles' "Hotel California"), I soon routed the field: the stone floor was littered with smashed cockroach corpses. But the victory was soon followed by a stale peace, boredom, and the first faint thuds of an emerging headache. Worst of all, I had no companionship. Take it all around, I preferred the lockup conditions down Mexico way. At least in Puerto Penasco, I'd had plenty of the fear-induced adrenaline that is the natural consequence of being alone and surrounded by the contemptuous glares of a couple dozen depraved banditos and tattoo-faced cholos. I even had food, after trading my polo shirt for a plate of tortillas.

While reflecting on this previous clash with Third World authority, I was surprised to hear the soft patter of footsteps outside the cell—and even more surprised to see the security door slide open. I was then left bewildered upon seeing a distinguished Thai gentleman, in sweat pants and slippers, stroll in with a casual but undisputed air of authority. Putting his hands together and with a slight bow, he greeted me: "Sawadee Khap."

I was clueless to the man's identity, but I greeted him in kind. In a state of confusion, I slowly tried to form my question, but he cut me off with a chuckle while explaining: "I am Rood's older brother. My name is Yose, and I am the commander of the police here in Kamala."

Aha! Wow! Just when I was beginning to cave into a hungover despondency, my resourceful buddy came through once again—and with style too! This was a fine surprise; my man's older brother was the big boss of police. Rood was leading me to believe that he had more tricks up his sleeve than even myself.

Humbled, I respectfully said, "I'm so sorry, Yose."

"That's okay. It was just a misunderstanding. Let's go. No pay money, no court, no judge, and no come back."

"Well, that's awesome, sir! Thank you so much!"

And with a shit-eating grin, I strolled out of the Kamala slammer with the big boss at my side.

As we hopped in his car, he handed me his mobile, and on the line was my old pal who made a half-hearted attempt at a scolding, before throwing in the towel with resigned laughter.

"Are you still going to Koh Phi Phi tomorrow?"

"Yep, but you're off the hook for driving us to the pier. I'll get a cab. Get some sleep. Thanks again, brother. See you in a couple of weeks."

And *that* should be the end of the story. But because I am as stubborn as I am careless, I insisted on having the last word. I just *had* to play that last trick still up my sleeve.

***

After Yose cordially dropped me off, I bounced back up those same creaking hotel stairs to the room where I was greeted by a stern look and a passionate embrace from my happily vexed Isan angel. I popped open a celebratory bottle, packed up all of our belongings down to the last toothbrush, arranged a taxi for 7 a.m. sharp, and retired out to the balcony with the bottle of hangover-killer to eagerly wait for sunrise, while staring with sinister intent upon the beach below.

Just as the first soft flares of light began to materialize above the jungle-choked inland mountains, I took a final swig of firewater, gently shook Mickey's shoulders until her eyes flashed consciousness, and then whispered, "Mickey, please get up now. We leave exactly at seven sharp. Be ready."

She drowsily started to speak, "Mark, where you go?"

But I was halfway out that door, and before she finished, I was already gone, with my backpack barely disguising the awkward bulge of an eighty-round octagonal ordinance, this piece being sometimes referred to as the MOAF (Mother Of All Fireworks). Coming out of the hotel, I cut left, walked purposefully back down the town's main drag, cut left again at the Children's Park, and slipped stealthily through the shadows of palm trees. While crouching down, I crab-walked over the white concrete bridge that spanned a wide tidal stream, and after stepping over deep drifts of sand, I reached the stone seawall which ran just underneath—and provided cover from—several beachfront structures. Among them were my hotel and a few tin-roofed domiciles of local citizens. Digging in, I improvised a sand launchpad, wedged in the artillery piece, and concentrated on deep breathing until my watch showed 6:55 a.m.

And then, under the slanting morning sun, I lit the fuse of the MOAF, watched the powder sizzle until I was confident that the fuse would burn to its destination, and then, turning back toward the bridge, I hauled ass, retracing my route back to the rally point. By the time I had gotten halfway over the bridge, the peace of a listless Andaman Sea morning was shattered in the explosions and screams of a devastating barrage of rockets and mortars, with sparks shimmering and arcing across the sky, while deep booms and piercing cracks thundered and echoed down, over, and all around the bay. The highest concentration of furious sound and light was directly above the abode of my nemesis: a scrawny societal menace who was now reaping the rewards of rapscallion's revenge.

I didn't sprint, but I certainly fast-walked it back through town. I gave a thumbs-up to the taxi driver idling in front of our hotel, bounded back up the stairway, and issued quick instructions to my confused companion. For good or bad, this young woman had gambled when she placed her future in my hands. Time would tell … later. Now was the time for clearing out. I slung our luggage over my shoulders, gave Mickey a sly smile, and quoting a famous character from a famous Western, announced, "Darling, I calculate that's the end of this town."

And out the door we went.

CHAPTER 7

GAMBLING WITH GUNS (2004–2010)

It takes two to get one in trouble.

—MAE WEST

In the previous stories, I ran into quite a lot of trouble that resulted from a combination of my overly trusting nature, carelessness, and an inordinate number of unlucky encounters with unsavory characters. At times, my freewill and the forces of Fate interacted harmoniously, but they more often seemed to be at odds. In retrospect, I picture the dynamics of this mysterious relationship as I imagine an intricate cloth pattern being created by two weavers working in accidental and reluctant collaboration. The pattern I discern is one of right angles, long and short corridors, a few openings, and a bunch of dead-ends: my personal history (particularly in Thailand) was an odyssey through this ever-changing pattern, a maze loaded with trouble. I narrowly escaped a few tight spots through quick thinking and good fortune. Through luck alone, I was not among the fatalities when the 2004 tsunamis slammed into Koh Phi Phi at an hour when I typically would have been sound asleep on the beach. A few times my luck held up just long enough for me to escape the labyrinth in Thailand, but then it abandoned me immediately upon my journey home. In the following story, Fate ensures me a lifetime of trouble by setting up a chance meeting with a fellow problem child, and my own carelessness lands me in the unemployment line.

In order to explain the circumstances of this tale (and a few others in this collection), I must necessarily introduce another character—a fellow hell-raiser and kindred spirit, Dr. J. McIntyre. To be clear, "Mac" is not an actual doctor, but he is a trained and certified member of the medical profession (so he affirms, and I mostly believe). At any rate, he has proven himself with sound medical advice and care over the years, and he has even demonstrated his skills on himself after various mishaps (mostly related to fireworks). However, his greatest talent is an amazing creativity mixed with fearlessness in the art of pulling pranks, in almost any situation and without prejudice. And to give credit (and blame) where it is due, I'll admit now that without his inspiration, this book would not be possible.

On Koh Phi Phi sometime in September 2004, after pulling an all-nighter at a local beach bar, I was celebrating the sunrise on Loh Dalum bay by launching bottle rockets from my balcony. A few Thai teenagers raking rubbish off the beach represented the only sign of human activity. Because of a worldwide prohibition against using industrious youth as objects of target practice, I looked about elsewhere until I sighted a strange shape approaching from the hazy white glare of sun-reflected sand. The figure became more defined as it advanced, and I soon discerned red hair and a white tank top exposing broad, freckled shoulders that supported a light blue guitar, which was being strummed none too delicately. The twang of the guitar was accompanied by an indelicate voice singing an indelicate song. The absurd lyrics detailing the proclivities of a cross dressing lumberjack seemed even more ludicrous in the cadence of a thick Dublin accent.

"Monte Python's 'Lumberjack Song.' It looks like we have a joker on our hands," I announced to the empty bar chairs below my perch.

I waited until the ginger troubadour was within range and then launched a succession of bottle rockets above and around the animated athlete as he dodged and danced forward. Within seconds, he was just below my hiding spot.

"Fireworks are your specialty, mate? Good to know," he yelled.

From my vine-shrouded position, I hastily dropped a water balloon, which exploded at his feet.

"I specialize in fire—and water!" I boasted.

He burst into an appreciative laugh accompanied by the flash of merrily mischievous eyes (the sort of look that promises trouble, then reliably delivers a double dose of it).

"Got any ganja, mate?" he called.

"Funny you should ask. I was just ready to toke on a number. Hang on. I'll let you in."

Such was the genesis of a scandal-plagued, irreverent, but rock-solid and lifelong friendship.

During that first morning palaver, Mac and I got acquainted out on the palm- and pine-shaded balcony. My second-floor porch was free from the haze of the withering sun, but it was infested with the haze of marijuana smoke. Between laughs, I learned that Mac was an itinerant medical practitioner from Ireland intent on settling Down Under (although he seemed to be taking his sweet time getting there). I remarked that an ex-criminal colony seemed appropriate for his kind. When I explained that I was a commercial fisherman on the Bering Sea of Alaska, he commented that a self-imposed isolation was probably welcomed by the rest of my countrymen. It turned out that Mac was also on Phi Phi for the long haul and was staying in the village. Although he had already attached himself to a very unfortunate Thai lady, she had just recently returned to her hometown in the southernmost province of the country. This left Mac unsupervised—and the rest of the island's population at his mercy. We spent many evenings—which often turned into mornings—on the beach at Hippies Bar where the ebullient Irishman entertained with his guitar, card tricks, magic shows, and assorted pranks. I mostly just watched and learned.

***

Although I managed to plan and execute a few decent gags that first holiday with Mac, I was still the apprentice. It was not until three years later that I met up with him again for my second semester at Trickster University. After the infamous fireworks fiasco on Kamala Beach and a bittersweet visit to Koh Phi Phi, I was dragging a now battle-hardened Mickey to her toughest test of the '07 trip. It was Mac's choice to rendezvous in the Thai coastal town of Ao Nang. I wasn't thrilled to be so close to the Krabi town docks, which might still be the haunt of that vaguely nefarious phantom whom I had struggled to shake from my tail and my imagination. But it had been three years since I escaped Long, and this time I had back-up in the form of Mac, who met us for drinks in the darkened bar of the guesthouse.

After three years, my always jolly friend had finally forgiven me for supergluing everything (including the shower head) in his apartment on Phi

Phi the night before my homeward departure. After a couple rounds, we moved the reunion party to my room, where we traded more solo stories of juvenile mischief. Mac laughed with genuine approval when Mickey burst into outraged hysterics upon discovering the rubber snake I had left curled inside the toilet bowl of the bathroom. And after I had related my tale of war-torn skies, incarceration, and revenge on Kamala Beach, Mac realized I was prepared to keep up with his shenanigans this year.

The next afternoon, I faked a stomach ache, and while Mac and Mickey were out at lunch, I took a peek at the professional prankster's party suitcase. Constituting over half of his luggage was an extensive stash of costumes and props for practical jokes. As I looked through the merchandise, inspiration struck; I stripped down to my boxers, put on the adult diaper, laid a sheet and pillow on the porch lounge chair, rigged one end of his IV kit to a can of Heineken and the other to my arm, then laid back and placed a call.

"Hey, man … I'm sorry … could you please hurry back? I've taken a turn for the worse—*OUHGGHH!*—seriously, I feel like I'm gonna die!"

Five minutes later, my friends were rushing up the steps carrying half of their lunch in a takeaway bag, only to find me groaning, pointing at the Heineken, and begging Mickey to hurry to the refrigerator because my "IV" was empty.

"Well played, mate!" Mac shouted between laughs, and he was even more thrilled when I agreed to tag along on his pilgrimage to Hat Yai.

This midsize town is located near the border with Malaysia in the deep south of Thailand, and its location provided Mac with two motives for the trip. The primary purpose was logistical. Because his visa was set to expire, Mac needed to exit and then reenter Thailand in order to qualify for a thirty-day extension.

The secondary motive was personal. His ex-girlfriend, Jan, lived in that area, and Mac had made plans for a brief visit with the young lady. I believe he was seeking "closure" for a relationship that had ended badly. At least, it had ended badly for *him*. In my view, Jan should have been thanking her lucky stars; she had been pardoned from what could have been a life sentence at the side of an Irish rogue. At any rate, Mac could hardly harbor ill will toward his ex-flame. His relationship with Jan was a primary factor behind Mac's continued existence on Earth. My buddy acknowledges *his* gratitude to those fickle and often unfair Fates: the reason he had been absent from Koh Phi

Phi on that tragic day in December 2004 was his spontaneous decision to make a weekend trip to Hat Yai for a romantic Christmas rendezvous with Jan. Freewill and Fate can take a backseat when a wildcard force like Love is added to the mix ….

Because it was just a quick jaunt to the border, Mac intended to grab a noon taxi to the immigration checkpoint, obtain another thirty-day visa, and be back for his dinner date with Jan. Mickey and I were going out to dinner as well; I was going to spoil my girl tonight as appreciation for her perseverance and patience these past weeks (while establishing goodwill for future foul-ups). As Mickey showered, I scampered off to the lobby for an impromptu meeting with the housekeeping staff. After bribing them handsomely, I gave strict instructions that the *dang* (red) haired farang must have his room cleaned every morning at 8:00 a.m. sharp. No exceptions! Just like me, Mac considered late-morning sleep a sacred right.

During dinner, I recognized there was a much different vibe in Hat Yai than I had experienced elsewhere in Thailand. Here, the engaging hospitality typical of the Thai people was non-existent. This was probably because the deep south of Thailand was mired in the civil unrest of a separatist campaign. This movement had started sixty years prior, when ethnic Malays (the majority in Thailand's three southernmost provinces) demanded self-rule. After 2001, this ethnic struggle had drastically morphed into a violent insurgency based on religious extremism. Radical Islamists had taken over the campaign and were wreaking havoc (between 2004 and 2015, over 6,500 people were killed and 12,000 had been wounded as a result of the conflict). This situation probably explained why the folks of the deep south regarded foreigners with either watchful distrust or condescending disinterest, often accompanied by a thinly disguised dislike. Hat Yai was not the ideal location for juvenile antics.

However, when Mac later discovered that I was behind three consecutive mornings of early wake-ups from the cleaning crew, and after a few rounds at the local bar, he challenged me to a duel. He even produced two snub-nosed cap guns from his pack. I had no choice but to defend my honor, and out to the street we stumbled, stood back-to-back, marched off ten paces, and then turned while simultaneously shooting. I was clipped in the shoulder, while my rival fell to the ground with a thigh shot. As a group of locals looked on contemptuously, we called a gentleman's truce, shook hands, and made for another tavern in search of a less-hostile audience. But the crowd in the karaoke bar we found was just as sullen, glaring at us in angry disgust as we downed shots and played Russian roulette at our corner table (a contest won by Mac three to one). Eventually, we became aware of the general animosity and called it a night, deciding that the deep south was just too uncultured for our Western brand of humor. The following morning, we jumped on the first train north.

I relate the Hat Yai foolishness because the gun play gave me inspiration in dealing with my usual enemies on the streets of Bangkok, the sinister stray dogs that lay about the streets in daytime but roam in dangerous packs after sunset. I do not exaggerate. In one panic-inducing scene, I was lost in a dark network of narrow alleys—with no escape route—as a dozen of the malicious mutts closed in on me. It was only by drawing down and firing off two cap guns in succession that I managed to scare them off. Because of this experience, I have always harbored a weary contempt for all unclaimed canines in the Kingdom, and several times I have been forced to resort to phony guns, real bottle rockets, or even pepper spray to keep them at bay.

My one-man war amused Mac to no end, and it was his idea to take a more proactive approach to the contest, as we began a policy of targeting those street wolves with water balloons or eggs launched from the balconies of our habitual hideout, the Watana Hotel in Bangkok's Ratchada neighborhood. Mac also introduced psyops to the campaign by using a high-powered laser to confound and harass the scabby hounds that hunted about the nearby streets and alleys.

Because these personal safety protocols had been routine for years, it did not seem particularly strange when, after a 2010 Songkran Festival reunion in Bangkok, Mac presented me with a parting gift of matching Yosemite Sam-style, long-barreled cap pistols. Besides the fine craftsmanship, their absurd size was spectacular, and I was extremely gratified by Mac's parting present. It was imperative that I transport the artificial artillery back home, even if I had no immediate use for shooting irons. At least this time, I had the common sense to pack my bags with care.

In a style fitting previous return trips, my itinerary left no room for error; I was to arrive in Seattle at 8:30 p.m. and leave Seattle at 6:00 a.m. the next day in order to fly to Dutch Harbor, Alaska, where a longline fishing boat was already awaiting my arrival. Apparently, I had stashed my assorted contraband properly, as it was a hassle-free connection in Seoul, and other than the usual suspicious looks and pointless questions of customs agents, reentry into the United States was uneventful as well. By 10:00 p.m., I was lazing about my ground-floor hotel room, drinking beer, and pondering my drastic change of environment. This change would culminate the following afternoon, when I would tramp down the fuel dock to where the *F/V Endeavor* would be resting, its black hull an insignificance to the grandeur of the snow-drifted Aleutian Mountains. I visualized slinging my seabags over the boat's rusted railings onto the slime-crusted grating of the hauling station, leaping over, and entering the boat's house—where I would be wrenched back into reality by the thick, blended odor of diesel fuel and dead fish. The first whiff of that unmistakable aroma always seemed to mark the official crossing of the dividing line between two alternative existences.

For now, I thought, "Deal with tomorrow when it comes. You know it's going to suck, but don't let it suck twice by thinking about it now."

In search of a distraction, I crossed over International Boulevard to the low-rent Silver Dollar Casino for a stiff drink and the steak and eggs special, thinking I could still squeeze in five hours of sleep before the next day's agonizing journey north.

***

I'm not sure why I decided to slide those long-barreled pistols into my jacket pockets on my way out the door …. Perhaps I wanted just one more playful moment, a joke with the friendly bartender, before enduring two or three months of perpetual drudgery. Rushing out (and forgetting to close the window), I bolted across the street, ducked out of the Seattle drizzle, fist-bumped the familiar Samoan bouncer, and strolled to the casino's bar, where Carlos was dishing drinks to the skeleton crew of customers

"Que pasa?" he greeted me with a smile.

"Nada mucho. Trabajo mañana."

"Going back to Alaska, huh? What do you want?"

"Absolute and ginger ale, and the steak and eggs special."

As Carlos walked off to the kitchen, I nonchalantly placed my pistols up on the bar, mimicking those Westerns in which cowboys must surrender their firearms when entering a saloon. Carlos returned with my drink. I sipped it while watching the action at the blackjack tables on the far side of the game room, and periodically, I shifted my gaze to the baseball game on the TV above the bar. Shortly thereafter, I saw Carlos approach with my food order. But just before he set the plate down, my arms were yanked suddenly from behind and twisted until my wrists were at my tailbone, while simultaneously I was jerked up and out of my seat and thrust headfirst against the bar.

"Stay still," a harsh voice barked in my ear while handcuffs were clasped to my wrists. Carlos stared in disbelief while a cop read my Miranda rights, while shoving me toward the door and out into the parking lot.

"What the hell is going on?" I protested.

"You are under arrest for brandishing a weapon and disorderly conduct," was the cop's cold retort.

"What? Seriously? I wasn't doing anything!" I fumed.

"Just get in the car! You can tell the judge all about it."

And off I went to King County lockup that Thursday night on a phony charge. Because of an inflexible police officer and a cowardly card dealer (I found out later a blackjack dealer mistook me for an armed robber and called the cops), I spent all weekend in a cell attempting to sleep through the stress. But I kept waking up and worrying about a lost job (no way the boat would wait at the dock for three days) and hotel charges for three extra nights, along with that open window, which actually did result in my room being looted. Well, life definitely sucked, just not in the way that I had anticipated!

That miserable Monday morning brought the court appearance, which was just a video monitor affair with an unsympathetic, fifty-ish schoolmarm of a judge. Luckily, she had a small bit of sense and agreed with my logic that a cap gun is not a deadly weapon. Although the "Brandishing a Weapon" charge was dropped, I did rack up another Disorderly Conduct for my resume, a (still unpaid) $1,000 fine, and a good scolding from the moralistic magistrate. Because the arrest was utterly unwarranted, my frustration was simmering under my respectful demeanor, and when the judge asked if I had anything to say for myself, I forced an earnest expression, and in my most sincere tone, I said, "Just a question, your honor: when do I get my guns back?"

Unamused, she prissily admonished, "I suggest that you quit while you're ahead, Mr. Thumann."

I slunk out of jail a very poor man, without a job, and had no prospects. I mumbled to myself, "Quit while I'm ahead … ? I didn't get a chance to play! Hell, I didn't even get my steak!"

CHAPTER 8

PYTHON ON THE PARAPET (2009)

Love is blind; friendship
closes its eyes.

—Friedrich Nietzsche

When I reflect on the previous incident, I am struck by the extent to which minor events or choices can influence future situations. What if Mac had not stumbled upon those cap guns online? What if I had not unpacked them from my sea bag? What if that card dealer had not called the cops in knee-jerk fashion, or what if the cop who responded hadn't been a total dick? I know. I know. I chose to take the six shooters to the casino. But the fact remains that if all of these small factors had not fallen into line, I may still be working for that same company, or my present situation may be completely different because of other circumstances that would have materialized if I had not missed that boat. My point is that the pattern of the maze in one's life is in constant flux because of the interaction of Fate and free will. If the reader is still in doubt about my assertion, this next story provides another clear example. This tale takes place in the summer of 2009 (less than a year before the previous escapade), and its circumstances and results run parallel to the 2010 casino catastrophe.

***

To get a full picture of just how many seemingly minor events can influence a story's outcome, I must begin this tale in Anchorage, Alaska, where I had a connecting flight to Seattle after the always delightful departure flight out of Dutch Harbor. At the time I was the factory foreman of a Bering Sea trawler, and I had enjoyed a very lucrative contract. But being the boss also came with additional obligations. In this case, I was charged with chaperoning a crew member with a broken foot back to Seattle. This was the reason that I was on the last flight off the island that day. It was also the reason why I, along with Dwight, missed the connecting flight to Seattle. This circumstance led us to sharing a hotel room in downtown Anchorage, and consequently it gave Dwight the opportunity to steal my wallet while I slept. Dwight was never heard from again, and I was left without bank cards. And because I had already purchased a non-refundable ticket, immediately after my arrival in Seattle, I departed for Bangkok with my passport but without debit or credit cards.

But this was no time to panic, and even if I had been tempted to get upset, I would have refused to give those Crazy Fates the satisfaction. So how does one spend most of the summer on remote Koh Phi Phi without an ATM card? The answer is a thing of beauty admired by many Bering Sea fisherman: the cash draw. In the Alaskan fishing industry, crew members often wait two to three months for final payment on their completed contract. The well-run companies alleviate the situation by allowing for a fisherman to draw cash from these future payments. I was fortunate because of two circumstances: the Subway restaurant closest to the corporate office was next to a Western Union, and the chief accountant was addicted to meatball subs. If I needed cash, I just called Frank, made my request, and then bit my tongue to keep from laughing, while he exclaimed in his thick Maine accent: "You already need money again? I just sent you $1,500 four days ago! What the hell are you doing over there in Thailand? Well, I guess I can send it to you at lunchtime. How much do you need?"

This was the logistical situation of my finances when I finally freed myself from the laid-back life of Koh Phi Phi in late August. I was on my way to rendezvous with Mac for a two-week blowout in Bangkok before my scheduled return to Alaska. As usual, Mac had come prepared with plenty of costumes and prank toys for wild times on Khao San Road and the various entertainment venues of Bangkok. One night out on the town turned into a surreal experience that lasted well into the next morning.

***

I—along with my Irish wingman—had been prowling about the late-night clubs of Sukhumvit, and at our last stop, I had been foolish enough to leave my drink unattended in the vicinity of assorted ladyboys. Several members of Thailand's transgender crowd (I know now) are infamous for playing predatory tricks, such as slipping drugs into foreigners' drinks. And that evening I was an apparent victim of that sly maneuver, because I was quickly under the influence of a substance with potent psychedelic effects. The hallucinations were definitely not the result of a few vodkas with Red Bull. This was pure carelessness on my part, as I had been forced to basically carry Mac home just the night before (for the same reason and from the same club). The difference was that while Mac was incapable of rational thought (more so than usual, I mean) and barely possessed any motor skills, I was able to walk under my own power, and I felt absolutely euphoric (thanks anonymous lady boy!). I was so energized that I did not get back to the hotel until after the searing glare of sunrise had morphed into the sauna of midmorning. And while smoking out on the balcony, I watched a wonderfully weird morning unfold on the street several stories below. As I scanned the surrounding area, I happened to notice that, just across the street, on the rooftop of the Coca Cabana massage parlor, there was an enormous black python writhing along the parapet.

This was astounding! I knew Thailand (and especially the capital city) was full of all kinds of magic and assorted weirdness—but wow! And then I thought, "Do they know it's there? Is it a pet? … If not, I should go warn them!"

Being a concerned global citizen, I decided to do just that. Upon entering and bypassing the reception desk, I was greeted by the sight of a glass partition; behind the glass, several ladies were elegantly arranged on a three-tiered seating area, primping, teasing their hair, and touching up lipstick with hand-held mirrors. It was 10 a.m., and beautiful women were on display in order to allow potential customers to assess their skill level in the ancient art of Thai massage.

"There is a reason the country is called 'Amazing Thailand,'" I mused.

However, I was immune from distraction: I had a duty to investigate this mystery of a serpent with a rooftop abode. So I went to the long, brass-railed bar and respectfully asked to see the manager. Shortly thereafter, I was greeted by an impeccably dressed, perfectly groomed older Asian man.

"Hello, I am Mr. Han, the manager. Would you like to have a look at the ladies?" he inquired politely.

"Hello, sir. No, thank you. I am here about the snake on your roof."

Raising his eyebrows in surprise, he asked, "What do you mean snake on the roof?"

"Sir, I'm staying on the eighth floor of the Watana Hotel. I was just looking down on your roof, and I saw a huge black snake up there—I think it's a python. Is it a pet or something?"

Frowning skeptically, he stammered, "Umm ... I am ... sorry, but you are mistaken."

Smiling conspiratorially, I half whispered, "Oh, don't worry. I'm not a cop. You can tell me. I won't turn you in."

He glanced around as if looking for the hidden camera of a TV comedy show, and then he said, "Sir, I am certain there is not a snake on our roof."

But I jumped in excitedly, "I saw it! It must have slipped away from captivity somewhere, and it somehow managed to slither up to your roof."

Now the gentleman fell into laughter. "No, impossible!"

I protested, "But can I just go up there and look? Just to make sure?"

"I'm sorry. Cannot. But if you want to look at something beautiful ...." he offered as he waved his hand toward the eye candy behind the plexiglass.

I dejectedly grumbled, "No, thanks, sir, but I'll keep an eye on that snake for you—"

He then produced his business card and said, "When you change your mind, I'll give you a very good price—the best girl in the house!"

"Thank you, sir," I admitted in defeat, and I then hurried off to get another glimpse of the fascinating creature before "they" could put him back in his hiding place.

Once back to my vantage point, I confirmed that the python was still slithering along the far wall of the parapet, but it also seemed to be flopping wildly about, as a freshly landed fish slaps the sides of a boat's steel hull. I then shifted my gaze straight down, and I was completely astonished to see two monkeys swinging from the cables drooped between the power poles lining the street. They seemed to be racing, like two kids on a jungle gym. Next, the twin acrobats swung their legs skyward as if to send me a signal—which they were. They were signaling that I needed to take a nap.

I awoke from a black, dreamless sleep to a fist pounding on the door, and a pounding inside my head. My brain groped about the dark, searching for a map back to reality. Of course, the knocking turned out to be Mac, lugging two bottles of booze and mixer, while announcing that it was happy hour. *Rise and shine!* I had no choice in the matter; I had tortured his hangovers in the same way, and these holidays were not for the faint-hearted or the pain-intolerant. By the second cocktail, Mac had finished relating the embarrassing details of my previous night's experience, and I finally had a chance to boast: I had spotted a python on top of the massage parlor's roof! Somewhere in the timeline of our association, I must have lost some credibility with Mac, because he immediately poked his head outside to look out across the rooftops.

"Hee, hee, hee, you puppet! That's not a snake. It's just a big drainage pipe!"

Alright, at least I was making progress on the road back to reality.

"Seriously? Shit! I swear that thing was slithering around like a huge snake!"

"Oh, I bet it was, mate!" Mac quipped.

I decided not to mention anything about the monkeys ….

And I also decided to take a quick shower, get respectably dressed up, make a humble pilgrimage across the street to apologize to the good-natured Mr. Han, and invite the gentleman to a drink. He graciously accepted, we both had a good laugh, and a tradition was born: every return trip to Bangkok, just after checking in, I visit Mr. Han and buy him a drink. And every time he gives me his best sales pitch, which I decline (almost) every time.

***

After a few more nights of mayhem with Mac, it was finally time to return to responsibility. As I packed my bags, Mac arrived at my room to give me another one of his parting presents. This one was a baseball cap with a large, plastic fist mounted on the lid. Attached to the fist was a section of rubber tubing, which was connected to a rubber air bladder. When the bladder was squeezed, the air pressure would surge up through the hose to the fist, which immediately extended its middle finger in a rebellious salute. Brilliant! That Irish rascal always had the best toys!

Once again, my flight schedule back to Alaska left no time to spare. After my Seattle arrival, I had a few hours at the hotel before heading back to the airport for a 6:00 a.m. northbound departure. And after a couple of ritual pre-flight cocktails, I was back inside SeaTac international airport. Unfortunately, I ran into a complication at the check-in station: the airlines had just instituted a policy of charging $30 for each check-in bag. Planning for a long contract, I had two bags for check-in but just $15 in cash in my possession. And (because of that thieving Dwight) I had no bank cards to access my funds or to charge the baggage fee. Unfortunately, the ticketing agent with Alaska Airlines was neither understanding nor helpful. We had a heated discussion as a line of vocally impatient customers behind me grew in size and outward annoyance. After another sarcastic comment from the lady behind the counter, I just couldn't resist—I squeezed the rubber air bladder (of course, I was wearing my new hat!), and the middle finger rose up in a sarcastic salute.

The ticketing agent seemed unfazed, saying she would phone a supervisor who could assist me. Satisfied, I stood to the side to wait. After just a couple of minutes, I suddenly had my arms grabbed from behind and my wrists cuffed behind my back. The airport bomb squad had arrived! Luckily, I was not arrested. But I was escorted off the premises and given a twenty-four-hour ban from airport property. That worked out perfectly, as it was just enough time to miss whatever chance I had returning to work on time. And once again I was given my walking papers from my place of employment, and a whole new pattern of the maze was presented in front of me—although this one did not have nearly as many options as before.

CHAPTER 9

BUMMED IN BEIJING (2014)

Don't carry a gun. It's nice to have
them close by, but don't carry them.
You might get arrested.

—JOHN GOTTI

No doubt Alaska Airlines has its share of customer service failures, and such rudeness invariably brings out the worst in me. But as awful as domestic airlines can be to deal with, they are amateurs in comparison to the governmental agencies in the airports of foreign countries. And one way to aggressively pursue the wrath of these authorities is to gratuitously taunt the totalitarian officers of airport security. These fellows aren't used to any feedback, and they are impervious to attempts at humor.

June was closing in on July back in 2014 when I once again defied the odds to make a narrow escape from the pitfalls of the Thai fun house, only to land in hot water just after departure. But at least I acquired another travel rule from this uncomfortable experience: don't ever book an airline reservation if the connecting flight must be picked up within the borders of mainland China.

It was another steamy Bangkok afternoon, and I lacked the patience to wait until the 5:00 p.m. resumption of alcohol sales at 7-Eleven, so I hiked across the overpass that crosses Ratchada Road at Soi 17. I had inside knowledge of a small general store that typically disregarded the Thai government's heavy-handed regulations. In my right hand was a mini Frisbee, and I tossed it in the air as I walked along the final stretch of sidewalk. I made one careless throw, and the Frisbee rolled sideways to a motorcycle-taxi stand, where it came to rest on the nose of one of Bangkok's surliest denizens: a scrawny, mangy, and shiftless stray dog. As I bent down to retrieve the toy, this cranky and possibly rabid cur jumped up and clamped its jaws onto my unsuspecting thumb. The mean little monster hung in midair as I shouted and attempted to shake myself free. This development was of great amusement to another group of Bangkok residents, the skinny, young troublemakers who work ostensibly as motorcycle-taxi drivers.

After disengaging myself and throwing an off-kilter kick that caught only air, I stomped off with blood pouring out of my thumb. Being an expert in the art of self-medication, I marched straight to a pharmacy and loaded up on antibiotic cream, bandages, and painkillers. Checking out, I glanced down at the glass counter top and was surprised to see two items that seemed quite out of place in a drug store: a plastic air pistol and a box of pellets the size of mini breath mints. Those Crazy Fates were obviously sending me a sign in order to assist with navigation in this part of the maze. I bought the pistol, loaded it, stormed back to the taxi stand, and blasted off a dozen rounds into that ornery canine.

In actuality, the mutt had done me a favor. I had been dreading a return to the grind of Bering Sea fishing, and this new circumstance provided a temporary solution. After visiting the local medical clinic and slipping a 1,000 baht note into the grasping hands of a pliant physician, I was in possession of paperwork stating that I had contracted rabies. I faxed the report to another lifelong antagonist and source of aggravation: human resources. I say "lifelong" because, no matter which fishing company I graced with my employment, I had always maintained a dysfunctional relationship with those fussy ladies charged with the exasperating task of overseeing my travel arrangements/ predicaments to and from Alaska. Over the years, I had become infamous for being the culprit behind last-minute complications and/or misbehavior that resulted in undue stress for the HR gang. If traveling were a game show, my entrance into an airport would be that moment when the contestant spins the big blinking wheel and waits for the result.

Anyway, I was successful in *this* battle with HR, and I reaped the spoils of another two weeks in Bangkok, time I spent in pursuits rife with both frivolity and danger. However, those mishaps are for another chapter. The action in this tale did not transpire until I was homeward-bound. My connection was in the unfamiliar confines of Beijing Capital International Airport. The facility was China's largest air-travel hub, yet it was characterized by the most convoluted and confounding processes in the history of airline transfers. The nonsensical signage and deplorable rudeness of airport staff caused a frustration that could only be alleviated by paying close and constant attention to the duty-free bottle of Smirnoff in my backpack. Aggravation surged again when I realized that—in a masterstroke of efficiency—the airline had made it necessary to retrieve my check-in luggage from baggage claim and then endure the security screening one more time. Things did not go well.

I was just as startled as everyone else when my luggage tripped the alarm system of the x-ray machine. The bright red flashing lights and shrieks of sirens mobilized over a dozen members of airport security, police, military personnel, and, I think, somebody from the fire department. An investigation immediately commenced, and I became the center of attention of not only the official personnel, but also the hollow robotic platoon of Chinese citizen-subjects. Apparently, a situation where the rules have been broken was pure novelty to the cogs of an authoritarian machine. As the assortment of commie henchmen rummaged through my luggage, jabbering and arguing, I impudently chuckled and inwardly remarked, *These guys would be pissed if they knew I was having fun!*

Just then, one of the uniformed scavengers shouted as he stood up with my "Bangkok special" pellet gun in his grasp. The ensuing scene resembled a pitcher's mound conference, a palaver of excited hand gestures and urgent debate. I watched the proceedings with half-interested amusement while furtively nipping from the bottle in an effort to preserve my equanimity. Eventually, the cluster of authority reached a consensus and elected a lieutenant as the representative who would apprise me of the situation.

The tall, well-built, young man had a respectable command of the English language, and holding up the weapon he announced: "Mistah Tooman, this item is not permitted in this airport."

"Oh, really? Well, no worries, I was just leaving anyway."

"Ha ha! I'm afraid you misunderstand. You are free to proceed to your gate, but you cannot take the gun with you."

"Whoa—hang on. Let me show you something," I said, and quickly grabbing the gun, I turned it so the bottom of the pistol grip was exposed. "You see that? It says, "Made in China,"! I already paid you fuckers for it! It goes with me."

I swear on a stack of Bibles that I was just making a joke; however, the Chinese authorities did not view it that way. Not at all. And quicker than you can say "Chairman Mao," my wrists were once again behind my back and fastened with zip-tie restraints. I made a hurried plea for mercy: "Sir, I was only joking!"

"Not funny! Now we are going to the airport jail!" he growled.

At that moment, my composure morphed into careless rage, and I began to unleash a barrage of complaints and threats laden with f-bombs.

Halfway through the terminal, the lieutenant suddenly stopped and shouted, "If you say 'fuck' one more time, I'm going to shoot you!"

He pointed toward the gun in his holster.

"Do it. I don't give a fuck," I said in a resigned tone with my eyes glaring directly into his.

He dropped his gaze, took a deep breath, and muttered, "Let's go."

Either my tone or my look disarmed the guy, preventing a bad situation from escalating into a calamity.

So we marched on, past a thousand shocked and confused faces, until we were out the security door, across the expanse of asphalt, and finally confronted with a concrete bunker in the center of the parking lot. The jail. I was placed in holding a cell, and while the police processed the paperwork, I pondered the charge and worried away the minutes. With the hands of the wall clock appearing to accelerate, I became convinced that I would now miss my flight back to the States. But, thankfully, the lieutenant had calmed down considerably, and he even seemed conciliatory when he sat down next to me and explained my legal status. I could leave now with just a warning and still make my flight—if I signed the confession he had just authored. The original was written in Chinese, but there was also a version clumsily translated into choppy English. If I chose to endorse the document, I would basically be admitting to attempted espionage, attempt to instigate an insurrection, weapons charges, threatening an officer of the Communist Party, and a few other gratuitous falsehoods.

I signed it with my only regret being that I lost my copy of that farcical confession. It was a masterpiece of absurdity. However, even though I quickly returned to the check-in counter, I missed my flight. And although the airline set me up with a room at a fine hotel, the staff botched my wake-up call, and I missed the flight the next day. I was then informed that I had illegally overstayed my one-day visa: this infraction resulted in a $500 fine. With my funds exhausted, I resorted to calling the US Embassy, and those fine folk were able to coordinate a wiring of funds. (A warning note: good luck locating a Western Union in Beijing on a Sunday.) And after two more dismal days, I finally departed Beijing, lighter by one pellet gun—and heavier by a few ounces of humility.

CHAPTER 10

HAVING A RIOT AT A COUP (2014)

When the going gets weird,
the weird turn professional.

—HUNTER S. THOMPSON

In the spring of 2014, Thailand was in the midst of another political readjustment, which looked like it would once again result in a coup d'état. In most countries, the overthrow of an elected government would be considered an Earth-shattering event. But in the Kingdom, with several institutional power brokers (the military, the police, Bangkok elites, populist leaders, and the monarchy), whose interests are at times aligned and at other times in conflict, and who are constantly engaged in subterfuge and shifting alliances, a game of political musical chairs and its accompanying civic disorder are inevitable. And because of these frequent outbursts of civil unrest, authoritarian crackdowns and coups are to be expected two or three times a decade (I attended the last big blowout in 2010, but I missed the wild party of the Thaskin removal in 2006). And these periods of political chaos are a fantastic time to visit the Land of Smiles (and street fighting). First off, the flights are dirt cheap, and secondly, the social unrest provides great cover for personal shenanigans and public misdemeanors; the cops (theoretically) have other fish to fry. This is wonderful—unless you happen to be an unlucky fish.

In late April I was scheduled to reconnect with a certain J. McIntyre at the Watana Hotel—just clear of the hot spots of political havoc in Bangkok—for another round of holiday mayhem. Squeezed in among the "soapy" massage parlors on Soi 17 of Ratchada Road, our hideout was not only safe from civil unrest, it was also within an easy cab ride to either Sukhumvit or Khao San Road, two major destinations for the other kind of civil unrest: the drunken, fun kind. I was a day ahead of Mac in my arrival, so that first late afternoon, when Bangkok's scorching heat was sealed in by smoky haze, I braved the thirty-second walk across the street to the Coco Cabana massage parlor to see my old friend, Mr. Han. I entered the vast two-story complex and stepped into the cool, dimly lit foyer, which sported a plush 1970s lounge decor, and inquired of the reception staff if Mr. Han was available. The distinguished Chinese gentleman soon appeared in a sharp suit, bowed, and flashed the wide smile of a genial game show host.

I had my customary chat with the "Big Boss" of the Coco Cabana, then returned to my room for some quality sleep prior to the arrival of my Irish-turned-Aussie sidekick. This was a wise decision; sleep was not on the menu for much of that socially chaotic reunion. Up in room 811 that first evening, Mac and I "planned" (whatever *that* word means in the context of holiday hell-raising) our attack on a metropolis roiled by political turmoil so unstable that martial law would be instituted within days. Because of the layout of the current protests, the best landing zone looked to be Khao San Road, an infamous walking street bustling with Western tourists and the sly locals who barter with them and cater to their assorted desires. The tourists are predominately backpackers and Thailand novices, indulging in the "bucket list" aspects of the Thailand experience. These folks were easy targets for two merciless mercenaries well-prepared for combat clowning. Mac had already devised our disguises for that first night: he was fully suited up as the red Power Ranger, and I was dressed in full leprechaun attire, complete with shamrock-studded vest, lime top hat, and hermit beard. I raised concerns: perhaps we should be more low-key? But Mac prudently pointed out that owing to our reputation among the local ladies and street vendors on Khao San Road, if we should show up looking normal, they would be even more suspicious. Sound reasoning.

And Mac was right. The usual gang of tuk-tuk tour guides, bar hostesses, trinket salesmen, and various carneys of the Khao San crowd welcomed us with open arms and knowing grins. I had brought along a toy fishing rod-and-reel combo spooled up with dental floss, and I contented myself with flipping the "bait" (a packaged condom) in front of ladyboys patrolling the thoroughfare in search of frisky farang. Mac—looking more like a superhero devil—walked off from the patio of the beer garden in search of victims, which he soon found at a foot massage venue. I should explain here that one of the sillier promotions in Bangkok is an outdoor foot spa consisting of a two-foot-deep pool of water filled with minnow-sized suckers that nibble off the epidermis of the foot-sore travelers who dabble their feet in the water, while cooing and taking selfies during this quaintly exotic experience. In comparison to other sordid novelties (sex shows, etc.), this activity is a rather innocuous pastime. Relaxing as well … until someone arcs a World War II replica hand grenade into the pool of exposed fleshy feet of jabbering European globetrotters. Apparently, the American GI's answer to the "potato-masher" was still a well-remembered weapon among the German contingent because the language of the Rhineland was the loudest and most hysterical piercing the nightair as Mac hightailed it away from the angry mob.

I caught up with the culprit about a block away, and we laid low for a while at another outdoor drinking venue. But then I spotted a self-important looking chap wearing a flak jacket a few tables away.

"What's his deal you think?" I asked Mac.

"I don't think he's joking, mate. He is really serious with that outfit," answered the Ranger.

We queried our waitress, and she confirmed, "Oh, that farang? French man. Not nice man. He write for a newspaper. Say many bad things about Thai people!"

"He tip okay?" I asked.

"No—no tip. No tip!" she complained.

I looked at Mac: "Lock and load?"

He smirked. "The puppet is wearing a flak jacket miles away from the action and acting like he's in a foxhole. Hell yeah!"

So he handed our waitress his camera. It was time for a photo op. We pulled our pistols and went in for an "assassination photo." Nothing says poser-journalist like donning your flak jacket at a street party only to have two bozos pointing plastic pistols at your absurd oversized melon!

After that, Mac was in the mood for a dance club, but I was in the mood for weed and the comforts of my hotel room. Therefore, we parted ways, and at the end of the street I approached a tuk-tuk driver who was engaged in waving glossy flyers advertising depraved strip shows.

"Ladies? Ladies? You want ladies?" he crooned.

"No, man. I just want some ganja. Can do?"

"Yes, can do," he replied. "Come on."

I jumped in the back of his exhaust-spewing, go-kart-like contraption, and we sped off into the Siamese side streets. We arrived out in front of a ten-story apartment building where the driver announced, "3,000 baht. I get you the best ganja. And a lot also."

I said, "Cool. How long you'll be gone?"

"Just five minutes only," he answered, as I peeled off three 1,000-baht notes.

***

I sat back to wait. And wait. And wait. After two hours, it was time to face facts: he was not coming back. Dude rolled me. There was no doubt about it, and nothing left to do but sulk on home ... or get even, and hold my head high on the homeward trip. After a long reconnaissance look in every direction, I pulled out a tube of superglue and injected its contents into the ignition slot of the tourist transport. I took another look around, then pulled out my pocket knife and popped both rear tires for good measure, and then bolted down the street until I located a taxi. I rode home feeling content that I was even in the dirty lowdown tricks department.

***

The next afternoon, I was surprised when my wake-up call turned out to have the soft-spoken Mr. Han on the line, instead of the obnoxious rantings of a half-mad Dubliner. This was an unprecedented development. To my good fortune, it had come to pass that one of the bespectacled director's top talents was smitten by the tall American chatting with her boss the previous day. Mr. Han was quite fond of this young lady and passed along her name (Nami) and phone number along with his whole-hearted recommendation and blessings. I decided that I might have to squeeze in some real actual dating on this trip; Mac was always adept at flying solo, and Bangkok could probably use a break from double trouble.

So I acquired a girlfriend to help pass the time on recuperation nights, while Mac either rested or carried on the fight all by himself behind enemy lines. Of course, those nights (and some days) when we were both on duty were spent nibbling at the edges of authority. I think we can both take creative credit for the maneuver whereby we stalked opposite sides of Sukhumvit Road, dressed in suit jackets over crisp oxford shirts pinned with phony intel badges. We were armed with sophisticated (for us) walkie-talkies, which we used to carry on urgent yet imaginary battle communications—sometimes protesting, sometimes whispering, but mostly issuing desperate commands for make-believe air support while looking skyward and pointing in the direction of whichever area was deemed in need of missile-strikes. I found it most effective to call in the strikes with a haughty expression of supreme authority and sideways glances of disdain while passing police or military checkpoints. Although this technique worked out to hilarious effect in Thailand where the rank and file are mostly impotent without an immediate commanding officer present, I would not would recommend trying it out in any other strife-torn states of the world.

One additional note: an unforeseen bonus of the CIA dress ensemble was that it also proved effective for buying booze at 7-Eleven after the store's midnight sales cut-off point. Just when the clerk would direct our attention to the sign reading "No Alcohol Sales After Midnight," I would brush my sport coat to the side, revealing a bronze badge, and coolly declare, "It's okay. I'm an FBI boss. Listen, the boys need a drink after today's action. Don't let us down here."

Seventy percent of the time I would leave with a bottle of Smirnoff under my arm—along with a huge helping of joyful satisfaction. Even when the gambit failed, there was still the priceless befuddled facial expression of the confused clerk to stow away for later laughs.

But as May's last days passed away, democracy died in the humidity-choked streets, rigid curfews and internet censorship became the norm, and I found it less bothersome, less costly, and (I hate to say it) less risky to stay in with Nami. Life was less stressful amid the comforts of room service, air conditioning, and a dozen channels of the "same-same" Thai soap operas, which must be the worst opium of the people any nation ever dreamed up in the history of the world. This was a mildly better choice than braving (convoluted) street demonstrations, (real) fire bombings, and (understandably) humorless junta gunmen posted behind sandbags stacked at every strategic street corner.

One day, following an uneventful (for anyone not intimately involved) evening home, I had my first scare involving an MIA Dr. Mac. I had been calling both his mobile and room phone all day to no avail, and my concern grew as the hours passed. By 6:00 p.m. I was passed concerned and going on worried. By 6:30 p.m. I was interrogating the always-recalcitrant reception staff. I was ultimately relieved—if somewhat vexed—when at 6:45 p.m. the phone rang and it was a perfectly intact but exhausted Mac, who informed me that he was zonked from painkillers. He had been at the dentist all day.

"Mac, you didn't say anything about going to the dentist."

"I hadn't planned on it, but you see, this Thai bird spent the night—"

"Yeah?"

"Well, she was boring the piss out of me! I couldn't get her to crack a smile—worse, I couldn't get her to leave either, mate! She wouldn't take the hints ... all morning long, damn it!"

"Okay, so ...?"

"So I finally told her I had a dentist appointment scheduled for this afternoon, but I just made that up!"

"But why did you—"

"Well, she insisted on going with me, and so I went ahead and got a check-up. It turned out I needed two root canals, and she was still in the waiting area. So I figured I'd go ahead and get it done right then."

"Ha ha ha! She was so tedious that you'd rather have root canal surgery? Stop it! Ha ha ha!"

"Oh, piss off! Talk to you tomorrow!

Apparently, my fears that Mac was hurt or jammed up somewhere turned out to be (for the most part) unfounded.

***

Although it appeared that my usually reliable intuition was out of whack, in actuality, the alarm bell was not so much inaccurate as it was just premature. Because just two nights after Mac's narrow escape from hook-up hell, I was knocking on the entrance gate to dreamland—having concluded another untroubled evening of basking in Nami's sweet affections and endearing platitudes—when my mobile rang the bell of consciousness (and conscience).

I reluctantly grumbled a greeting into the receiver and was met by an outburst of vague information.

"Mate, I need help now! Bring an army if you have to! I'm in a bathroom stall, and there's like eight Thais that have me trapped here! They're going to kill me!"

I jumped straight up, and I was already hunting for shorts while asking "Okay, where exactly are you, buddy?"

"Khao San Road in the men's room of a bar—" he blurted, while simultaneously hushing his voice.

(A bar on Khao San Road? That was like somebody relaying their coordinates as a taco stand in Tijuana!)

"Mac, what's the name of the bar?" I shouted.

"I don't know! Fuck—I don't know!"

Suddenly, I heard a crash, scattered shouting, and the crack of his mobile hitting tile. There was no more time to wait on directions—only time to haul ass, and hope for the best! *Whoa, ease up Mark, go prepared!* I grabbed my backpack and stuffed it with my only available weapons: NATO-issued pepper spray, pocket knife, deck knife and belt, titanium flashlight, binoculars, and two empty SangSom bottles—just in case. With phone and wallet in hand, I yelled to Nami, "Call you later!" as she looked on with shocked and amazed eyes (it must have been quite a bombshell that the old man could move so quickly in an activity not related to last call!).

I flew through the Watana lobby, past the always-disapproving stares of the receptionist coven, and straight to my crew of juvenile delinquent motorcycle-taxi drivers across the street.

"Khao San Road now!" I shouted, and three of the boys were already jumping for their bikes.

But Ay was quickest, and before you could say "200 baht tip," we were flying through the backstreets and bouncing along the motocross course that is Bangkok's blacktop. I hung on tight while trying to focus my thoughts on the most likely bars or clubs to be holding Mac, while also keeping my brain waves away from the distraction of other less important subjects—such as my lack of Traveler's Health Insurance.

Luckily, of those crazy teens, Ay was the most dexterous driver, and also the smartest and most trustworthy. We jammed through curfew-empty streets and passed by bored and drowsy troops, until Ay dropped me off at the northernmost end of Khao San Road. My plan was to speed-walk up the thoroughfare while quizzing the closing staff if they had seen Mac (many knowing us both by sight and deed). I zigzagged my way up the street, weaving through late-night stragglers and prowling ladyboys, while shouting, "Mac!" and questioning any familiar faces.

No one had seen him.

Finally, I was facing the facade of the local Burger King. I had reached the southern end of the road.

I was about to reverse and make another pass when a gaudily decorated tuk-tuk cruised by, and upon spotting me, the driver's eyes flashed wide and furious. He slammed on his brakes and came to a smoke-screeching stop twenty yards away. I could see him reach down, and then his arm flew up with a flash of silver and black in his right hand.

Uh oh—dude's got a gun! And it's for me! I heard my own voice shouting inside my skull.

Yes, it was the previous week's weed dealer—the scammer who had rolled the wrong white man. He did not seem too happy about the street justice that I had rendered him. He slammed his ugly, yellow junker in reverse, but I was already hightailing it, feet flying and arms pumping, back down Khao San Road (and because only foot traffic was permitted, I had the advantage). Heart pounding and secreting a sheen of SangSom sweat, I realized that the dude would already be waiting for me at the far end of Khao San, so I cut a hard right onto one of the road's side alleys. These mini-sois are shoulder-width tight and make various twists and turns. Some have outlets, while some are dead ends. I was gambling on the former. But, hell, that sonofabitch probably already had a gang on foot scouring the area for me. This thought set my heart to "Bangkok kidnapping speed" as I ducked behind a blind cut in the alley, crouched down, took huge gulps of refuse-and-piss flavored alley air, and assessed the desperate dilemma.

Obviously, my hands-on, search-and-rescue activity would have to be cancelled. Besides, at this point, I would be more effective calling hospitals and police substations from the hotel. I decided to hunker down and prepare a defense, in case my adversaries approached from either end of the alley. I unpacked and placed my weapons in strategic locations about my ad hoc ambuscade. With my ears intently alert for the sounds of an approaching enemy, an empty whiskey bottle in my right hand, and the NATO mace in my left, I crouched, ready to spring and start swinging. After a few minutes, I heard the sound of Thai voices getting increasingly louder down the alley. Adrenaline began to pump overtime as the voices began to argue, but then the utterances got fainter until they were gone completely. I was inhaling huge gulps of the alleyway's foul fumes, while soaked in sweat so thick that I could have been resting inside a rain shower. I needed calm, so I chanced a smoke and a long pull from my silver hip flask.

After another quarter-hour, things were quiet, and I was calmer, but I wanted to assure myself that the crucial can of pepper spray was functional, so I sprayed just a tad toward the far wall. And I discovered a new travel rule: never spray mace in a windless, enclosed alley that possesses the dimensions of a Hobbit's house! I attempted to keep silent while coughing, sneezing, and crying until enough time passed that my respiratory system and vision were once again operational.

I decided to make a break for it. I crept down the passageway in the opposite direction of Khao San. My gamble paid off; the route egressed directly on to the next major street, where (even luckier) a metered taxi idled just twenty feet away. I dove in head first, issued directions, laid way back out of sight, and I was soon back in my room phoning every hospital and cop substation in that section of Bangkok, but nobody claimed a bruised middle-aged Irish maniac. The dispatcher at the substation closest to Khao San Road was memorably adamant in his denial. Discouraged and out of my mind with fear, I laid back to rest my brain, but I was startled back up thirty minutes later when my cell phone rang and it was Mac. He was at that same substation closest to Khao San Road. Lying bastards!

Mac gave me the rundown. He had been chatting up a gorgeous Thai lady, and she was very friendly to him in return. Mac was unaware of the other dynamics pertinent to his attempt at romance, mainly the eight young Thais sitting at the adjacent table. They were all off-duty cops, and the flirtatious vixen was engaged to one of them. And instead of accepting Mac's profuse apologies, the entire gang followed him into the restroom, trapped him, and then beat the holy crap out of him. They then arrested him and dropped him off at the substation, where he was worked over once more by night-duty cops intent on getting a piece of the action. Deflated and demoralized, Mac pressed me.

"Mark, they just want 3,000 baht, and then they will let me go—no court or anything."

"This is complete bullshit, Mac!"

"Mate, I'm begging you. I am literally begging you! Please just bring 3,000 baht and pay them. Please don't start any trouble. It's not worth it. I can't stay here—I gotta get out of here!"

Oh, boy! The poor fellow. I felt so miserable for him—and so damn angry at those power-abusing pricks! But I assured him, "Of course, Mac, be there right away! I'll take care of these fuckers!"

He cried out, "Mark, please, no—" but I had already hung up.

I quickly showered and then pieced together an outfit that I call "The Cowboy Lawyer"—brown penny loafers, pressed Levi's, a crisp, white button-down shirt, silk tie, gray sport coat, and a brown Stetson cowboy hat. I arranged some paperwork in a manila folder, grabbed my camera, cell phone, and print-outs of US Embassy information—while almost forgetting to grab the 3,000 baht from my emergency fund.

At the station, the desk sergeant was either overwhelmingly ignorant (likely), or completely mendacious (equally likely), because he still denied any knowledge of Dr. J. McIntyre. This ceased to be a problem; I could now see Mac behind the plexiglass of a conference room. Flanked by two cops, he was slumped over with his head resting on his arms, sound asleep.

Finally, a lieutenant came along and escorted me to Mac, who upon hearing the opening door bolted his head awake, looked at my ensemble, and about flipped out. He started to violently shake his head from side to side, while muttering, "No, please, no ..." and then looked into my eyes with the terrorized resignation of an abused puppy.

Damn it! Oh, damn, damn! I cursed inwardly.

I had wanted to go a few rounds with these puppets, but that poor, pitiful look on Mac's bruised and battered mug was too much. I set my folder down, pulled out the wad of 3,000 baht, and said, "Gentlemen, thank you for taking such good care of my wayward companion. My most sincere apologies for any trouble he may have caused. I will be sure to set him straight so that he never causes you any more problems. I admit that he is a stubborn jackass, though."

With that humble yet completely disingenuous apology, and payment of the shakedown cash, the Royal Thai Police (enemies for life) allowed us to exit the precinct as free men.

Outside, a grateful but dejected Mac thanked me with a choked-up voice.

I just muttered, "3,000 baht? Big freaking deal. I owed you at least that much anyway! But goddamn it, Mac—I just wanted a few minutes to terrorize those idiots. Shit! I had a dozen bluffs all ready to go!"

***

And even now in the summer of 2020, as I pen this tale of the trouble caused by carelessness, bad timing, and bad actors, I ponder the payback due those pathetic police. Payback for Mac, for myself, and come to think of it, for the scandalous scheme that those shakedown artists executed just days ago in an attempt to jam me up here in Phuket Town ...

PART 3

PHUKET TOWN PRANKS

When you stop doing things for
fun you might as well be dead.

—Ernest Hemingway

CHAPTER 11

VOLUNTEER WORK (2008)

You're only given one little spark
of madness. You mustn't lose it.

—ROBIN WILLIAMS

From the white sand of Surin to the cascading breakers off Kata Beach on Phuket's western coast, all the way down to the subtle splendor of Rawai Beach, which spearheads the island's southernmost thrust into the blinding blue expanse of Andaman Sea, Phuket astonishes all with its beguiling coastline and surreal sky. Sunsets are streaked with fiery cloud wisps, and the fading light of dusk paints the darkening horizon with pastel hues as children's chalk colors a suburban sidewalk. Immersed in the encroaching twilight, a person can feel his soul melt and transform into the promises of the uncharted horizon. In Patong Beach, a wayward soul can sin seven times before 7:00 p.m., and another seventy times before the next sunrise. In Kata Beach, family vacations are promoted, and with luck and prudence, they might even be possible. But tourist beaches are overrated, overcrowded, and as humorless as the editorial page of an imported German newspaper. For real fun (a.k.a. trouble), I recommend getting acquainted with the underbelly of Phuket Town.

Ever since my first trip to Thailand, when I arrived in Phuket Town sweaty and shirtless after desperately attempting to shake the tail of that gang of grifters from Krabi, and almost as desperately trying to escape the lingering effects of an inadvertent yaba trip, I have stayed at the upscale Pearl Hotel. I remember being comforted by the beauty of a spotless polished lobby, and a kind and competent staff, particularly the bellhops. The cool, dark lobby announced order and civility, while the bellhops were classy barriers to intrusion. But it was Mr. Bow, a young man I first came to know in the summer of 2008, who was the best of the bunch. With a broad smile and stellar attitude, he was the epitome of empathy, generosity, and ingenuity. He was slight even for a Thai—perhaps ninety pounds after a fully clothed swim—but affable, insightful, and most importantly, resourceful. Bow was a man who knew how to get things.

We became fast friends outside of our guest/host relationship, and often after delivering "supplies" to my impregnable yet comfortable eighth floor suite, he would hang out and entertain me with tales of his life in that mysterious Kingdom. One day, he described his former employment as a clerk at one of the six million 7-Eleven stores located in the Land of Smiles. He must have interpreted my expression as incredulity, because he returned the next day and proudly presented me with a gift: his green and white pinstriped 7-Eleven uniform shirt.

Being alone in Phuket Town on a dull day can be a challenge to free spirits. We retain an expectation of *some* excitement regardless of circumstances. So it should come as no surprise that when a shiftless prankster like myself possessed too much idle time, along with too much whiskey, devilment—or at least foolishness—would be the result. That scenario did actually come to pass the day after I received Bow's pinstriped present. The stifling stillness of the tropical air and the monotony of the empty afternoon had assailed me with soul-killing boredom, but I did not surrender. Instead, I was inspired to seek employment in the exciting field of Third World convenience store salesmanship. I squeezed and writhed into the uniform shirt and managed to fasten one button, while the rest popped off during the attempt. I rode down the elevator, past the puzzled glances in the lobby, and then strode across the street into the nearest 7-Eleven.

"Sawadee Khap!" ("Hello!") I greeted the young woman behind the counter.

I smiled, strolled around the counter, and then attempted to operate the cash register. I fooled around with the buttons for a minute, then, looking up pleadingly at my new coworker, I said, "I'm sorry. This is my first day. It looks like I am going to need some training."

There is a facial expression unique to Thais, which they display when confronted with a situation or information that they find incomprehensible. I would describe this singular countenance as somewhere between "deer-in-the-headlights" and "catatonic." The expression on the face of this unfortunate young woman was from seven to eleven levels past "catatonic." It was exquisite in its absurdity. And it was also addictive. Like a free-wheeling bank robber, I hit all six store locations in Phuket Town that afternoon. But because of the language barrier, my lack of a work visa, or the unavailability of an XL-size uniform shirt, I was never offered a full-time position.

CHAPTER 12

WHERE THERE'S SMOKE, THERE'S TROUBLE (2009)

If you had great time someplace,
it's not as though you can go back
and get it. If you had a really great
time, a warrant is probably still out.

−P. J. O'Rourke

Spending the majority of the 2020 COVID-19 lockdown "stranded" in Phuket Town enabled me to engage in one of my favorite leisure activities: dropping out of the demanding daily grind in order to reminisce about Times Gone By, and to reinforce and organize these memories into a semi-accurate timeline: keeping events, emotions, people, and arrests in line with corresponding years. Every few days, I would summon the energy to brave the cloying humidity and go for a short stroll down memory lane, as I traversed various parts of the historic downtown. Some streets and sois I had never explored. Some I had run roughshod over with regularity. And some I ventured down, believing them to be virgin territory, but then—to my happy surprise—some detail of the terrain sparked the damp fuse of a firecracker in the crumbling arsenal of my memory bank.

This is a special phenomenon. Unlike the remnants of shared adventures with friends, these memories are an endangered species; they stubbornly survive in the harsh environment of a solitary, fifty-year old mind. Besides, they are much more polite than their distant cousins who tend to burst upon the scene whenever Mac, or some other hooligan, gets a booze-inspired fancy to ring me up and reminisce about one of my past idiocies or misdemeanors. If lost, my solo memories are buried for eternity (unless, of course, they are connected to any outstanding warrants), and the precarious hold they have on existence is mocked by their infamous relatives who have better survival rates than a clan of cats.

I was particularly thrilled one night when a previously forgotten anecdote jumped back to life. I had left my condo for a walk in the monsoon dusk so that I might forget then-current troubles concerning an unwanted, but mandatory, engagement set for the next morning. On a whim, I ambled over the uneven pavement heading east—instead of my usual westward route— and, after threading through street vendors and motorbikes, I happened upon a large public park bustling with the joyful activity of newly released coronavirus captives. Two life-sized, concrete-cast dinosaurs stood watch just behind the park's entrance, and the image of those stone reptiles provoked my subconscious to the extent that I decided to take up the invitation of the captivating old-growth tropical hardwoods that towered over an elongated, twisting lake. *Damn, this place looked so familiar!* But did the image in my recollection even exist here in Thailand? I received nothing but static confusion in answer to this question, until I followed the twisting track that ran along the curvatures of the lake.

And then I heard the "crack!" of a solitary firecracker shocking dead memory back to life, and the images and storyline roared to the forefront of my conscious mind, which then caused me to physically burst into laughter. Several of the nearest Thai fitness fanatics looked queerly and suspiciously upon my spontaneous outburst, while distancing themselves socially from an obviously unhinged old farang.

I *had* been to this park before, and it was the curved asphalt track that jogged my memory. It was a Saturday eleven years prior, and the sprawling park had been packed with people: drivers, groupies, sweethearts, and spectators to an amateur car race. There had been a carnival-like atmosphere. The owners and drivers were showing off their souped-up sports cars in a pre-race preening contest. Officials made preparations for the big event, and the young ladies showcased the latest fashions, while feasting on snacks bought from food carts wedged under the shade of tropical pine trees. That was the festive scene this American scoundrel had stumbled upon, out of happenstance and a Smirnoff-saturated personal guidance system. I was lugging a backpack jammed with the spoils reaped from a misdemeanor offense: "Shopping While Sauced"—which is also known as "Shopping With a Mission!" I had been killing the boredom of a sluggish Saturday by winning a wager from my old buddy, Bow, who was still working at the Pearl Hotel and still the coolest bellhop in town. He had bet that I could not fulfill a certain boast: that I could find and buy fireworks in Phuket Town. And it was this particular challenge that carried me so far from my usual stomping grounds.

I had recently developed a theory, which soon became a technique, for locating fireworks anywhere in Thailand—whether they were legally for sale due to holiday, or if they were technically off-limits. Of course, it would have been an easier task if any of my Thai friends were willing to assist me. But after the catastrophe in Kamala, any mention of pyrotechnics in the vicinity of Rood was met by his Clint Eastwood-like scowl. I was better off finding the contraband on my own initiative, and after some trial and error, I discovered an effective method. The gambit was just a modified version of my off-hours, booze-buying scheme in Bangkok: impersonate American law enforcement. The outfit was simple: dark sunglasses, fake US Marshal's badge pinned to a white, button-down shirt, cowboy hat, and—if showboating—phony pistols and fake handcuffs. Once confidently attired, I would seek out the section of town with the most Chinese-owned general stores, and then canvas them one by one.

Typically, I would enter the premises, stroll about in an authoritative manner, and then begin a slow, sign-language-assisted interrogation of the owner. Of course, they would all deny having an inventory of pyrotechnics, but I would just remove my sunglasses and suggestively wink an eye, or raise an eyebrow, while talking in a soothing tone of camaraderie: *Sure, I was with the FBI, but I was here on holiday with my kids .... I just wanted to buy a few fireworks for fun .... I wasn't looking to bust anyone!* Sometimes they stubbornly maintained their denials with angry pride; sometimes they held out with amused smiles and outright laughter; but sometimes they glanced out at the street to make sure that the coast was clear, and then they escorted me to the *back room*, which was where the coveted contraband was always stashed. After breaching the hallowed *back room*, it was all over but the wheeling and dealing. I would put my success rate somewhere between 17 percent to 23 percent for all shops visited. No problem! I merely had to assail a maximum of six stores in one afternoon before scoring. Chiang Mai, Kalasin, Khoen Koen, Udon Thani, Bangkok, and Phuket Town had all been—or would be—conquered.

When I inadvertently stumbled upon that high-octane celebration of personal automotive pride and civic unity, a singular opportunity almost immediately became obvious to my booze-buoyed intellect. I understood clearly that those Crazy Fates had purposely arranged this afternoon for my own amusement (sometimes those sadistic bitches throw you a bone just to keep you in the game). This belief stemmed from the earlier shopping experience. Although I had found fireworks and won the bet, the reality was that the selection was substandard—anemic to an enthusiast. Aside from basic bottle rockets, flares, and Roman candles, nothing else was even in the ballpark of what is universally known as "the good stuff."

However, I did notice a product line that might prove useful when playing pranks in an urban setting: golf ball-sized, waterproof, industrial-grade smoke bombs. The packs of a dozen came in a rainbow selection of colors. Instinct instructed me to purchase ten packs; worst case scenario, they would make for decent defensive weapons against the stray dogs of dirty sois. So, any reasonable person can understand the immediate connection I conceived concerning fifty finely-tuned race cars firing up their engines in a combination of bravado and due diligence ... and a backpack of 120 colored smoke bombs. Who wouldn't?

I figured purple would lead off the action, as I squeezed through a tight cluster of racing groupies, while stealthily preparing a test run. Up ahead I saw an ideal drop point where an apple-red Honda was revving hell next to a giant hulking fern. After slipping behind the tree, I casually kneeled as if to fix my sandal strap. Instead, I lit both wicks and side-arm rolled both bombs under the Honda's hood, snapped to my feet, and circled back the other way. The red Honda was quickly lost in a dense cloud of violet fumes, and within seconds I heard a terse shout bite the air, the unmistakable sound of a Thai distress call. The single cry soon became a chorus of chaos, while perplexed mechanics struggled through the smoke. Take it all around, the first salvo was a success. But, I realized with disappointment, I had no device for visually documenting this criminal immaturity. Damn it! Where was Mac when I needed him? There was going to be no method of conveying a true picture of the obscene subterfuge. The only option was to put the pedal to the metal, shift the attack to the gear labeled WFO (a.k.a. Wide Fucking Open), and foment enough panic for this event to become infamous the old-fashioned way: through Word of Mouth.

I slithered behind another tree trunk, made a quick assessment of the entire field of targets, and created a hasty mental map of an inconspicuous and expedient route through the maze of metal and clustered humanity. I took one carefully focused look for the presence of potential tails, then set off with the speed and casual confidence of a master shoplifter. Zigzagging through the triple columns of hyper-engineered Hondas and tricked-out Mazdas, I mixed colors and locations, flipping bombs either under the hoods or beneath the exhaust pipes. Glancing back, I saw clouds of red blowing into masses of smoky blue, while a fog of orange mixed with bubbles of yellow haze. But soon shouts could be heard inside the rainbow fog and became a rising tide of voices: some confused, some frightened, but most fighting mad.

I knew that my goal of shock and awe have been met, so I ceased dropping bombs, and fast-walked toward my planned escape route. Unfortunately, there was a hyper-alert vigilante type dead ahead, and he had already discovered the word "guilty" written large across my forehead. He had his right arm extended and pointed at me, as I hustled now in a slanted direction. This tattletale must have been a fisherman, because he observed perfect "man overboard" protocol: shouting alarm while keeping his eyes always directly aimed at me, and his arm stretched outward with his index finger pointing at the guilty depravity of a rascal on the run.

Fuck it—this was no time to worry about exiting in style! I broke into a sprint towards the small spillway that exited one of the lake's lagoons. This overflow shoot flowed into a rock-walled canal, which dipped under the bridge of the main road. I leaped down into the knee-high brown soup of swamp water and slow-ran with high-stepping legs and flailing arms. I knew the posse must be close, but in no way was I going to turn around to gauge their progress. By the time I had gotten to the other side of the thoroughfare, I was soaked in the spray of primeval muck, but I push-upped myself out of the canal and kept up the paranoid pace of an escaped jail-breaker, while enjoying the silver lining of this drunk and dirty exodus. I encountered no human resistance: my swamp stench and ragged hobo appearance cleared the way back to the Pearl Hotel, where Bow waited for me to collect my cash.

CHAPTER 13

SHE'S SO COLD (2009–2012)

When women go wrong,
men go right after them.

—Mae West

Phuket Town has certainly been the scene of many outrageous adventures. They were mostly solo escapades, which typically make for incomplete memories. Yet such stories are also treasures, because they are unique to my own consciousness and a challenge to preserve. And it's okay if the imagery is fragmented: some details are best forgotten! A few days after my stroll through that park and its happy memories of hell-raising, I went exploring in the direction of the town center. Just south of Old Town, I again encountered an image that jump-started my memory.

I was taking a shortcut through a back alley that ran parallel to one of the town's filthy, mosquito-infested canals when I came upon a section of steel scaffolding that rose up about twenty feet, until it abruptly stopped. It looked like whatever used to be at the top of the structure had been cut off—just as if someone had snipped a flower off its stem. I lingered a bit longer, because this place both looked and *felt* familiar. Soon a past episode of idiotic brashness was replaying in my mind: that scaffolding used to rise up another twenty-five feet, and on top was a platform of steel grating that supported a huge, blue, plastic cylinder for water storage. Yes, this was the place where eight years ago I staged a minor act of revenge after being double-crossed.

As I have described previously, Phuket's island neighbor Koh Phi Phi exists in a state of splendid isolation. However, one minor inconvenience is that there is a limited variety of nonessential products for sale. So when, in the summer of 2009, I tired of losing money playing pool at Sunflower Beach Bar because of warped cue sticks (and a sand floor that made for an ever-shifting slope to the playing surface), I decided to make a run to Phuket Town to load up on billiard supplies as a surprise gift to the bar's owner, my old friend Ben. The inspiration for this plan happened to strike me while I relaxed inside the tattoo shop of my wayward buddy Bob. After I indiscreetly announced my plan aloud, it took about two seconds for Bob to be swept up with a bright idea of his own: he really needed a holiday from the island as well ... why don't we go together? Even though Bob's inspired ideas always ended up costing me (financially or otherwise), I agreed to his request. At least Bob's goofy anecdotes would provide entertainment for the boat ride.

Soon enough, we were checking into the luxury of the Pearl Hotel as I bankrolled a massive cash security deposit with the latest Western Union transfer that just so happened to coincide with accountant Frank's latest relapse in his battle with meatball-sub addiction.

"Mark, why you waste money for two rooms?" Bob asked.

Underneath his dopey expression, I could almost read the scheming mind of a mushroom hustler as he imagined other ways we could spend my money.

"Because we have a great friendship, Bob—and I want it to stay that way."

Later, Bob was at my door and looking like a kid at his parents' bedside early on Christmas morning:

"Ready to go out, Mark?" he said, with his deep brown eyes sparkling through the curly locks dangling over his forehead.

"Bob, I am getting some rest tonight. Here—" I answered, while handing him 1,500 baht. "Go have fun."

***

A few hours later, I answered the rapping at my door to find a stumble-drunk Bob, along with two local ladies who, from all appearances, "worked evenings." Although I have many faults, being a lame wingman is not one of them, and I followed the unspoken dictates of the code: I agreed to entertain one young lady, and the other guided Bob back to his room. And this was how I came to meet Neung. Without the least attempt at subtlety, those

Crazy Fates had just dropped a wildcard of a woman off at my front doorstep. Freewill didn't have a chance in that surprise attack.

***

Neung was a beautiful Thai lady who worked at a massage parlor on Phuket Town's Phoonpon Soi 11. Every city has its one infamous area, its red-light district, or that vice-ridden street, where the cravings of the unholy are satisfied. Soi 11 is Phuket Town's pathetic version: a dark, dirty, and decrepit hundred yards of cramped alley lined with massage parlors, smoke shops, and seedy guest houses. I had never been there before meeting Neung, but because of our ongoing friendship, I eventually became familiar with some of that street's shady characters, and I gained a vague understanding of the illicit activities that characterized the area.

With long, dark hair flowing down past her Daisy Duke-style denim shorts, high cheekbones, and dark, gorgeous eyes (which were both enigmatic and cynical), Neung was a gem of that forlorn street. She had a wicked sense of humor, an appreciation for irony, and the jaded street-smarts of a Vegas hustler. We were "friends" in the same way that Charlie Brown and Lucy were football teammates. I always managed to fool myself into believing her phony stories, and I "loaned" her cash while she played me like a fiddle.

For the next three years, whenever I was in Phuket Town, I ended up reconnecting with Neung. I knew going in that I would end up dropping cash in her company, but she was like a sister fallen into a hard life: I felt the obligation to do what I could for her welfare. I happened to be in Phuket Town during the Christmas season one year, and I located Neung so that I could take her on a shopping trip. She was intent on acquiring new shoes, and upon finding a classy black pair with "Ho, ho, ho!" decorating their tops, she asked my opinion.

"Oh, they are perfect, Neung! You must have them!" I said. (I felt, considering her occupation, the inscription was perfectly appropriate.)

***

But our relationship eventually came to a sour end. In November 2012, I was on my way home after a violent incident on Koh Phi Phi. It had left me with a deep scar down the left side of my cheek, and a hospital bill that had left my holiday funds in a very shabby state. I had a two-night stay at the

Pearl Hotel as I awaited my flight back to Bangkok, and I called Neung to arrange a farewell meeting. I was expecting some sympathy for my situation. But instead of sympathy, I was the victim of a cynical maneuver on her part: she swiped my cell phone and about $150. Even for Neung, this was an exceptionally unsentimental act. I had always been a very kind and generous friend! It was hard to believe she would sacrifice our friendship for such an inconsequential price, but I had no way to approach her for redress; the criminals who controlled Soi 11 were hostile to me over other outstanding issues. And yet, I was too incensed to let it go without some protestation.

The previously described water tower happened to be located just a few yards away from the northern end of Soi 11. At midnight the day after the robbery, I climbed to the top of the tower with a backpack of rockets from an old fireworks arsenal. I spent the next hour raining missiles down upon the massage parlor/guest house where Neung resided. When I heard police and other assorted mafia scouring the area, I just laid flat upon the platform, completely unseen from below. It was the closest thing to revenge possible. Of course, that was the end of my relationship with Neung, and it was also the end of my association with Soi 11 … for the next eight years, at least. Little did I know that in the year 2020, Soi 11 would come to play a huge role in the most dramatic and life-threatening adventure of all my Thailand experiences.

CHAPTER 14

INSECURITY GUARDS (2007–2014, 2020)

No one can build his security on the
nobleness of another person.

—WILLA CATHER

Before I get to the heart of this particular story, I believe that it would benefit the reader to be provided with a brief background of the peculiar characteristics of employment in the field of private security in the Kingdom of Thailand. The most striking observation is that on a per capita basis, Thailand (with over 450,000 private security guards) is a world leader in the number of positions available for this unheralded, yet important vocation. With such an omnipresence of watchmen, one might believe that Thailand is rife with petty larceny and grand theft. However, the Kingdom has a relatively low property crime rate, and this nominal level of criminality wouldn't seem to necessitate such a leviathan-sized private security force.

And yet it is most likely not the presence of this massive security force that keeps the criminal element from running rampant here, because at any given moment between the hours of 11:00 p.m. and 6:00 a.m., approximately 87 percent of "on duty" security personnel are not consciously engaged in the act of safeguarding the private property to which they have been entrusted. On the contrary, these night rangers are devoting themselves completely to the security of those absurd images and discursive plot lines of the subconscious that constitute dreams. If sleeping on the job were an Olympic sport, a

Thai private security team would join women's volleyball and badminton as Thailand's perennial medal contenders. I have always been astonished by the brash—almost entitled—attitude these snoozing sentinels have toward racking-out on the job. In fact, I believe that extra sleep must be an unspoken, but de facto, component of the compensation package. Every once in a while, I ponder the mystery of what these fellows do during their off time. Do they lay about their homes, resting up for a hard night of napping?

Perhaps these descriptions sound mean-spirited, but they are not exaggerations. For those skeptics in the audience, I will direct your attention to the curious case of a Siamese serial killer. In November 2007, I happened to be in Bangkok when the Royal Thai Police (in a rare case of semi-competence) arrested a serial killer who had been terrorizing the city's community of security personnel. According to the *Bangkok Post*, after a five-month-long manhunt, Wittaya Jaikhan, age thirty, was arrested for beating to death eight security guards who slept on the job and badly injuring eight others. A former security guard himself, Wittaya confessed to the killing spree, attributing his rampage to "professional outrage." He was quoted as saying: "I hate guards who fall asleep on the job and don't perform their duty."

Heavy stuff. After almost thirty years of commercial fishing on Alaska's Bering Sea, I have seen my share of slackers and screamed at those shiftless bums until my voice was worn out. I have an intense intolerance for their ilk; however, I do not advocate for the extermination of the chronically unproductive. The application of strict training measures or outright dismissal from employment are much more humane and effective solutions.

For instance, as factory foreman on the *F/V Gulf Prowler*, I was once cursed with two young deckhands who had the temerity to arrive ten minutes late for work for five consecutive days. This was simply unacceptable on every level. The remedy was extreme—perhaps akin to hazing—but it proved effective. Using an aluminum product pan as a drum, I wailed on it with a small crowbar about two feet away from the eardrums of the snoozing delinquents as they lay in the black chasm of absolute sleep. The bottom of this chasm is the exclusive territory of commercial fisherman, and to be yanked so violently out of its depths is a torture only they can understand or endure. Yet, afterward, the two offenders were not only early for every shift-change, but both Kieran and Calvin approached me on separate occasions to express sincere thanks for instilling in them the importance of a consistent work ethic. Tough love, not serial killing, is the proper procedure for curing complacent indolence.

But let us return to the autumn of 2007. When this killing spree came to light, I was still a frequent patron of the billiards sections of several of Bangkok's all-night dance clubs. In fact, my waking hours generally coincided with the sleeping hours of the city's nightwatchmen. And although the pathologically hypercritical hitman had already been apprehended, I was still concerned about the possibility of a copycat killer—particularly when the potential victims insisted on making themselves such easy targets. So, on my evenings out on the town, I became a one-man caffeine/Red Bull supplier for the inadequately vigilant seat-warmers on duty. There were several security booths located along my usual nightly route through the Sukhumvit Road sector, and it was a fairly cheap yet conscience-soothing activity to drop in at a 7-Eleven and procure a supply of caffeinated beverages, which I would distribute to the lucidity-challenged guardians of nocturnal society.

And ever since that strange time, I have retained an amused affection for these gallant warriors who struggle valiantly against drowsiness, ennui, and inverted life schedules. Through the years, I have endeavored to show my appreciation for their efforts by keeping conventional security guards, bar bouncers, and other informal guardians of public safety alert and even entertained. In addition to free Red Bull and iced coffee, I also kept them occupied with conversation, and frequently inspired them with either annoyance or amusement through various practical jokes. I firmly believe that busting the chops of a friend is a great way to demonstrate your affection for that person. This is a quirk of character that I acquired from my father (although I somehow missed out on inheriting the genes that produce responsibility, foresight, financial restraint, sobriety, and respect for authority).

I wish that I could report that the average security guard was skeptical and a challenge to outwit, but the truth is that they would fall for the most obvious ruses. For example, one standard joke followed the same pattern: I would buy a cheap toy cell phone and go through the motions of having a real phone conversation as I arrived outside a club or parking garage security booth. I would be conversing earnestly with an imaginary friend as I made my approach, then fake an outburst of frustration, and anxiously plead in broken English for the guard to take my phone and speak to my friend in order to give him directions. Without fail, the guard would oblige the request, put the phone to his ear and repeatedly offer up the Thai greeting of "Sawadee Khop" while I would light a cigarette and stare off up into the sky in order to keep my unavoidable grin from broadcasting the prank. The ever-helpful, yet gullible, guardian would repeat the salutation up to a dozen times before taking the phone off his ear and examining the device—only to find a pink Barbie design or a red Spider-Man flip-phone. He would then glare at me with wounded pride, and I'd finally succumb to spasms of laughter.

Of course, this sort of silliness would be rewarded with a slap upside the head anywhere in the USA, but one of the endearing qualities of the Thai national character is an abundant appreciation and tolerance for humorous antics. Besides, I always made it up to them with either a Red Bull or a financial reward, but only after they insisted on having the phone and immediately performing the same prank on their nearest crony.

On other occasions, I would approach the attendant in a serious manner while flashing a fake US Marshal's badge, point my flashlight into their security booth, and imperiously demand to see their identification and credentials. Or sometimes I would hand the guard a walkie-talkie, show him that I had the other, and in a tone of strict authority, order the perplexed sentry to keep it turned on and to stay alert. I would be patrolling the inside of the club for any fights or drug dealing, and I expected him to be ready to knock down anyone trying to escape into the night. (Although I usually saved that routine for a beautiful bartender inside the club; handing her the walkie-talkie, and explaining that I would be over at the corner table and I would call her on the radio after I decided on a drink order.)

***

In the last few years, legislation has been passed to regulate the security profession. Age restrictions, licensing requirements, training, and other common-sense rules are now codified into Thailand's labor laws. However, one of the endearing (yet sometimes frustrating) characteristics of this country is that, while so many aspects of life elsewhere in the world are changing at extraordinary speed, change in Thailand comes slowly and, often, not at all. Of those cultural conditions that are impervious to change, two stand out in my mind: unsupervised dogs still harass and attempt to intimidate foreign nationals in the night, and security guards still sleep on the clock. And both of these features played a role in a recent trouble-making episode in Phuket.

There was a hundred-yard stretch of unlit, unpaved lane that connected the main road to the condo complex where I resided in the summer of 2020. In keeping with the "one per twenty-five-yard" rule of thumb, there were four unsupervised and impudently aggressive four-legged bullies that I was forced to contend with in order to access the main road. So, in the year 2020, as a pandemic terrified the world, and America self-imploded as it set the world on course for an encore of the Dark Ages, I found it imperative to purchase an eight-shot, revolver-style cap gun. I test-fired the weapon (with an absurdly loud report), but I had not yet been compelled to fire it in self-defense. The very sight of the pistol intimidated the scabby mutts enough that they crawled back to their hiding spots. I did, however, find it advisable to always employ the concealed carry philosophy.

I had just recently moved into the condo complex, and although it was a gated facility, and there was card key access to the building, management had deemed it necessary to install one of our intrepid security heroes at the front gate. Although the young man did not seem entirely focused, he had managed to at least ward off sleep (having a second-floor balcony, I was able to survey the guard shack)—at least for the first week of my residency. But then late one night, I was returning from drinks and billiards at the local pub when I was confronted by an all-too-familiar sight. My man was asleep, very deeply and lovingly asleep. Sitting on a lounge chair with his head laying back limp, his snores were loud enough to drown out the crickets blasting their tune from the overgrown jungle. I watched, almost mesmerized, as his head would begin to roll itself back up-right, only to flop back limp, his mouth open and drooling, and his eyes oblivious to the waking world. This was a vintage performance, perhaps the most intriguingly original one I have ever witnessed.

This was such an exquisite example of the previously described phenomena, it just had to be documented. I quickly retrieved my laptop from my room, set it down on the parking lot, and had an impromptu photo shoot, putting myself into the action by mimicking a desperate intruder with a cap gun pointed at the guard in the firing position, along with other absurd poses. I soon had enough material and left him to his guttural snores and whatever images flash through the dreams of night watchmen (no doubt, the nightmares consist of brutal beatings by former guards). At the time, I did not know the photographic evidence would soon prove helpful.

Just two nights later, I returned from the same pub—this time with company. Boom, the raven-haired bar manager, accompanied me home for the relaxation of after-work cocktails. Apparently, she had been charmed by my adolescent foolishness; she did not even get upset when I introduced myself to her bar staff with a phony robbery, demanding vodka with the cap gun pointed directly at her elder sister. Afterward, I explained to her that this was not a real gun; it was a cap gun intended to fend off the local hounds who were my arch enemies. But apparently, I did not communicate effectively the exact nature of the toy. After navigating the canine gauntlet, we arrived back at the condo complex. Upon arrival, we were treated to the spectacle of the snoozer-on-duty, who slept through our entry into the complex.

Everything was going quite well. The young lady with the sexy, sweet smile sat next to me on the balcony, while charming me with subtle Siamese endearments. However, after I returned from a bathroom break, I was startled to see Boom fooling around with the pistol. Unfortunately, I had fallen victim to a common problem for foreigners in Thailand: the failure to understand that usually a Thai person finds it more polite to say they understand something than to admit they actually do not. More specifically, when I previously asked Boom if she understood clearly the inner workings of a cap gun, she failed to understand that the cap gun spoke her name, "Boom," when the trigger was pressed. A spits-worth of smoke scorched the air, my ears were ringing, and Boom's face was a helpless picture of transfixed shock. Absolutely, this was the loudest cap gun I had ever heard!

Boom looked at me with such worry—bordering on panic—that she obviously believed this was a real gun, and that she had shot a real something. I, of course, was laughing my ass off. But our now semi-alert security officer was not. Down below, the suddenly sentient guardian was furious, as he castigated me in subdued tones. And I could not really blame him. That cannon might have woken up the entire population of the condo community. *Shit!* I thought. *I did not need this trouble.* This was too nice of a place for too nice of a price to allow myself to get tossed out.

However, a little quick thinking provided me with an easy fix. After soothing my sweetheart, and shuffling her to the living room couch, I grabbed up the laptop and went to have a chat with the posted sentry of the condo's barricade. After I presented him with a brief slideshow, I was able to convince the guard that it would not be an advisable career move to notify management of this evening's gunshots. He understood that in this anemic COVID-19 economy, job security was a priority, and he promised to keep his mouth shut. And I promised not to email his bosses any incriminating photos of him confusedly crashed out in the dark. But creating memes and posting them on social media was something we did not discuss—and thankfully, I'm quite certain he will never see.

PART 4

AN ODYSSEY OF CHANCE AND CHOICE (2020)

It is not Justice the servant of men,
but accident, hazard, Fortune—the
ally of patient Time—that holds an
even and scrupulous balance.

—JOSEPH CONRAD

CHAPTER 15

DEAD END (EARLY AUGUST)

In the middle of the journey
of our life, I came to myself
within a dark wood where
the straight way was lost.

—DANTE ALIGHIERI

"Why would I want four people who are 15,000 miles away on my visitors list? Stupid!" I muttered.

The guard exploded in self-righteous rage and began roaring insults in calculated hysteria, while pointing his index finger an inch from my nose. In my confused frustration, I reflexively snatched up his finger in my right fist and bent it backwards. Instantly, a flash-bang grenade exploded inside my thick skull. Lightning flashed in my peripheral vision, and the thumping "whaw, whaw, whaw" sound reverberating in my eardrums had the intensity of a beach ball's worth of inhaled nitrous oxide.

The foot of the other guard (standing behind me) had connected perfectly to the soft part of the skull just above my right ear. My interrogator, having recovered his finger, squatted low with knees akimbo, and then delivered an equalizer blow with a hard palm slap to the left ear—causing the flash-bang/ *whaw whaw* sound effect to double in intensity.

Humiliated, I wrapped my arms around my knees and stared stoically ahead, while feeling the cumulative gaze of forty Siamese cellmates who were condensed into the 250-square-foot room. Now arrived the full force, the concrete reality, the nightmare answer to an enigmatic question: were my deep-seated fears and impressions of the past four months just the inevitable consequences of an overly paranoid imagination, or was I in *real trouble*? I humbly finished my interview, then stoop-walked back to my spot underneath the plywood mezzanine deck and laid my newly shaved head back upon my "pillow," a folded bath towel, which, along with cotton trouser shorts and loose T-shirt, were the only items issued to me when I arrived in Phuket Provincial Prison two days earlier.

Opposite to this cell was another unit of the same size, housing an additional fifty-odd rejects of Thai society, all with shaved heads and tattoo-graffitied bodies. These more seasoned convicts cracked jokes and conversed at top volume, in order to compete with the sappy dialogue and trite musical score blaring from the community television. In the US, the programming itself would have been considered cruel and unusual punishment; in the evening hours, the TV cranked out one dumbass Thai soap opera after another. Through the bars of the nearest window, I watched packs of prisoners—hundreds—moving about the courtyard and open-air bathing facility.

If not for the thumping of my head, I may have fallen into believing the soothing (yet credible) idea that I was in the midst of a nightmare from which I would soon awaken. Something else gave this a dream-like feeling: the déjà vu—a quality to the atmosphere that was so much like some former experience. Not the confined space, I thought. It was the cloying humidity at 8:00 a.m., the unfamiliar animal smells, and the proximity of dense, intruding vegetation. Yet the most strikingly familiar aspect was that these lively features of the natural world were enveloped by an urban environment. I could hear the honking of stubborn motorists, and I could smell car exhaust and the oily blacktop of city streets. I could not pinpoint the memory, but the *feeling* in my soul recalled a hopeful and carefree epoch of my life.

I looked up higher and spotted the familiar sight of the mammoth Gold Buddha Statue at the pinnacle of a mountain of blinding green jungle. How many times had I looked upon that idol, unmindful of my position of freedom? Could it really be that I would have to endure *four years* here before gazing at that magnificent sight from a liberated perspective? I closed my eyes, and I felt a slight fan breeze brush over my boiling body, while my shell-shocked mind attempted to follow the twists and snarls of coincidence, missteps, betrayal, petty greed, and incurable corruption that had led to this dead end of unrivaled misery and fear.

CHAPTER 16

A LUCKY LOCKDOWN (MARCH–MAY)

Two key rules of Third World Travel:
1. Never run out of whiskey.
2. Never run out of whiskey.

—P.J. O'ROURKE,
ALL THE TROUBLE IN THE WORLD

I first entered this labyrinth the moment I serendipitously encountered my friend Lek immediately after my arrival in Phuket Town in March of the unexpectedly chaotic year 2020. At least it certainly *seemed* lucky to have collided with my old friend that night; the next day, the COVID-19 virus compelled the authorities to completely lock down the island of Phuket and to shut down all hotel operations. Stranded foreigners were required to stay at government-managed facilities and kept under observation. But because Lek had just recently rented a neglected four-story building, in order to renovate the property and open up a boarding house, I immediately obtained accommodations, which enabled me to fly under the radar of provincial police and other bureaucratic enforcement brigades.

And, for the first three weeks, the domestic arrangement was wonderful. Lek and her sister insisted upon cooking, cleaning, shopping, doing my laundry, and essentially spoiling me to the extent that I had plenty of time to begin transcribing this collection of personal adventure tales, with only the occasional interruption. Most of these disruptions were caused by Lek's adorable nine-year-old daughter, Nok, but she was easily appeased by an inflatable swimming pool, peanut M&Ms, and colored pencils. Life was grand in comparison to the experiences of almost everyone else on the island. The Phuket economy is (or was) 75 percent dependent on foreign tourism. And this one-dimensional economy quickly crumbled under the onerous lockdown restrictions imposed as a result of the Chinese Communist Party's callous malfeasance. Every afternoon, I watched from my window as the poor of Phuket Town lined up for the daily food handout, until eventually the mass of humanity assumed serpentine form, wrapping around several city blocks.

The sight caused me to realize just how lucky I was, despite the lack of freedom of movement. But the longer I stayed in such close proximity to Lek, the more it became obvious that she wanted more than friendship out of our relationship. She was becoming romantically attached to me; however, I did not share in the feeling. I did my best not to give her false encouragement, but the more I disregarded her hints and overtures, the more intent she became on a romantic conquest. She also wanted me to be her business partner.

And as Lek endeavored to expand her business, her desire for a romantic/business relationship became more intense and suffocating, despite my very clear position on the subject. We were great friends, and I cared for her deeply, but I was in no position—financially or professionally—to make such a commitment. She said that she understood the situation, yet she persisted with constant requests for financial assistance, which I often resigned myself to render, until I realized how much of those funds were actually used for what had devolved into an overwhelming drug addiction. Eight years prior, I was aware that she was acquiring a habit (along with her former boyfriend, Sak), but although he had been forced (by confinement in the Thai prison system) to clean up his act, Lek had been driving in the fast lane at ever-increasing speeds. Having had my own share of "speeding tickets" tacked on to my record, this environment was no longer a viable living situation. Additionally, I would soon be in financial distress, if I continued to provide the girl with the "loans" necessary to keep her afloat financially.

But the most disconcerting consequence of continuing this charade was the moral component; Lek was still convinced of the illusion that I would have a change of heart, and that we would soon be business partners and lovers. Lifelong happiness was just around the corner. The knowledge that she continued to wholeheartedly believe in this fairy tale fostered a sickening guilt that penetrated my bones. She had her hopes still set on me—and by the scars on my own heart, I know that false hopes should never be encouraged. To do so is a sin of selfish pride and careless cruelty.

Despite my deep desire, I was unsuccessful in my attempts to move out. I had been handcuffed by the shutdown of the hospitality industry, and by Phuket's absolute ban on travel between "tambons" (roughly, the equivalent of townships in America). On five separate occasions, I had made a reservation for a new room through Airbnb, only to have it cancelled at the last minute. And to make matters even worse, local authorities instituted a total booze prohibition. For the most part, Thais are relative lightweights when it comes to the effects of alcohol consumption; actually, Thais are easily rattled when consuming any mood-altering substance. For this reason, the authorities find it necessary to arbitrarily regulate alcohol sales for the entire population. Thus, I sensed danger after reading about recent alcohol bans in other provinces. These had been enacted in order to combat the virus (because nothing makes it easier to stay home in self-isolation than to also be deprived of the company of your best friend!). And although my instinct warned me that Phuket's bungling bureaucracy was about to enact another useless law, the nannies pulled a fast one: the decree was issued at 10:00 p.m. on April 11 and went into effect at 11:00 on the same night.

And just like that, I was stranded in a dry lockdown without a war chest of whiskey. However, I was an old hand to the underbelly of Phuket Town's black market, and a situation that could have been unbearable became a mere inconvenience. Although there were several options for purchasing alcohol, Phoonpon Soi 11 was the sure thing, and it was just around the corner from Lek's boarding house. As I mentioned in an earlier story, I was familiar with the illicit nature of that particular street. And although I had abruptly burned my bridges with the midnight rocket barrage of 2012, Soi 11 was under new management now.

***

During my first shopping trip to Soi 11 during prohibition, I became acquainted with Kris, a young Thai man who facilitated in the purchase of Hong Thong whiskey. Over the ensuing weeks we became friends, and I came to know his wife and young daughter. The toddler always shouted "Farang!" when I approached (I never forgot to bring treats from 7-Eleven).

At the time, I wasn't suspicious when Kris asked if I wanted other illicit items, even sending me explicit messages online. I figured he was just trying to hustle as much commission cash as possible. I also assumed he was just being neighborly, because throughout April, my daily visit was as regular as a newspaper route. But then came the month of May and her monsoons, which thundered in from the sea, bringing heavy rain, wild mushrooms, and *change*. I was finally able to leave Lek's house and move into a choice condo on the outskirts of town. Although I was no longer within walking distance, motorbike taxis became my transport for Soi 11 shopping and social calls to see Lek and my little pal, Nok (peanut M&Ms had become a dietary staple by then). And if I was particularly unmotivated, I just made one call, and Kris would deliver whiskey and smokes right to my doorstep.

CHAPTER 17
SET UP (JUNE)

Perhaps life is just that ...
a dream and a fear.

—JOSEPH CONRAD

Eventually, the prohibition ended. About the same time, travel between Phuket's tambons was again permitted. I was thrilled to ditch city life and get over to the coast, where I spent two weeks lazing about Kamala Beach and enjoying the company of my old friend and fixer Rood. But when there was an interruption in cash flow, I was forced to move back in with Lek until funds were restored. This was not an ideal situation; Lek's drug abuse was running rampant, and her clarity of thought was extinct. In fact, I came to suspect that she was also selling the illegal product in order to finance her personal use.

Apparently, I was not very keen-minded either. One afternoon, I agreed to a very stupid course of action. Because I was temporarily boarding for free, I felt obligated that fateful day to help Lek with a request. My landlady was desperate to trade a small amount of ice for a small amount of yaba, and she asked if I could accomplish this with my contacts on Soi 11—she was busy entertaining her family who had come to visit. Sure. Easy enough. I would just call Kris. He had always advertised his willingness to help out, just as I had always helped him out with cash loans, free advice, and other assorted favors.

Early in the afternoon on Wednesday, the eighteenth of June, I called Kris and informed him of the situation. Sure. Easy enough. He just needed some time to get it arranged. After we traded phone calls throughout the afternoon, Kris finally told me exactly where to meet him at 5:30 p.m. Curious enough, the meeting point was not on Soi 11, but at a spot just fifty yards from Lek's boarding house. I wrapped the pinch of ice in a piece of plastic and, using black tape, stuck it between two (long defunct) credit cards.

At 5:20 p.m. I left my room. My intent was to buy a pack of cigarettes from the corner store prior to our meeting. In flip-flops and T-shirt, wearing a fanny pack carrying my passport, cash, and the goods for trade, I exited the building. I walked twenty yards, whereupon I heard panicked shouts and commands from three different directions. At least eight individuals in civilian clothes swarmed upon me—two with drawn pistols. I was immediately smothered and handcuffed, threats and commands screamed into my now-shuttered eyes. I began shaking convulsively, heart thumping, incredulous .... I stood there in the blinding sunshine and roiling heat—a few idle bystanders gawking—as I was wildly manhandled and searched by undercover police.

After two long minutes, their frustration was palpable: they had nothing. But just when I thought I might get out of there with my skin, one of the faux protectors of distressed tourists found the piece of black tape stuck between the two credit cards. Upon opening it up, the crowd of plain-clothes cops instantly became an imitation of the infamous simian bandits on Krabi's Monkey Beach, as they shouted in triumph and cackled their mockery at the freaked-out farang. Now, the Fear seized instant and total control of my shocked soul, while the crumbling shell that houses it quaked with involuntary spasms.

Just then, a forty-something female cop emerged from the ranks and seemed to take command, while the rest of the gang deferred to this matriarch of the vice squad (oops! I mean *tourist police!*). It is a scientific fact that all Thai women are born with the acting gene, and this lady performed wonderfully: she expertly transitioned into the role of "good cop" in this twisted version of a daytime drama. Reaching up to pat my shoulder and soothing me with motherly tones, she explained that this was "no big deal." It was "nit noi" (just a little). I was "a nice man who just made a small mistake." She offered the assurance that "everything would be okay" and tossed out other life rings of hope. Now that we had ostensibly become allies, she eased into a light interrogation: "Where are you staying in Phuket Town?" My mind jumped into high gear: *Shit! I can't let them know that I stay at Lek's house. Jesus, she could be screwed for life! ... As careless as she is? And on the one day that her family is visiting from Isan! ... And how happy and proud she had been last night ... showing her Mom how well she was doing for herself ... and now to have her place ransacked, and her hauled off to jail in front of them?* I flipped the switch to bullshit mode.

"I don't stay in Phuket Town. I just came here for the day—from Kamala Beach."

"What? You no stay here in Phuket Town?"

"No. I stayed here during the lockdown, but I already moved to Kamala Beach. I only come here today to shop and see some friends ...."

"When you stay here before ... for lockdown, where you stay?"

"Oh, I stayed at the Wide Condominium ...."

"Really?"

"Yes, first I stayed at the Wide Condominium. Then I went to Kamala Beach to stay with my friend Rood. Do you want to call him?" (*Ready to cover for me, old Buddy?*)

"No! You stay in Phuket Town! Don't lie!" erupted the closest cop.

"I'm not lying! I do not stay in Phuket Town. Everything I have is at Kamala Beach with my friend. I've come here only for the day!"

The lady cop wrapped her arm around one of the guys, and they both walked off, speaking in subdued whispers. As soon as her back was turned, the other goons quickly shuffled me over to a black sedan with black-tinted windows, and then squished me into the middle of the back seat. My wrists were wrenched behind me and screaming the pain of flesh on fire as the steel cuffs burrowed into bone. One cop sat on my left side, and another squeezed in on my right. And then two more cops sat down in the front seat—all humanity hidden behind four pairs of dark shades. This wasn't going to be good. Not at all ...

The foot soldier in the driver's seat suddenly twisted his torso, until he was fully facing my front side, and then he jabbed his finger into my cheekbone while malevolently shouting, "Where you fucking stay in Phuket Town!?"

I became indignant: "I don't stay in Phuket Town!"

Whomp! A Charley-horse was delivered to the top of my thigh with the precision strike of an old school butcher. This was the retort of the agent to my right. "What you say?" he snarled, while twisting my neck, using my ear as the crank.

I played tough one more time: "I don't stay in fucking Phuket Town!"

Thump! Thump! Thump! Three heavy thuds were the sound effects of three closefisted shots to my sternum, compliments of my fans in the front seat. The third blow pushed out what little air was left in my lungs.

"Where you fucking stay in Phuket Town?" screamed the guy at my left as he tomahawked another Charley-horse to my other thigh.

The cop in the driver's seat raised back his fist and shouted, "Where you stay, motherfucker?"

"Okay! Okay! Okay … Stop … Okay? Moment please?" I begged, while panting like a luckless hound kicked on an August afternoon.

(It should be noted here that, while the Royal Thai Police are universally recognized as grossly incompetent, they are absolute maestros in the infliction of maximum pain while leaving a minimum of *visible* physical damage as evidence.)

"Tell me now!" shouted Front Seat.

"There! There! For fuck's sake! There—" I coughed, and I pointed and nodded my head in the direction of Lek's boarding house, which sat just twenty-five yards in front and to the right of us.

"Where, exactly?" was the question that accompanied another sternum shot.

I offered in numb defeat: "There! Look right there—you see the one with the pink sign right there? The one that says 'Nok's Guesthouse'?"

"That's better!" someone replied, and a thumbs up was shoved in front of my face, while they all laughed like jackals, basking in the primitive joy of nasty brutes.

How is it that evolution still produces humans who get their kicks from inflicting pain and humiliation on another soul, an individual made powerless only because of numerical superiority? Do they understand that their strength is a phony thing, attributable to nothing more than an accident of circumstance?

They yanked me out of the car, whistled and yelled to their comrades, and pushed-dragged me into the lobby of Lek's house, where her mother and sister sat in perplexed terror, while her brother looked utterly displaced, the picture of confusion. They were treated to the unwelcome drama of city life, as their daughter's fantasy—a Prince Charming of the West—was manhandled by a gang of plain-clothed, half-witted mafia underlings who took pleasure in their victim's obvious shame, fear, and paralyzed anger. Barking commands, they dragged me up the second flight of stairs to room 201 where I had been staying for barely two days. In fact, my bags remained unpacked, and I had just a few personal items lying about, along with some clothes hanging in the closet.

"Squared away" was the condition of the premises, until six or eight vultures of the phony vice squad worked over the premises. They clumsily ripped the place apart, digging through my bags, throwing clothes all over, and searching every crevice and corner, while cracking juvenile jokes and chattering away. But they were coming up empty-handed, and the clumsy fools were completely incapable of disguising their shocked disappointment. It was obvious they fully *expected* to find a treasure-trove of illegal materials. Unlike their lady-leader, these mugs had no thespian talents, and their lack of self-awareness was almost comical. Their exasperation was so apparent that, even in my shock, I knew there was more to this. It was also obvious that they *already* knew I was staying in Lek's building. They just needed me to admit it, in order to legally search the premises. This was their justification for resorting to the "enhanced interrogation" in the sedan—to force my cooperation.

The buffoons were as deflated as America's mainstream media just after the election of Donald Trump to the presidency. Confident expectations had been destroyed. The only illegal item discovered was a homemade bong, which was clearly an accessory of Thai construction: it was far too intricately designed and expertly built to be the handiwork of a clumsy farang. After twenty more minutes of foolish persistence and no results, the collective emotion changed. Now they were pissed. And I was pissed. I was so infuriated that I could no longer restrain my mouth from unleashing the indignant sarcasm that had been percolating since the enhanced interrogation in the car. I got the attention of the actress cop by shouted out this question: "Hey! I have an idea. Why don't you order these goons to give me another beat down? It worked out in the car. What? Are you afraid of doing it in front of witnesses? You only beat people in secret—must not be legal!"

Face. Saving face. It means everything in this convoluted culture. And now, although physically powerless, I was in possession of the strategic high ground. I clearly had the psychological upper hand. I could see in the lady cop's eyes that *she knew* that *I knew* that this entire encounter was not some random police action; this was a highly coordinated operation with a specific goal. Being well-educated on the subject of Thailand's tradition of condoned corruption, I knew the goal of this whole fiasco must be the acquisition of a financial prize. Although the script is well-worn, its results and rewards are reliable enough that it will forever remain the boilerplate guide to the Siamese Shakedown.

Storyline #1: Set-up/bust (supposedly) rich tourist and intimidate/terrorize the tourist with threats of prison—unless financial demands are met right there on the spot.

Storyline#2: Tourist is unwilling or unable to pay the immediate bribe. This necessitates working (and—ouch!—*sharing*) with corrupt officials in the judicial/penal systems who will help terrorize/intimidate family and friends of said tourist, until an exorbitant financial penalty is paid.

It was undeniable that these proceedings had devolved into the clean-up stage of protocol for a failed shakedown attempt. Even the good country people of Isan knew the score, understood the implicit rules of the power game, and pretended that the situation simply did not exist—Thailand's version of the Jedi mind trick. So while Lek's family ducked and hid behind their feigned ignorance, the crestfallen cops recovered enough to pretend this shit show was just a typical law enforcement operation. Sure! It is common practice to devote an eight-member task force, countless man-hours, and considerable public resources for the sole purpose of apprehending an absolute nobody of the criminal class! ("Citizens! Behold the dangerous farang outlaw! Pay no attention to the obvious fact that he is just a careless fool in the wrong place at the wrong time ….")

And to ensure my goodwill and cooperation in the keeping up of appearances, the entire squad had adopted the role of "good cop." My handcuffs were loosened—with apologies! I was given a cigarette, and I was included in their silly jokes and general fraternity. They all encouraged me with promises that I would be in and out of the police station in no time at all (quicker than you can say "botched drug raid!"). All I had to do was play along and earnestly pretend this wasn't just another criminal racket of the Royal Thai Police, an extortion swindle facilitated by their cohorts on the other side of the tracks. I refer to the street mafia, my acquaintances on Soi 11 who wheel and deal, lie and betray, and pay off the pathetic parasites disguised as police so that they can run their rackets with impunity, and squeeze the tainted baht out of every sordid business in Phuket Town. Those petty thugs operate their shakedown schemes with an audacity that would make a Sicilian blush.

And if this were Rome, I would be wearing a toga! Of course, I played along. I considered myself quite lucky that Lek hadn't gotten any other part of her premises searched—and *incredibly* lucky that Lek had been out running errands during the search. She would have been up to her skinny shoulders in shit, if she had been present for the raid. For the moment, it looked as though I just needed to smile and play the part of dumb buffoon tourist. If I could manage to do that, I would be able to get out of this with, perhaps, just a midsize payoff to the appropriate boss man of the RTP.

I was also lucky that it was the least perceptive, and most complacent cop, who searched the fridge. He made the foolish assumption that the large reusable container on the bottom shelf was filled with leftovers from lunch, completely missing his opportunity to discover almost two pounds of magic mushrooms; my refrigerator was sometimes used for storage by my scatterbrained buddy, Bob. We'll get to Bob and his antics here shortly ....

CHAPTER 18

LIBERTY IN LIMBO (LATE JUNE–EARLY JULY)

Only the fool, fixed in his folly, may think
He can turn the wheel on which he turns.

—T. S. ELIOT

The speedboat cut a smooth streak over the sublime expanse of sea, a flat field of pure Andaman blue, which was closely mimicked by the lighter tones of an unblemished sky. The vast uniformity of color gave a passenger the sensation of flying through a tunnel into a world of unbroken beauty. My body was stretched out on the cushioned bow, with a life jacket padding my spine, and a bottle of Smirnoff padding the rest. Kiki, a Florida girl, was assisting me with the vodka disposal and listening to my lecture on the societal, cultural, and historical aspects of our island destination—my estranged mistress, Koh Phi Phi. My original traveling companions, Kat and Alicia, sat in the shaded stern, engaged in their own private conversation. They, undoubtedly, remained unconcerned with my social maneuvering, even though my new friend was another stunning single lady.

In need of a translator, I had hired Kat three weeks earlier, just after my release from the Phuket Town jail. She had comported herself with admirable poise, insight, and competence in my first meeting with a Thai "advisor" (Lek's friend and an alleged ex-cop) who was willing to help me navigate the legal process for a cash payment of 10,000 baht. Kat had also accompanied me to my first appointment at the courthouse. She had proven to be an excellent chauffeur, trusted confidante, and a first-rate dinner companion. I was quite fond of her. This short trip to Phi Phi was a thank-you gift for her invaluable assistance. And because her good friend, Alicia, was visiting from Bangkok, I began the trip with two lovely ladies for an entourage.

When conversation between us Americans slipped into silence, I began to contemplate the enormity of the horizon and the mystifying plot twists of my unconventional life history. I was soon engulfed by a swarm of memories and emotions. With my harrowing legal situation falling further behind at every bounce of the boat, I drifted into a reverie of joy and hope. I was returning to my former sanctuary, where I would see my dear friend, Ben, for the first time in seven years. I also knew that I would be treated to sights of unspoiled grandeur: the island had been cleansed of the unwholesome blight of mass tourism. The COVID-19 virus had taken care of that problem for now. Poignant memories and images flashed about my mind and stirred my imagination. When the vessel smacked into a small swell, a slight spray misted over the two of us up forward. I looked down at my glistening forearms to discover goosebumps were bubbling up in a physical expression of the sentiments of my soul. I looked over at Kiki and remarked, "What an amazing day!"

It was a day I would have thought *impossible*, if I had considered it from my seat in the conference room of the Tourist Police Station in Phuket Town just three weeks earlier. Surrounded by my new best friends, the Shakedown Squad of the Royal Thai Police, and blessed with a box of fried rice, a bunch of dwarf bananas, and two bottles of water sitting in front of me, I stared with incomprehension at the large whiteboard on the wall. My full name was written large across the top, and my two mobile numbers were neatly printed underneath. Beneath my contact info was a hand-scrawled map of the four city blocks surrounding the immediate vicinity of Lek's boarding house. Several arrows were drawn to indicate travel patterns (obviously mine) between Lek's place, the 7-Eleven, the mini-mart, and Soi 11. Below this crude diagram, I noticed several notes scribbled in the esoteric characters of the Thai alphabet. Incredulous, I pondered this revelation: I was here because of a sting operation targeting *me* specifically—I had been watched, followed, and scrutinized for quite some time. How could this be? And why? For buying bootleg whiskey during the prohibition? No. That was impossible. Somebody had been feeding the police false, yet incriminating, information about me. Who? Who could be so maliciously motivated?

My benefactress, the Queen Bee of Vice, sat down next to me with a notebook and pen and spoke in her soft and soothing tone.

"Okay, Mark, this is really no big deal. If you just tell me the exact truth, you will spend probably just one night at the jail, and your friends can get you tomorrow. But you must tell me the truth"

I answered in a cooperative yet assertive voice, "I understand. And I am willing to tell you the exact truth. But before I start, I need a question answered for me—truthfully."

"Okay. What is it?"

"Obviously, somebody has been informing on me. Who is it?"

"Well ... the truth is we do not know the person. They called the anonymous phone line with information about you. We do not know who the person is."

I grasped for some clue. "Okay, but was it a farang or a Thai person?"

"Oh, he was a farang, for sure. Not a Thai person."

"What about an accent? American or European?"

"Oh, yes, he was European, for sure."

One half of my mind wrestled with this confusing information, while the other half conjured the spirit of that clever scoundrel, Huckleberry Finn, in preparation for a soft interrogation surely laced with booby traps. I was going to need to fabricate a convincing story woven of non-contradictory "stretchers," a narrative which would minimize my exposure, yet also protect Lek, her friends and family, and Kris.

***

And over the next twenty minutes, I deftly answered every question with sincere eye contact and credible half-truths. Apparently, I satisfied the suspicions of the detectives. I was soon signing off on a statement, in which I admitted (falsely) to buying the narcotic from an unknown person on Soi 6, with my own money, solely for my personal use, and with no intent to sell the contraband to another party. The report also stated the officers' conclusion that because of the small amount (less than half a gram) and because of my forthrightness, it was clear that I was not trafficking in drugs. (At least, that is what they told me it said.) After a friendly cigarette break, some fingerprinting and photo ops, two phone calls (one, of course, to my man Rood in Kamala Beach, and the other to Lek), I was respectfully repatriated to the city jail, with superficial goodwill demonstrated by all parties.

Lying on the bare concrete floor with a water bottle for a pillow, and a dozen or so friendly Thai cellmates for company, I concluded that this lock-up was tolerable—except for the uncertainty of release. But the involuntary downtime allowed my mind to focus on the task of peeling away the layers of clues and contradictions that enveloped the enigma at the core of my predicament: Who the hell had a grudge against me? Who was so full of venom that they would resort to such a dirty low-down trick? He was a foreigner, yet I had virtually no contact with foreigners since my arrival in March ... except Marcel. He was a drunk from Switzerland whom I had met through Rood. I had stayed at his guest apartment during my excursion to Kamala Beach. We had an argument late one night when he was sloshed, and I was annoyed. And I still owed him 2,000 baht for my stay. That's it! I decided he must be the one. He was the only farang I knew in Phuket, he had a grudge, and he was unpredictable when hammered—which was often. I concluded that I could be 95 percent certain that he was the culprit, and I began to stew with silent fury.

***

On the morning of my third day, I was called out of the cell and escorted to the offices on the building's second floor. There sat Rood and a farang attorney. Lek arrived about five minutes later. I could read the expression on Rood's face: he was annoyed—not at me, but at the fact that this problem had occurred in the jurisdiction of Phuket Town. This was not his turf. If this had gone down in Kamala Beach, the whole episode would have been over two hours after my arrest. Lek's face showed her honest and intense concern for my well-being. For whatever reason, that young woman believed that I walked on water. Thankfully, it was her devotion, and her mystery connection with an influential member of the police department, which resulted in my release from jail later in the afternoon. In lieu of bail, Lek had signed a personal guarantee that I would appear in court two weeks later. I was still uncertain what charges or penalties I was facing. The cops all said I would *most probably* just have a possession charge. But the likely penalty was a matter of total ambiguity. A short jail term? Just a fine? When would my passport be returned? This was Thailand, where "justice" has always been completely arbitrary.

As I clung to the back of Lek's motorbike, an approaching monsoon blew the wild wind of freedom through my hair, and every street was a fleeting streak of beauty as the town lit up with the vivid-colored neon piercing the descending dusk. A profound gratitude for my deliverance flooded my heart. Perhaps, every few years, everyone should get jailed for a three-day stint— there would be a lot less bitching in the world, and a lot more appreciation for the state of grace that is human liberty. My gratitude was compounded when I discovered a large deposit to my checking account. I immediately moved back to my bachelor pad at the Wide condo complex, despite Lek's ill-concealed dejection. I knew she intended on keeping watch over me at her boarding house. But how could she possibly expect me to stay with her, while under a microscope of police surveillance?

I already felt eyes upon me, and I suspected almost everyone of having hidden motives. Suspicions and theories of low probability spun in my head with the plodding inconsistency of a battered secondhand washing machine. With every idiosyncrasy of daily life or slight change in ordinary behavior of my acquaintances, I privately analyzed in my increasingly paranoid thought processes. The Fear was tightening its grip on reason and rational thought, and was reinforced by its partner in the destruction of the human will: uncertainty. This was, after all, Thailand. I had always loved that beguiling, yet exasperating land of wonders. However, I realized a long time ago that this is a country where you never know the real truth. The biggest fools on Earth are the expats who brag about the number of years they have resided in Thailand, and, consequently, know everything there is to know about the Kingdom. The more an expat brags, I become more convinced that he is full of shit. The only rock-solid 100 percent truth is that a farang *cannot* put absolute trust in anything, or (almost) anyone in this Land of Duplicitous Smiles.

So saddled with the weight of uncertainty and the shackles of pervasive fear, I hunkered down in my condo and shunned personal contact with almost every one of my friends and acquaintances. My communications over the phone or social media were rare, terse, and business-like. I unleashed a horribly unfair message to Marcel, which was laced with accusations and threats, an indictment and conviction of him as the villain behind a vengeful frame job. I contacted Kris to explain my absence from our meeting, and to announce that I would be needing to keep my distance from him because of the obvious danger of associating with anyone on Soi 11. He seemed to have understood at the time. But after just one day, he resumed calling several times a week with offers of support or offers of business transactions.

I spoke to Lek only on the phone, and solely for the purpose of acquiring professional advice from one of her police contacts. Finally, I contacted the incredibly helpful (and stunningly beautiful) Kat, in order to hire her for translation services. Navigating the pitfalls of an unfair and confounding legal process is harrowing enough, but to endure the ordeal without understanding any of the communications is about as anxiety-ridden a tribulation imaginable. I was lucky to have found a competent translator, and I was extraordinarily lucky that she would also prove to be a lady of personal integrity, compassion, and loyalty.

CHAPTER 19

WHAT ABOUT BOB? (LATE JUNE)

The free soul is rare, but you know
it when you see it—basically
because you feel good, very good,
when you are near or with them.

—CHARLES BUKOWSKI

The one exception to my policy of isolation was my loyal, but bumbling, buddy, Bob. I relied upon this old friend's visits to my bunker. His unintentional hilarity kept me sane, entertained, and in a positive mindset. The two of us had been friends for a dozen years. We had first met on Koh Phi Phi, where Bob demonstrated his artistic skills by inking the tattoos on my shoulders. We had been through plenty of adventures and mishaps together and had alternated roles in bailing each other out of trouble. He was an exception to my previously stated axiom that warned of placing complete trust in a Thai native. I trusted Bob completely. He would always have my back ... but I also had full confidence that he would be scatterbrained and careless enough to stumble into trouble of his own on an almost daily basis.

Although he lived on Patong Beach, Bob often stopped by my place either before or after his daily mushroom hunt to the north. It was still Phuket's monsoon season, during which the heavy rains drench the dung of grazing elephants with enough water to spur the growth of wild mushrooms, the "groovy kind" craved by hippies, college kids, and other assorted free spirits. A good portion of Bob's annual income depended on his mushroom harvest and selling the crop (for a hefty profit) to Phuket's sizable backpacker set and a few weed-friendly beach bars. Tragically, the year 2020 was shackled by the COVID-19 crisis, and the crippling lockdowns had torpedoed demand. Bob could only harvest, hoard, and hope for a timely rebound of Thailand's tourism industry. Realizing that my friend was in potentially spirit-killing financial distress, I knew that I had to step up and make periodic purchases of the mind-altering mycelia, just so that my income-bereft buddy could attain some level of liquidity.

Besides, when you are lying low from the law, hemmed in by curfews and travel restrictions, and you spend your time researching and over-analyzing an alien system of jurisprudence, slumming on social media, and succumbing to the torture of Thai television, it can be therapeutic to drink a cup of freshly brewed mushroom tea, ride the elevator up to the rooftop pool, and ponder the panorama of a tropical sea surrounded by the lush flora of a half-tamed jungle sprawled out with lazy calm under a gentle sky peppered with listless puffs of ragged white. From that elevated perspective, you gaze with wonder as Mother Nature and her supporting cast of characters all suddenly explode in a fit of kaleidoscopic animation. A grove of mature palms rises up as one unit; a synchronized battalion of tree creatures capable of fluid movement begin to march, as if they were Tolkien's fictional Ents on the warpath in Middle Earth. The thick jumble of sagging clouds transforms into purple and pink holograms, with fluctuating shapes and expressions against a background of shifting yellow and orange ...

Well, you get the idea. I gained a few hours of distraction from the legal fiasco hanging over my head, and Bob gained some much-needed baht for his wallet. And I also reaped the reward of an immaculate condo; Bob was a cleaning dynamo! Well, there was one exception: he could probably stand to attend a workshop on identifying and using the right type of cleaning agent.

Just a couple of days after I had moved back in, Bob stopped by to tell me all about his politically powerful uncle, who was going to look into my case and determine if he could help. Wonderful news! Any hopeful sign of assistance was certainly welcome. Bob was really excited about the development, and he demonstrated his energy by speed-cleaning the condo—while also speed-telling his story. I listened, simultaneously researching attorneys on my laptop.

Suddenly, Bob let out a yell and followed it with a string of panicked f-bombs. Looking up, I saw him rubbing his eyes with one hand, while he shook his head from side to side. Overcoming his distress, Bob muttered, "Mark, this one supposed to make the room smell good—but not do! What happened?"

I looked at the small, green canister labeled NATO, which he held up with an outstretched arm, and thought, *Jesus Christ, Bob!*

But I collected myself and said, "No, Bob. That's not air freshener. That is pepper spray."

Looking puzzled, he asked, "What you mean?"

In a tone of resigned amusement, I explained, "That is NATO-issued pepper spray. Mace. It's for protection—which I no longer have."

As I stated before, my man was a friend of guileless loyalty, but also apt to do some really stupid shit!

***

At that time, the curfew for Phuket was still 11 p.m., so if Bob were visiting, the prudent time for him to leave for Patong would be about 10:15 p.m. (although Bob and the word "prudent" should never be used in the same sentence). On a typical night, the start of curfew would also mark the arrival of the heebie-jeebies: the twisted nerves caused by the encroachment of the Fear and my angry anxiety produced by total awareness of total vulnerability. I would be alone again with my thoughts, suspicions, and regrets. How did I stumble into this mess? Had it been a mistake to travel to Thailand with a pandemic just beginning? But how had everything seemed so prearranged? I had stayed literally one day ahead of every lockdown, and when I finally was locked down, I just happened to run into Lek, who just so happened to have accommodations. It was like a trap—a trap arranged by those Crazy Fates.

I would often creep back to the bedroom, which fronted the main thoroughfare running along that edge of town. Then, slightly cracking the curtains and using binoculars, I would scope out the streets and sois closest to the condominium. Hours could be spent attempting to differentiate shadows from potential police, or deciding if parked cars had living occupants staring back at me. Despite my self-knowledge of an overtaxed imagination and a weakening grip on reality resulting from a lack of quality sleep, I was still confident in the strength of my mind and spirit. I still trusted my instinct and my logic-based conclusions.

After a few days, I was convinced that a certain white van, which I had seen every night, was a surveillance vehicle. It would be parked in different alleys on different nights. And I was almost certain when looking through the binoculars that I could see a person (or persons) inside. Or maybe these "sightings" were just the phantoms of a paranoid imagination that had been doused with the accelerant Monsoon Mushroom Tea.

A few days later, Bob stopped by early in the evening. He had been to Lek's place to pick up my court documents (and, probably, less wholesome items). I was fine with this, however, I advised him to refrain from going directly from Lek's house to my condo, because I didn't need to look at any more whiteboards indicating my involvement with certain people and locations. I lectured Bob on the importance of taking extra precautions, and he agreed to them. Although agreeing to a policy, and then actually implementing and adhering to said policy, is not a strength of Bob's. He started off in fine shape, leaving my place at about 9:30 p.m. However, twenty minutes after his departure, one of my mobile phones rang. As I walked to the bedroom, I debated the pros and cons of answering the call, but The Responsible Side won out. I picked up the phone. I immediately regretted that decision.

In a subdued tone of voice—almost a whisper—Bob said, "Mark. I need 15,000 baht."

Amazed and almost speechless, I said, "What the fuck are you talking about? Where the hell are you?"

"I stay at police station. I need 15,000 baht. You must come here! Or they lock me!"

"You gotta be shittin' me, Bob! It's 10:15—okay! I'm going to walk to the ATM and see how much money I can get out. Call me in a half hour."

I probably looked like a schizophrenic off his meds as I shouted curses at myself while fast-walking to the closest ATM. As I suspected, I could only withdraw 10,000 baht for that day. *Too bad, Bob. Sorry.* Five minutes after returning to my hideaway, Bob called.

"Bob, I only have 10,000."

"Okay, maybe that's enough—"

"Bob! It doesn't matter! The curfew starts in ten minutes. I do not have time to get there!"

"Oh, no problem. No problem, Mark. The police can come with me to your room—"

"No! No! No! What the hell is wrong with you, Bob? Do not bring police to my room! Ever! Never ever! Understand?"

Bob muttered something unintelligible, and the line went dead.

Good God, I wanted to strangle him!

Twenty minutes later, I answered the ringing phone to hear Bob say, "It's okay, Mark. Everything clear! My uncle wired the police the money already."

"Thank God. Where are you?"

You know…. Mark, I'm in the hallway."

"What hallway, Bob?"

"The hallway outside your room. I knock on the door right now."

Hell's Bells, I might just go to jail for homicide.

I took a look through the peephole and recognized Bob's curly mop in sweaty disarray, hanging over and partially hiding the kind and crazy features of his bronze face. I took a deep breath, prayed for patience, and opened the door. Bob rushed in with his mouth motoring full-throttle, as he recounted his ninety-minute adventure: the police roadblock, the lack of ID or insurance for his motorbike, the yaba pill in his sock, etc. I remained silent, allowing him to get his story out, but I soon tired of his ramblings and cut him off.

"Bob, you must understand something. No matter what you do, you do not send cops to my place!"

"But, Mark, I know one policeman. He a good man. They not do anything to you. They only want 10,000 from me!"

"Damn it, Bobby, listen! Do you think that if you brought those cops here to see your farang friend in this really nice condo that they would just let it all go? No. They would set me up, and they would shake me down. You know I'm not rich, but they would think so because of where I'm staying! And I don't have $100,000 or $200,000 baht."

"But, Mark—"

"No buts, Bob! Just do not bring cops to where I live! And do not tell them you came here from Lek's place. That's nothing but trouble for all of us. Did they follow you here when you left?"

"No."

"Sure?"

"Yes! I made sure."

"Alright. Sleep on the sofa chair. I'm going to bed. You really wear me out, Bobby."

"Goodnight, Mark. Thank you."

Back in my bedroom, I laid down in the dark, desperately hoping that this incident did not somehow get into the gossip mill of Phuket law enforcement. The last thing I needed was another coincidence used as proof against me. But I had a strong intuitive notion that there was someone in power (or close to power) who was proactively fucking with my fortunes. Well, I had two more days until Kat and I met with the police contact, and six more days until I had to appear at the Phuket Provincial Court. I held out hope that I would just have to pay a modest fine. I could put the whole ordeal to rest, and make preparations for a post-lockdown exodus from the island. But the disturbing vibes radiating from my instinct were telling me that there was more trouble up around the bend.

CHAPTER 20

STRATEGIES AND SURPRISES (LATE JUNE)

Never turn your back on Fear. It
should always be in front of you, like
a thing that might have to be killed."

—Hunter S. Thompson

P-Chang was middle-aged, sturdily built, and stony-faced, but this rough exterior seemed to obscure a humble and empathetic spirit. He sat next to me, with his thick hands resting on the glass kitchen table, chattering away in rapid Thai, eventually reaching the velocity at which my understanding of the conversation typically goes from lost to utterly befuddled. But Kat was a pro; she could translate the concerns and questions written on my changing facial expressions as effectively as she translated the languages of East and West. As an added advantage, she had the ex-cop (or actual cop, or liaison, or outright fraud) smitten with her stunning physical beauty and her attitude of confident independence. Although I was (and remain) unsure of P-Chang's exact role, it became clear that he had inside knowledge of "the system."

After an hour-long conference held in the friendly confines of my condo, his advice consisted of the following recommendations:

1. To go through the process of attending each of three court appearances that would be spaced two weeks apart.
2. Keep myself out of trouble, and my body free of forbidden substances, as I would be taking a drug test at the court.
3. Be aware that I was being followed and watched by the police—even here at my upscale condo.
4. Expect to pay a fine of between 20,000 and 40,000 baht, and then my soon-to-be expired passport would be returned, and I could be on my way.

As the meeting ended, P-Chang asked if I recognized him, and I replied that he looked quite familiar. Chuckling, he then asked if I remembered saying hello to him at the 7-Eleven. I answered that, yeah, I remembered him now, but at the time, I thought he was just an acquaintance from years past, someone whose name I could not recall. It turns out that he had been following me as part of the surveillance team. We both laughed, and he became even more joyful when Kat informed him that she and I were not romantically linked (which was not *entirely* true, technically speaking).

When the meeting concluded, I was in high spirits. I now had a solid strategy, a surefire ally in Kat, and a vindication of my suspicions— confirmation that I was not in the throes of a paranoia-induced psychological breakdown. The police really were outside in the dark drizzle of 2 a.m. and surveilling my condo, as I peered out through a crack in the curtains. Although I was not guilty of anything that would require such a degree of surveillance, the cops were still *hoping* that I was guilty of something, which could increase the size of a potential payoff. (Welcome to Thai "justice"!)

***

Four days later, sharply dressed and acutely stressed, I rode on the back of Kat's motorbike for what I assumed would be a formal, morning-long court proceeding. But we were both surprised when the clerk behind window number three simply slipped us a certificate of attendance form. I provided my initials and signature in the appropriate places, and the clerk gave us instructions to return in two weeks. I was astonished, and, of course, incredibly relieved at this development. In fact, I was in a state of disbelief at the simplicity of the proceeding. I had spent so much time in anxious preparation for a potentially catastrophic outcome of the hearing that this result seemed too good to be true.

As an added bonus, Kat was free for the rest of the day and was willing to spend it hanging out with me. Over a late breakfast, we discussed strategies for continuing this apparent success, and also discussed the logistics of keeping me out of sight and out of the mind of local law enforcement. My mind was already racing with possibilities. Actually, my mind was focused on one course of immediate action. Along with Phuket's roads being reopened, the surrounding sea was now accessible. This meant that I had the perfect opportunity to shed the surveillance of Phuket's spies, take a boat ride I had put off for far too long, and return to a special place, an island that would always occupy territory in my heart, as well as provide the dreamscape for innumerable adventures of my subconscious during the sleeping hours of my life. Suddenly exuberant, I asked Kat if she would like to go on a short holiday with me as an expression of my gratitude. "Of course," she said. She would love to go with me on a boat ride to the currently tourist-free paradise of Koh Phi Phi.

Although I thoroughly enjoyed my residence at the Wide Condominium, I had to face the fact that continuing to live there would be a stupid and unnecessary risk. I packed up all of my belongings and made preparations for a mini-vacation. The reservations would be for a party of three, now that Kat's pal, Alicia, would be joining the pilgrimage. I knew that upon returning from Koh Phi Phi, I would be seeking accommodations in another Phuket location—far from Phuket Town and its multitude of potential pitfalls. I was going to put an end to this surveillance shit. But before I made my exodus, two unexpected events provided new and crucial information that changed my perspective, my understanding, and potentially my battle-plan concerning this possibly life-ruining legal situation.

The first development was an urgent message that I received from Lek's sister. Lek's boarding house had been raided by the Crime Suppression Unit, with the result being that Lek, along with five tenants, had been hauled off in the paddy-wagon, and now the lot of them were having an impromptu slumber party as they enjoyed the amenities of the Phuket Town jail. As much as I felt duty-bound to come to Lek's aid, basic logic convinced me that contacting her was a logistical impossibility. She was the guarantor of my "free on bail" status. Common sense and deductive reasoning clearly indicated that my status would be immediately revoked if the guarantor of my freedom was locked up herself. I figured that if I went to visit Lek at the jail, I would not be coming back out.

Secondly, I had no real idea what the total amount of my own fines/bribes/court costs would be, and so it was clearly necessary to save as much of my modest cash supply as possible for any eventuality.

Finally, the fact that her business was raided made me question Lek's supposed "powerful friends" on the Phuket police force—particularly P-Chang, who had become a slippery eel when Kat tried to contact him with follow-up questions. This put everything that I learned in our meeting into the category of questionable information. How could I possibly believe he could help me if he could not even help his close friend who was native Thai? There were many angles from which to view this situation, but they all pointed to dirty deals and institutional corruption. I imagine that there must have been double-crosses, triple-crosses, and even quadruple-crosses going on behind the scenes. Surely, a spider web of deceit and betrayal existed within the ranks of Thai law enforcement, a web I could not hope to escape if caught. Clearly, I needed to remove myself entirely from Phuket Town and everyone I knew there.

The second perspective-changing occurrence was a phone call I received from the Shroom Tycoon. Once again, Bob was on one of his wild runs of irresponsibility, and he was calling me for the phone number of Kris. No doubt, Bob was on the hunt for yaba. I complied, but with a warning: "Okay Bob, I'll give you his number, but don't come here with anything, and if you get caught don't say a word about me."

He agreed and I went back to packing, cleaning, and hoping that I would make my escape before any more absurdities arose from unexpected events. When I finished my chores, I laid down for a nap, although my rest was soon cut off by the ringing phone. It was Bob, and he spoke with agitation and babbling excitement.

"Mark, I must tell you something really important! You must understand. Your friend, Kris, knows many police!"

"Why do you think that?"

"Listen, Mark, I buy yaba from him. This one not same style. This one old style yaba. Not same they have now. Mark—this one really strong. Only police have this one. I not smoke this one for long time. The only way to get this one is if police give back to the mafia."

I considered this, and then attempted a bit of dry humor: "Bob, when you say old style, what year vintage are we talking about? The super high-grade from '08 and '09? Or is it the premium of 2012?"

Being a bit tone-deaf in the irony department, Bob continued with focused enthusiasm: "Mark, I'm not sure, but I know this one nobody have for long time. Your friend, Kris, get this from police! Sure!"

Finally, the revelation! In an instant, I had the answer to the most persistent and maddening life mystery in a decade!

"Shit, Bob! You know what this means?"

"Yes, your friend work with the police."

"Right. But son of a bitch! That sack of shit, he's the bastard that set me up!"

"Mark, listen. You must not contact him again."

"Exactly, Bob. I don't want to have a murder charge on top of everything else! And you have to delete his number and his messages—and don't call me or message me until I contact you after I get to go to Koh Phi Phi."

"Okay, okay, yes, Mark. But leave right away!"

"Tomorrow. Tomorrow morning. Bobby? Great job, brother. Awesome! Thanks man!"

I hung up the phone, poured a drink, lit a cigarette, and began absorbing this astonishing revelation of betrayal. I undertook a diligent memory search for every detail of my relationship with Kris, and several overlooked items, which—when put together—reminded me of the fact that the clarity of hindsight is far more powerful than 20/20 vision. It is more like gazing at a view through high-grade binoculars. The amount of evidence that Kris (and the police) had used to set a trap for me was overwhelming. I was also smacked by the undeniable realization that the motherly voiced vice-squad leader was, in actuality, just a typical woman of Siam, steeped in mendacity and deception. She had lied to my face about *the one truth* that I had asked for in return for my total cooperation; actually, it was compliance to the extent of self-incrimination! And, of course, she couldn't just admit that it was a Thai who had called the anonymous tip line. No, this is the culture of saving face—even if it means sacrificing truth and justice, or scapegoating the innocent.

RULE NUMBER ONE: Always scapegoat the foreigner, whether it is (preferably) a Malay or (ideally) a Burmese or (reluctantly) a Westerner.

I sulked in shame at what a gullible dupe I had shown myself to be, and I once again cursed my unreliable instinct. The signs had been right in front of my face: Kris had pathetic English skills, yet he sent me messages with explicit language (spelled correctly) offering illegal substances for sale, and he had sent many of these messages over the last month. In addition, I knew that he had legal issues of his own because he had "borrowed" money from me in order to make payments to the court for a previous arrest. Also, Kris had disappeared on two separate occasions, both for three-day periods, and when I inquired of his whereabouts, another contact on Soi 11 told me that he had been taken to jail.

But the most powerful piece of evidence was the manner in which he acted the day of my arrest. For one thing, he kept postponing the time of our meeting as he stalled me all afternoon long, which indicates that he was also making arrangements with other interested parties (i.e., police). Next there was the fact that this was the first time that Kris volunteered—no, *insisted*— that we meet at a location other than Soi 11. Finally, the most damning aspect of Kris's behavior was the fact that, during those afternoon calls, he doggedly attempted to convince me to engage in a far larger transaction than simply making a small trade for the benefit of a friend. He continually requested that I bring him a larger amount of ice because (he boasted) he would quickly be able to sell it for a big profit, which we would split. I had shot this idea down, explaining that I was just doing a favor for the lady who managed the building where I was staying.

When I consolidated these various pieces of information, I arrived at the following reconstruction: Kris was in deep trouble with the police, either before I met him or shortly thereafter, and he was keeping himself out of jail by promising a bigger prize (myself) or prizes (maybe he was setting up others). Shortly after I met him, he began to use me as bait by promising the cops that I was a big-time player, and he just needed time to gain my trust and to gather evidence. And this is when he began to send explicit messages, in order to entrap me with a documented conversation as evidence. He was surprised and unprepared when I called on that fateful day to ask about making a trade, and that is why it took him all day to arrange our meeting. He needed to coordinate with the vice squad so that they could ambush me in a location unobservable from Soi 11. It would have been inconsiderate for the goon squad to make a bust on the turf of the *actual* criminals who paid them good money for their operations to remain undisturbed. This explains the high expectations of that pathetic posse of police, and also provides the reason for the inordinate anger and disappointment when the belligerent dopes failed to find anything illegal in a significant enough size to orchestrate a proper Royal Thai Police shakedown. There was no doubt that Kris was the ungrateful fraud who was so unscrupulous and dishonorable that he could betray my friendship and pay back my kindness with the potential loss of my freedom.

***

Betrayal. There is nothing quite so painful as the shock of a sharp dagger driven between the shoulder blades, and the knowledge that it was delivered by the hand of a trusted friend, or a person who—solely out of human kindness—you had attempted to help. This type of wound unleashes the poison of cynicism into the blood stream, and it also begins to infect the soul with the pathological ailments of rage and revenge. That evening all of these malignancies began to assail my spirit as I tried to fall asleep and rejuvenate mind and body before the trip across the sea. Of course, the dominating thought, and the one that morphed into violent fantasies in the mind, was: *revenge.* I desperately wanted to walk to Soi 11 and give Kris a well-deserved beat down in front of the mafia, his wife ... but no! I could not hurt him in front of his young daughter, the adorable little girl who had just had a birthday a few weeks earlier. Kris had had no money for her present, and he called me about this problem at 9:45 p.m. With the curfew at 10 p.m., I fast-walked to 7-Eleven, found the best thing available (I think it was a toy tea set), and made sure to get it to Kris via my regular motorcycle-taxi driver so that the little girl would have her present for her birthday.

Revenge is a horrible transaction, and I was lucky that those mean, spirit-killing thoughts dissipated before I boarded that boat to a place where I could forget about it all.

CHAPTER 21

FROM PARADISE (EARLY JULY)

Where a man feels at home,
other than where he's born,
is where he's meant to go.

—ERNEST HEMINGWAY

With a tight knot of anticipation in my stomach, I had threaded my way through the paved paths leading home, noting both the familiar and the foreign; additions and subtractions to businesses and buildings had tweaked the appearance of Ton Sai Village since my last visit seven years prior. But it was the shock of the surreal solitude which one could experience everywhere on Phi Phi Don that was the most conspicuous change of the island's character. I had returned to an island left almost empty of humanity.

The village thoroughfares now had: no young locals shoving two-wheeled carts of farang luggage to and from hotels; no young women of the Western world lugging comically overstuffed backpacks, grimacing with sweaty faces, and chattering an exasperated commentary of complaints; no drunken Aussies or English boy-men stumbling in packs from pub to pub; no natives with faces of barely concealed contempt going about their business or hustling baht from the mass of intruders; no uniformed harems of local ladies singing from shopfronts the same lyrical offers of Thai massage; no foolish kids financing extended stays by pressing paper flyers (boasting of cheap booze at bars) into the hands of passers-by. I had seen three people (two of them I knew), since I had left Kat and the other two ladies back at the guest house for my solo mission. I never imagined that I would experience so much joy from seeing the island free from the self-absorbed masses. This was the most spiritually fulfilling view of emptiness since my last trip to the Grand Canyon.

But on the less-trodden back road to the beach, the territory was essentially unchanged. On the left were a handful of shuttered shops, and on the right lay the swampy jungle of the upper reaches of the tidal stream, then the four-story tsunami evacuation building (or as Ben calls it, the "Corruption Memorial")—its aesthetics apparently influenced by Cold War Era Soviet architecture. Just a few feet further, a sad, unkempt, little "garden" lay lonely between the encroaching jungle and the sea, the villain responsible for its creation. This hodgepodge of vegetation, and a collection of plaques engraved with the names of victims, was what remained of the previous memorial that had been, at least, a respectable and respectful remembrance of the victims of the 2004 tsunami.

Just a few strides farther, on the left, stood the Sunflower Beach Bar and Boathouse. It was closed down, along with 75 percent of Phi Phi's business operations. The open-air entrance had been blocked by a barrier of ropes and tarps, but I slipped in through the back gate and crept in silence until I spotted my prey: a shirtless, wiry, bronze frame of a man with long, gray tangles of frazzled hair dangling over and obscuring his face. He was methodically marking pen strokes upon the pages of a ledger while sitting cross-legged upon the same familiar seat—the bow section of a busted long-tail boat.

Without looking up and in a deadpan voice, Ben said, "Uncle Mark, so you get out of jail."

Ben's prescience and intuitive powers had always astonished me, but this was something else.

"How are you, my brother?" I asked as I put my right arm over his shoulder in a half hug.

In a mellow tone, he explained, "I change everything, Uncle Mark. I am good. Now I just take it easy and meditate. No more drinking or smoking."

"Awesome! And you are not sick?" I asked.

"No! Never sick. I'm seven!" and we both chuckled at his old joke.

My friend's self-medicating practices had long ago become self-destructive binges—often resulting in dramatic (sometimes violent) outbursts. I understood very well his pain-driven choices, as the personal devastation he suffered from the '04 tsunami would have driven almost anyone to insanity or suicide. But Ben's chemical-based coping mechanisms had outlived their shelf life, and the change in lifestyle was already showing positive results in my friend's equanimity and physical health. He seemed to have found an inner peace, which my instincts told me was surely the work of his wonderful daughter.

"So then you know about my ... legal problems?" I stammered.

"Of course! But I knew it was a small thing. You didn't need my help for it. If you did, I would have come to Phuket," he answered.

"Thanks, Ben. I didn't want to bother you with it."

Ben waved his hand complacently in the air, saying, "Enough about police. Police boring me every time."

He drew out the words and flashed his crooked pirate smile.

***

Although his operation was closed, Ben insisted that I go get my stuff and move into one of his guest rooms. He reasoned that it made no sense to pay for a room in town, especially when I would be needing that money to bribe the police. I replied that I would—after my female guests went back to Phuket in a couple of days. And so we sat and enjoyed each other's company, sometimes chatting a bit, but mostly in silence, as we still retained a unique bond of understanding which rendered speech unnecessary. Ben meditated while making small marks in the ledger, and I wrote and watched the effects of the setting sun, which colored pink and purple streaks upon the narrow bands of clouds stretching across the horizon outside Lo Dalam Bay. And I once again felt the familiar peaceful easy feeling of my former sanctuary.

The next day was that rare day in a person's life: a day so impossibly perfect that the memory is often confused with a ridiculous dream. I had arranged to take the ladies (with the addition of Kiki, my harem now numbered three) on a long-tail boat ride to Phi Phi Leh, the sublime national park that was in a robust state of rejuvenation as a result of the tourist-free conditions. Free from the constant traffic of speedboats, dive-boats, long tails, and the multitudes of often-careless tourists, the beaches, coves, coral, and aquatic wildlife had been given the chance to return to a more natural state.

These were the ingredients of the ideal open boat excursion: one ganja-smoking local guide, three lovely ladies in bikinis, vodka and ginger ale, a soft blue sky, a smooth sea, and the astounding natural beauty of the island's limestone cliffs, caves, and inlets of clear placid water flashing yellow and pink from the massive streaking schools of fish. And all of this was amplified by the amazing fact that there was no one else around. Not a soul.

When the girls swam to one of the small stretches of sand for an impromptu photo shoot, I raised my smiling face to the sky, and thanked the Creator, acknowledging my ignorance that I had no clue just what I had done to deserve this day, and promising that I would always remember it for those times in the future when Fate was not in my favor. Back home in the States, people were being violently assaulted, and cities burned because of the pernicious Marxist lie of white privilege expounded in the aftermath of the George Floyd riots. But I was living in an alternative universe, where ridiculous concepts became realities, and that day I had a triple serving of white privilege.

After soaking up several hours of paradise, we eventually made the run back to Phi Phi Don—with just one quick stop at Monkey Beach, where we encountered our first humans of the island tour. A lone father was attending to his three young sons. Two of them were playing in the sand, while one clung to his father's arms as they waded in the slight surf. As our long tail cruised towards shore, the man continued to stare at the three gorgeous ladies sitting about the bow. When we anchored up, just a few yards away, the man was still transfixed by the three sexy sirens.

I decided to break off his revelry: "Hey, I know what you're thinking, but I'm not making any trades today! You got your three, and I've got mine!"

Kiki—who had done more than her part in draining the fifth of vodka—burst into laughter, but unfortunately the expressionless man was either a non-native English speaker, or simply a German who suffered from the typical Teutonic handicap of a non-existent sense of humor.

That night would be our last together, as the girls were booked for the early morning departure. I was planning an early night in, but Kiki invited me to join the ladies for drinks. Remembering that this circumstance was a once-in-a-lifetime stroke of good fortune, I rallied, agreed to meet them, and asked if they needed anything. This was a rather innocuous question, but while sitting and sipping sangria with my girls, I received a message from Kiki, who sat directly across from me.

The message said, "Yes, I need something. I want ice."

I immediately handed my phone to Kiki and asked, "Did you just send this?"

"No! Absolutely not!" she replied in confusion.

Well, it was a message to my account from her account, and she clearly did not send it. *Nice try, Phuket police. Now I know you have hacked my phone and social media accounts, you greedy bastards!* The cops must have been convinced that I was engaged in serious criminal activity, or more likely, their greed for a big payoff led them to this fairy tale. At any rate, I was disgusted by the whole sordid mess.

For three days I had been free from the clouds of apprehension, ambiguity, and The Fear, but this intrusive remark had penetrated my peace of mind—here in the place that used to be my fortress and sanctuary from the anxieties of life. And that night, I had my first thoughts of an escape, an unsanctioned exodus from the Land of Smiles. I could hole up here with Ben until a sailboat or other sea-going opportunity presented itself. Or, with Ben's many connections, I could even pay to be smuggled to Malaysia. But with no passport, and the severe pandemic restrictions in place everywhere, I was looking at a dead end. I shelved the foolish fantasy.

But I did stay on for the island for a few more days. I was able to revisit my old stomping grounds, remember, and reflect on past and present. Residing at my former home, I spent much needed time with Ben; I was aware of, and dreading, the possibility that the court could ban me from ever returning. Perhaps Ben had also considered that possible outcome, but we did not discuss the issue. Finally, I was able to catch up with the few friends that remained on the island, hanging on to a hopelessly emaciated economy. The coronavirus had proven to be a double-edged sword for Koh Phi Phi. The economic shutdown was acutely painful for my friends, but it provided the conditions for an environmental regeneration, and possibly a renaissance of the spiritual and cultural components of the Phi Phi experience. My hope is that this "time out" will spur the island's decision-makers to institute a managed tourist trade and decide on reasonable controls to keep the island from being overrun by wasted jackasses, while allowing considerate and appreciative folks the opportunity to enjoy the beauty and spirit of this paradise.

CHAPTER 22

TO PURGATORY (MID-LATE JULY)

You gonna get used to them chains,
after a while, Luke. But you never
stop listening to them clinging.

—THE WARDEN, *COOL HAND LUKE*

O n the side of a rounded hill, the Phuket Provincial Court stands partially shaded by the canopy of intruding jungle. It is served by a gravel parking lot at its base, and on the path between the two, there is an open-air snack shop, which is where Kat and I were having a palaver prior to entering the court. Not only had my trusty translator picked me up in Phuket Town after my return from Koh Phi Phi, but she had also spoken to our "police contact," P-Chang. He had confirmed that today's appearance was just another check-in appointment, and nothing for concern. Kat had also located and negotiated the price for a top-notch condominium in Rawai Beach to serve as my new hideaway.

After finishing our coffee, we began walking up the steep path, which was now populated by far more customers than our last visit. "Farang!" I heard a little girl's voice ring out, and I looked over to see Kris's wife and daughter strolling past us, the youngster smiling and pointing at me, while her mother hurried her away, pulling her by the hand, keeping her own head down. *Okay, so the black heart still has business at the court,* I thought. Now my formerly relaxed feelings switched gears into anxious suspense. *Where was Kris? Sitting in jail? Inside the courthouse providing false testimony about me?*

Reading my face, Kat asked me about the pair who had just passed us by in a rush. I replied that they were the family of my betrayer.

"Mark, if you see him, do not say or do anything to him," she ordered in that even tone of authority used sparingly, but effectively, by women of extraordinary beauty.

"I know, Kat. Don't worry. I'll control myself," I assured her. I also tipped my hat to those Crazy Fates who loved to tease me with "coincidences" such as this random encounter.

But there was no sign of the back-stabber, and this appointment took just seconds. My paperwork was stamped, and Kat and I were on our way to Rawai Beach, the location of my new hideout in a just-completed eight-story building. Kat stuck around to make sure I was satisfied with the spot, and then returned to her fast-paced career. I was on my own, and new to Rawai, which was just the scenario that fit the needs of my situation. My only crucial task was to contact the US Embassy in Bangkok to confirm my eligibility for an emergency passport. I was assured that it could be done hassle-free. I then called Rood to inform him of my whereabouts and status. I had a long-standing policy of keeping my most trusted friend posted whenever I changed accommodations in Thailand.

My final call was to Bob; I wanted to make sure he had not gotten lost mushroom-hunting in an elephant sanctuary, jammed up in jail, or under a house arrest order from his long-suffering saint of a wife. I then imposed a communication moratorium—total silence with any other contacts on Phuket.

***

For two weeks, I relaxed in my new refuge and made myself comfortable to the point of complacency. I befriended the cute, always-smiling, manager, Nan, and her staff at a dive-bar just up the street—an open-air joint where I played pool in the evenings. Most mornings I ventured to the specialty bakery down the street for egg-and-cheese croissants and had late lunches at the burger joint across the street. In the afternoons, I put in the time relaxing at the rooftop pool, which commanded a stunning view of Phuket's southern shores. And after spontaneously buying a fishing rod, I decided to try my luck off the Rawai pier, but on my first angling opportunity, I made the mistake of guaranteeing a fish for my new friend, Nan, to cook for her crew. After three hours of futility, I decided to throw in the towel, yet I felt obligated to keep up appearances, and at a beachside market I bought a fresh, whole fish of the snapper variety and delivered it to Nan at her bar, while confidently claiming that I had caught it just minutes before. And then I shamelessly absorbed the adoration of Nan and the ladies on her staff.

For those readers shaking their heads in disapproval, I can confess that the precedent to this little trick was even more objectionable. Several years ago, I and that Irish instigator, Mac, had planned a fishing trip out of Koh Phi Phi. Prior to the trip, I had been boasting to anyone who would listen—and especially to the anti-fishing zealots of the island's dive shops—that Mac and I would soon be returning with coolers full of fish. As it turns out, Mac's fishing talents extend only to laughs and ladies, and I … well, I just had an off day. By 3 p.m. Mac had caught nothing but a wicked sunburn, and I had landed nothing but an enthusiastic beer buzz. While Mac marched home Frankenstein fashion because of his scalded skin, I slipped down a side alley that terminated at the island's fish market, where I purchased a four-foot shark for 1,000 baht, along with a section of light rope. Lashing one end of the rope to the monster's tail, looping the line over my right shoulder, and with the fishing rod in my left hand, I proceeded to stroll through town, and past every dive-shop, with the dead shark trailing behind me in the dust. If it were true that the eyes of humans could kill with the focused energy of their heart's hate, I would have died, at least a dozen times that afternoon. Oh well, screw them. The shark was already dead, the shopkeeper got 1,000 baht, and I found a family of Thais who enjoyed the dual pleasures of a seafood feast and the company of a half-tanked fisherman. (Unsurprisingly, I have never hooked up with a female dive instructor on that island.)

Those memories of fishing and telling "fish stories" are pleasurable to recall, but now I must return to the story at hand, which is, unfortunately, in the painful category. The morning of July 30, I awoke early and still lightly buzzed to set out for my third appearance at the Phuket Provincial Court. This time I was much more relaxed and went about my preparations with nonchalance. I was so confident my legal situation was under control that I had stayed out late with Nan the night before, and that morning I dressed casually in cargo shorts and flip-flops. From the information provided to me by P-Chang (via Kat, of course), at this appearance I would either be assessed a moderate fine that would clear up the issue, or there would be another continuance of up to three weeks. In my confidence (or ignorance), I chose not to bother Kat with the chore of accompanying me to the court. Instead, I arranged a ride with my neighbor, a cab driver who lived across the street from the condo. In my mind, the worst-case scenario would be that I did not have enough cash on hand to pay the fine. I might, perhaps, be inconveniently tossed into the courthouse jail until Rood or Bob came to sort it all out. I was wrong. Terribly wrong.

I felt the first pangs of bad vibes when approaching the security entrance to the courthouse. The uneasy feeling increased when I was denied entry because I was not wearing long pants. This was odd, in that on the other two occasions, I had felt overdressed: most people had been dressed in shorts or other casual wear. Perhaps this day was designated for official court proceedings. Fortunately, my taxi was waiting down in the parking lot. I was also lucky in that I had left my warm-weather clothes at the manager's office of the Wide Condominium, which was just a few minutes away. After a quick run there and back (and changing clothes in the van's back seat), I was able to enter the courthouse. I immediately encountered a scenario vastly different from my two prior appearances: two court officials had been waiting for me. One was a bailiff/guard and the other a thin, young Thai in civilian clothes who was to act as my interpreter. I instantly regretted not asking Kat to be by my side that morning. The young man explained that I was scheduled to go before the judge this morning and this process could take a while. A sudden second wave of bad vibes overwhelmed me. The bailiff escorted me to the parking lot, where I paid off the taxi and told him I would see him later today for my clothes.

Once back inside, the interpreter took me aside to an alcove where we sat as he explained the situation: the prosecutor had examined the evidence, and he had decided to raise the charge against me to possession of a category 1 drug with intent to sell. This is where the bad vibes transformed into the Fear, the dark terror of a nightmare come to life. I almost doubled over as if I had been punched in the gut, and I entered a state of total disbelief that manifested itself in a throbbing headache and spotty tunnel vision. I almost couldn't function. Everyone, including the police who arrested me, at least a half dozen citizens working in the legal profession, and another half dozen friends with "experience" in these matters had told me that because I had less than one gram of the substance, I could not be charged for trafficking drugs. The interpreter informed me that after the purity test, it had been determined that I had 0.41 grams of ice on my person when I was arrested, and that the actual threshold for being charged with intent to sell was 0.35 grams. Now my heart began to race, my throat felt like it was closing up, and my breath came in gasps. I barely managed to ask the interpreter what was going to happen next.

And then the hammer came down. The shy young man explained my options. My first choice was to go before the judge today, plead guilty, and if it went well, the judge would *only* impose the minimum sentence of four years in prison. *No! No, he did not just say four years, did he?* Having had one prior panic attack in my life—on a terrifying flight from Phoenix to Las Vegas—I recognized the same symptoms of that situation were now overtaking me. I had a strange thought: I was now in a place and time so far away from that previous ordeal that it was inconceivable that I was even the same soul. Now my heart was *galloping*, my vision became blurred with red and yellow spots, and my windpipe felt like it was going to close completely.

With a concentrated effort, I finally regained control of my breathing and focused my mind on the task at hand. The second option, the young man explained, was that I could plead not guilty, post the 500,000 baht ($16k) bail, and I would remain free until my next court appearance. And behind door number three: the choice to plead not guilty, and wait for my case to be resolved (typically a four-month process) as a guest of the Phuket Provincial Prison, which, for my convenience, was located just two football fields away. Option number one, obviously, was not an option at all—unless my goal was spiritual suicide. Option number two also was not within the realm of realistic choices: I didn't happen to have sixteen grand in my bank account, nor any way to obtain it. Option three it would be! I was afforded fifteen minutes to make my phone calls.

I first called a bail bonds company, and the representative informed me that it was too late in the game for them to assist me. Next, I called Rood, and he briefly spoke with the interpreter. When I got back on the line, I froze in a perfect panic: the voice of my most powerful friend was quavering with worried frustration and fear. But he composed himself and told me to hold tight. He would get working on the situation. My final call was to Lek, and I spoke to her with barely concealed outrage: she had guaranteed me that

P-Chang would have everything settled, I had paid him 10,000 baht for his help, and I had given Lek herself tens of thousands of baht since my arrival back in March. It was her contraband I was taking the fall for! I had never once said anything that could possibly implicate her or her business, and I was still keeping my mouth shut. Lek and I had an awful communication problem resulting from her almost nonexistent English, the effects of drugs on her brain, and my lack of patience. These factors were magnified during phone conversations. She could only interpret the meanings of my words through the emotions in my voice, and by the time we hung up, I knew that she was in tears.

After my calls, the guard took my backpack for safekeeping, and pushed me along into the court's holding cell, where a dozen defendants were lying about and staring at me with mild curiosity. An adjacent cell was occupied by another eight prisoners: these were the inmates from the prison who had court appearances that day. One of them—an apparent degenerate—spent an hour mockingly calling out to me: "Farang! Farang! Are you ladyboy? Farang, you ladyboy?" while I stared in the opposite direction and debated whether I needed to verbally jump his shit to send an immediate message of, "Don't fuck with me." (Hey, it had worked down in Puerto Penasco two decades ago.)

But I decided that it was too early in the game to engage in a dramatic display, which may prove to be unnecessary. Instead, I paced away the day in a tense inner skirmish between resignation and hope. Because Rood knew of my situation, losing faith would be foolish; he had performed miracles before, and he would never give up. That was a certainty—and a comforting one at that. And there was always the chance that one of my other friends would show up and put a halt to this waking nightmare.

CHAPTER 23

TO THE MONKEY HOUSE (EARLY AUGUST)

The degree of civilization in a
society can be judged by
entering its prisons.

—FYODOR DOSTOEVSKY

On the south side of the cell, there was an open-air view of the service lot, which was located behind the courthouse. This was used primarily for the loading and unloading of inmates going back and forth between the prison and the court. As the afternoon waned, and the shadows from the jungle stretched out and spread farther upon the pavement, I began to prepare myself for the probability that the cavalry would not be arriving today. And when the dusk descended into darkness, the final fleeting hopes of my heart died with the day. I was officially in the system. By now, the shock had melted into resigned exhaustion, and I was almost relieved when the prison bus pulled up to haul us reprobates on the two-minute drive to the prison. The guards cuffed us person-to-person, wrist to wrist, so that we had to synchronize our movements as we snaked awkwardly through the lot and clumsily boarded through the bus's back door. A guard had handed me my backpack on the way out, and I placed it between my knees as I sat down.

Next came the gang of eight scrawny offenders that had been on a blessed holiday from the prison. These sorry souls had the added luxury of ankle manacles. These accessories forced each inmate to hunch over and hold up the connecting chain with one hand, while waddling from side to side as they attempted forward movement. Their hunched backs and lurching legs immediately brought to my mind surreal scenes from the classic sci-fi film, *Planet of the Apes*. It looked humiliating. Later I was given the opportunity to discover firsthand that the ankle shackles did not just cause humiliation, but the awkward postures needed for movement caused excruciating back pain as well.

When the back doors slammed shut, there was an eruption of activity—one of the new arrivals produced three or four smuggled smokes, another pulled out a lighter, and the cigarettes were puffed on and passed among the passengers. My neglected stomach reminded me that I might just have provisions in my pack from my last fishing trip. I dug inside the bag and found a plastic water bottle. I quickly raised it to my mouth and began to gulp down its contents. My lips instantly signaled to my brain an amazing accident, and although my throat was burning, I drank deep and drained half of the 12-ounce water bottle of straight vodka. Sometimes absent-mindedness is a real blessing! One of my closer companions witnessed my sudden good fortune and looked at me with hopeful expectation. *I might as well start making friends,* I thought. I handed him the bottle, and it was passed along in an egalitarian process, while I received the last third of a cigarette for my contribution. I speedily sucked in the smoke as the bus rumbled over the rough asphalt, until it came to a harsh halt at the unimposing prison entrance.

Backed up against a mountain of tangled green jungle, the Phuket Provincial Prison is fronted by busy Damarong Street, and its entrance is at the termination of Montri Street, on which, three blocks away, stood my old headquarters at the Pearl Hotel. (I thought, sardonically, of the movie, *The Shawshank Redemption,* in which the warden threatens the protagonist, "I will take you out of that two-room Hilton, and cast you down with the Sodomites!") According to *The Phuket News,* the prison was built in 1902 and originally designed for 750 prisoners. Additions over the years had raised the recommended maximum capacity to a total of 1,328 inmates. However, when the beat-up shuttle bus backed up and parked just outside the oversized double doors of the prison's entrance, the population had swelled to over 2,830 prisoners (not exactly coronavirus-compliant!). I had observed the entrance from street level dozens of times, and from that perspective, the penitentiary looked like just an ordinary administrative building, with a facade adorned with tributes to kings, and mounted with poles on which the flags of Thailand and its royalty lay limp in the dead air. But behind those double doors and wrought iron gates is a primitive, sloppily constructed complex of squat, rectangular bunkhouses, a dining hall, central courtyard, open-air bathing/ toilet facilities, and a perimeter of tall chain-link fence laced with razor wire.

We hobbled and stumbled out of the bus, while several guards prodded, shouted, and lined us up. We marched in through the iron gates and then spread out on the courtyard like a platoon of marine recruits reporting for drill. Unable to understand any of the commands, shouts, or hand gestures, I was always one move behind the other outcasts in the step-by-step induction process. We placed our personal belongings in a pile in front of us as guards came by to inventory the items, then have us sign off on property-description vouchers. We were then issued the latest in prison fashion—light tan T-shirts, maroon string-tied shorts, along with a towel, which was also supposed to serve as a pillow, mattress, sheet, or blanket (pick one!). Next, we were ordered to strip naked, and we were given one final search.

Then, we were marched to the collection of half-walled, waist-high, water troughs that serve as shower facilities. Here we rinsed, scrubbed, rinsed again, and dried off as the guards practiced their comedic talents, mocking and deriding the lot of us, but having particular fun with the six-foot, three-inch tall, white-skinned farang with blue eyes. Surrounded by shorties with dark hair, dark eyes, and dark skin, I hadn't felt so demographically outnumbered since the six weeks I spent in the hood of west Las Vegas. Apparently, the white privilege I so much enjoyed on the long-tail boat cruise around Phi Phi Leh had just been a one-day pass. I briefly reflected upon this irony with bitter sarcasm.

We were then directed along in separate groups to cells, which were just rectangular rooms with a wooden mezzanine deck running along the entire course of the room. This deck served no purpose (other than providing a perfect point of contact for my upper forehead), as it was forbidden to sit or sleep on top of it. Upwards of forty young Thai men had been crammed into this room, which was about the size of a shipping container, and almost all of them stared in my direction with curiosity. I stood self-consciously looking around—attempting to find what might be an available sleeping spot—when our "dinner" arrived in tin trays. Tonight's fare was a rice gruel, along with something that may have been meat, covered in curry sauce. I was famished, and I ambushed my tray, finishing before tasting the meal.

Luckily, there were a couple of (rudimentary) English-speaking Thais who were sympathetic to my situation. They explained to me some simple rules of the communal living arrangement, then issued a few orders and arranged a place where I could lay down for sleep. It was against the back wall, which seemed to be the most inconspicuous, and thus the most desirable, location. I made sure to keep my feet far away from the head of any other inmates. I folded my towel for a pillow and laid down. It was now time to employ the same tactic that I had used in previous conditions of incarceration. Believe it or not, I had been to jail(s) before, and I had found that a concentrated effort at hibernation was unquestionably the most effective coping mechanism. Of course, one-night stands for disorderly conduct, spent in modern facilities, in a country with a Bill of Rights, were weak preparation for what Rood always referred to as "the Monkey House." I now completely understood his meaning.

Of course, there were some major obstacles to the hibernation strategy: lack of a mattress and pillow, forty chattering roommates, humid air in the high 80s, and personal space consisting of just a tiny rectangle on the cement floor. I mostly overcame these challenges because the mental blackness of sleep was far preferable to wakefulness and worrying to the point of acute anxiety. After three days, a tedious schedule was established and ingrained into the cloudy consciousness of my mind in the same way that lower back pain was ingrained into my spine.

***

At dawn every morning, the entire prison population woke and stood respectfully for the Thai national anthem. After a quick roll call/headcount, the first rice-gruel meal of the day was served. Afterward, almost everyone went back to sleep until sometime around midmorning when the guards opened up the gates of the cages, and the courtyard and toilet facilities were flooded with inmates taking advantage of "recreation time." Although, of course, there was no room for sports or exercise, other than walking in a packed mass as thick as the mob of spectators on the infield of the Indy 500. For some reason—perhaps the conformist nature of Thai society—the flow of traffic was unexpectedly structured and peaceful. It was fortunate that the inmates maintained such collective calm, because any sort of disturbance could cause a human stampede with tragic results. Undoubtedly, several people would be stomped to death. I considered going out for some air, but decided against it: I would have needed a crowbar to pry myself into that miserable mass of humanity. Besides, the case of claustrophobia I would surely suffer from being crammed into a crowd of criminals would negate any benefits of breathing open air.

One positive thing I can say about Thai prison life is that other than getting my head kicked in by the staff, I had no fear for my physical safety from fellow inmates. Thai prisoners reflect the same characteristics as the majority of the Kingdom's population: 90 percent of the Thai people are kind-hearted, respectful, and usually just curious about foreigners. The prison experience would be much different in an American prison where the insane racial attitudes and omnipresent, ultra-powerful gangs would have chewed me up and spit me right back out.

Another (slightly) positive part of the experience was receiving a free haircut; however, due to the language barrier, the barber shaved my head just as bald as everyone else. I did not complain, though. (I had learned quickly that unsolicited criticism was not appreciated at this facility).

Those moments when sleep eluded me were full of dread and disbelief. From what had been explained to me at the court, it seemed to be a certain fact that I would be here for four months before even going to trial. I did not have, nor could I arrange, the 500,000 baht needed to bail out of there. Also, I had no way of communicating with anyone until a visitor showed, and because of the miscommunication that resulted in the head-knocking, there was no one in Thailand on my list of permitted visitors. I did not know when I would see an attorney, or when I would see someone from the US Embassy. I did not want to think about even four months of incarceration, and to consider the possibility of four *years* would have put me into such a tailspin of depression that I successfully and completely blocked that thought from my mind.

But what I could not stop thinking about was the stupidity of this situation. Of course, I realized that there were far more egregious cases of injustice in the world—but they don't mean a damn thing when an injustice is perpetrated on *you personally!* Imagine spending four years sleeping on a concrete floor with forty strangers in a shoe box of a cell, within another slightly larger shoe box of a prison located 15,000 miles from your birthplace. And all of this misery and waste would be the price of a "crime" I did not commit! I had done absolutely nothing to harm another person and had, in fact, spent, "loaned," and given a large sum of money to the locals of Phuket trying to do my part to alleviate the suffering caused by the COVID-19 lockdown. Certainly, the figure would have been enough to hire a decent private lawyer. And now I was high and dry because of dirty cops and a dirty rat. (Oh, how I wished to see Kris in here! I would break his neck!)

I realized, though, that I could not continue with this train of thought. I was there because of my own poor decision-making, regardless of motive and circumstance. I had spent enough time in Thailand to have learned not to trust anything—or anyone. On several occasions in the past, I had placed my trust in people here, and I had been badly burned. Now I just had to face my final and harshest consequence. With this thought in mind, I'd finally fall asleep.

CHAPTER 24

ROLLING UP (EARLY AUGUST)

It takes a special sort of man to
understand and enjoy liberty,
and he is usually an outlaw in
democratic societies.

—H.L. MENCKEN

When I awoke before dawn on that fourth morning, it was because I heard my full name being repeatedly called out: the unexpected wake-up call was so strange that I believed I was merely transitioning from one dream to another. A guard of the night watch was struggling to refrain from shouting, and also struggling with the pronunciation of "Mark Ervin Thumann" as he peered through the bars of the cell. I snapped awake and immediately processed the situation. There were only two possible reasons for being called out individually at this hour of the morning. One of them had the potential to end with a happy result, and the other would be incomparably disastrous. From what I had learned from books and old movies, it was at dawn that prisoners were brought out before the firing squad to be shot. But it had also been my experience that being singled out from the crowd often meant special consideration on the positive side.

Fortunately, the authorities were unaware of my *actual* crimes, and I was spared the firing squad. However, I was not spared the ankle manacles and the torturous hunched shuffle. After I had been retrieved from my cell and escorted to the "shower" (along with two other candidates for court), we were given a change of clothes and then taken to the corner of the courtyard. That was the spot where the medieval mechanism for the installation of the shackles sat as an awkward reminder of primitive justice. A person had to sit down and place his ankle on the curved cut-out at the bottom of the contraption. One half of the cuff was placed on top and one half on the bottom. Next the heavyset guard took the long wooden lever from chest high and thrust it towards the ground causing enough pressure to cinch the iron semicircles of the cuffs into an excruciatingly tight ellipse. The cuffs on each ankle were connected by a thick iron chain that inmates were forced to hold in their hand while moving around. It must be admitted that this primitive method of applying restraints truly added to the purposefully dramatic and symbolic show of force by the authorities while simultaneously heaping misery and shame upon the prisoner. I almost admired the authorities for having such an obsolete machine still operating and out in the open for the intimidation of all, even if there must be a hundred quicker and better ways to restrain an inmate. I imagine the warden must have started out at the Immigration Bureau.

After another hour of waiting, we were loaded back onto that same bus, then taken to the courthouse holding cell where we waited through the morning and midafternoon. I passed the time speculating about whether Rood had once again pulled me out of trouble, or if someone else had intervened on my behalf.

Staring out to the back service lot, I remembered—with regretful irony—the time just three years ago when Rood and I stood out there joking as we waited for a friend to be released. A Bering Sea brother had gotten pinched at the DUI checkpoint between Kamala Beach and Patong. On my request, Rood had once again come to the rescue, using his connections to retrieve James from jail with only minor psychological damage. And here I was on the wrong side of the fence … and laughing no longer.

Finally, I was taken to the conference room for an interview with the judge (the same shy young man serving as the interpreter). The judge explained the situation: a friend of mine had signed a personal guarantee for my bail, and the judge had agreed to my release because of special circumstances (i.e., the fact that while a global pandemic was raging, I was incarcerated in a prison with triple the number of inmates than the facility was built to house). I would be able to live in liberty until my next scheduled court appearance three weeks later.

This was amazing! The COVID-19 crisis had worked out to my benefit all year, and now it was saving me from the tropical gulag! But underneath my joy was the Fear. Surely this was too good to be true .... Someone was just about to change policy and crush my hopes. Everything that had taken place all summer seemed to have happened in a purely arbitrary fashion. What was to stop those Crazy Fates from indulging in more capricious behavior? I would not feel at ease until I was free of these shackles and out of the custody of bureaucrats, cops, and corrections officers.

I was taken back to the holding cell to wait out the entire afternoon, because it simply runs counter to sacred Thai bureaucratic methodology to do anything in an expeditious manner. All tasks must take at least seven times longer than necessary.

***

We were returned to the prison late in the afternoon, just in time to play more of the waiting game. I do believe the command staff of the Phuket Provincial Prison relishes dragging out the process of release: they were milking the operation for all it was worth, and every passing minute, the anxiety increased. I was dreading the possibility of a mistake being made with my paperwork, or perhaps orders from the court could change. I would be erroneously sent back to the communal cage. Those last two hours of getting processed out were probably the most stressful of the whole experience. The desire to be on the other side of those walls was maddening. I longed to be anywhere else, so long as I was away from those fatuous administrators and petty dictators disguised as corrections officers. I do believe that the strongest craving of my entire life overwhelmed me right there in the courtyard, the craving for pure freedom! In my head I could hear the loud, unmistakable voice of the real decision-maker of my existence. It spoke with total authority: *I am never coming back here again. No matter what I have to do—I will NEVER step foot inside this monkey house again!*

Finally, all the tedious steps of the process (multiple fingerprinting exercises, photo-documentation, handwritten descriptions of tattoos, and the inventory of returned property) were completed. I even got *all* of my cash back this time! (After my initial arrest, the cops at the town jail had made off with a crisp Ben Franklin I had stashed in my wallet). But then, *damn!*, another part of the process made itself known: the Big Boss of the operation felt it necessary to grill all eight of us individually. The interrogation was more about showing off. The pot-bellied and pompous commandant insisted on asking inane questions, ridiculing the guys with petty wisecracks, and generally exhibiting to everyone the ugly face of bureaucratic tyranny. When I had my turn with the self-important fraud, he attempted to be chummy with me by joking about Thai ladies and "boom-boom." I played my part by fake-laughing at his insipid innuendos.

But when he finally tired of toying with us, I walked through the twelve-foot iron gates and out into the dark of early evening, where Lek stood smiling next to another new car. This was the third time I had seen her with a new car that summer, and I began to seriously question whether I truly knew who this woman was, or if she had an agenda of which I was unaware. I had "loaned" her well over 100,000 baht this year because of her supposed dire financial situation and single mother status, yet she kept showing up with new cars and new clothes. However, I would have hugged the Devil himself if he were the one responsible for arranging my release, and he was standing there with a pitchfork in his grasp ready to drive me home.

I walked over and hugged Lek tight. I quickly climbed into the car's passenger side, while still looking over my back for the possible pursuit of captors who had reconsidered my release. Besides thanking Lek several times, I said very little. Still overwhelmed with incredulity, I considered not just the twists and turns of the past week, but I also recalled the highs and lows of the entire "holiday," which was now over five months long. As we pulled out from the darkness and onto the lights of Montri Road, the stereo kicked in with the straining voice of Don Henley, as he sang about a forlorn highway and the illumination of an oasis on the horizon. Upon once again hearing the first haunting lines of Thailand's unofficial national anthem, I stared out the side window with a sardonic grin. Several times, I had experienced a dramatic adventure in this country with this very same soundtrack flavoring the encounter, and I knew exactly who was sending this ironic message through the airwaves: those twisted jokers that I refer to as the Crazy Fates.

***

Despite the new car, Lek was, once again, in desperate need of 10,000 baht—right away, of course.

"Stop at the next ATM," I said without hesitation.

The true value of release could not be measured by baht or dollars. Besides, my intuition had just informed the accountant upstairs that this would be my last payoff/ loan/gift to Lek. Later, I would begin to seriously question Lek's motives and connections. Twice now I had walked right out of custody because of her mere signature, and both times I made a direct payment to her. And her house had been raided, with herself and several tenants arrested. And she *actually was* selling drugs! How was she out of jail and driving around town in a new car?

I had her drop me off in Rawai at a hotel located a few blocks away from my condo. My caution now extended to almost everyone—and especially to a mystery woman who could accomplish the momentous task of springing me from prison with just a stroke of the pen. I did not want her to know my exact location because, for all I knew, this could be a revolving door operation. She could be working with one of the authorities to ensure I was in and out of jail and paying every time. But who could know? This was Thailand, and I wasn't any closer to understanding the truth from the machinations and illusions of a fundamentally deceptive people. Lek could be one of several spiders spinning the web in which I had become entangled.

Once she was out of sight, I hustled back to my castle, mixed up a (mostly) vodka and ginger ale cocktail, and started calling and emailing in a flurry of communication. I needed specific information and a strategy if I was going to beat these phony charges perpetrated by corrupt police. And I had to win this case. Going back to that prison—for *any* length of time—was not an option to be entertained.

I discovered that several of my Phuket friends had been trying to find me. I had multiple messages from both Kat and Bob. My mailbox was also filled with emails from the few friends in the States aware of my ordeal. Bob and I had a long talk during which we speculated about the various scenarios that could explain my strange circumstances. Bob was all but convinced that Lek was involved with the police, and that she was deceiving me for her own benefit.

I did not sleep that first night, but I did intensely appreciate the many comforts of condo-living while I considered and prioritized every aspect of this desperate situation: who to trust, how to get more cash, how to hire a lawyer, the constraints caused by my confiscated/expired passport, and the risks and rewards of various courses of action. The Crazy Fates must have been having great fun because I just could not decide upon the proper route out of the insane labyrinth that those meddlesome creatures had constructed. I still had three days before my lease expired, and I would take every minute to enjoy freedom to the fullest, and to protect that freedom by bearing down hard with every analytical tool at my disposal. I might not find the answers to all the riddles, but I hoped to at least find the key to the exit door.

CHAPTER 25

AND ROLLING OUT (MID-AUGUST)

A man who has blown all his options
can't afford the luxury of changing
his ways. He has to capitalize on
whatever he has left, and he can't
afford to admit—no matter how
often he is reminded of it—that
every day of his life takes him
farther down a blind alley.

—HUNTER S. THOMPSON

About an hour before he arrived at the hotel, a heavy and fast-falling rain had enveloped Kamala Beach, and the streets were already streaked with streams of sand-stained water. I waived him over and then swiftly loaded the three bags into the open trunk. One was a small camo backpack of essentials, and the second was an authentic US Army-issued backpack leftover from an adventure on Alaska's Kodiak Island—seven months and a lifetime ago. The third was a heavy-duty garbage bag stuffed with all the possessions that had become impractical for my present mission. I hoped that Rood might find, at least some of them, useful. It had become evident that I needed to travel light, for the dual advantages of speed and stealth. However, there were still three hours until the scheduled departure of the northbound bus, leaving us plenty of time for the trip to the station. The rain made a good excuse for slow driving. Neither one of us was in a hurry to say goodbye.

We slipped past the still-closed Fantasea entertainment complex and its vast parking lot, which lay empty, except for the company's fleet of buses and minivans, vehicles that had not moved for months. Rood's fruit stand was set up on the shoulder of the street just thirty yards from Fantasea's entrance, and he slowed down to a crawl so that I could say my goodbyes to his wife and daughter. My friend's tandem loves were holding out hope for a few customers to come straggling through the rain on a mission to buy some mangoes or coconuts. That day, Kamala was flooded with rain water, but the entire island of Phuket had been suffering from the devastation of an economic landslide. The genesis of this calamity was, of course, the arrival of the COVID-19 virus in late February, and there was still no end in sight for this island of vast natural beauty and incompetent governance. The economy of Phuket was almost completely dependent on foreign tourists, who were long gone (excepting vagabond outlaws) and not coming back for a long time. Phuket was unquestionably the province in Thailand hardest hit by the regime's panicked overreaction to the threat, and yet small business owners like Rood had still not received the financial aid promised by the self-serving Bangkok elites.

This had been a sad summer for Rood. The first hit was the coronavirus lockdown. The second strike occurred when two family members passed away during the very same week. And then the Fates finished the beating with the untimely deaths of two of his most treasured farang friends during July's final days. Now I was leaving. The unspoken fact—that it was highly unlikely I could ever return—hung over us, just as the dull and sagging rain clouds smothered the jungle-choked hills ahead. As the car climbed, and Rood negotiated the tight turns of the coastal highway, I looked over my left shoulder to gaze over the elongated ellipse of beach and the storm-churned stew of seawater boiling in the bay. This grand view had always been a joyful sight, particularly when we drove in from the other direction after an airport pickup—both of us anticipating the good times ahead. Now it was doubtful that I would view this panorama of Andaman coast ever again. Despite that depressing idea, I was grateful for the opportunity to secure my liberty. Rood's face showed sadness (as another loved one departed), but also relief: I was getting off the island and out of the country before the police were aware that I had lit out for parts unknown.

During those last three days in Rawai, I had gathered enough intelligence to reach a definitive conclusion: if I stayed and fought the legal system—even with the best attorney—I was going to be spending the next four years in prison. The only alternative was to turn outlaw and make a run for the border—but which one? Malaysia had potential; Bob was a native of Thailand's deep south, and he had people who could help me crawl across the border in a dead-of-night jailbreak through a rubber plantation. Cambodia was a possibility, and my Bering Sea shipmates had connections in Vietnam. But because of the severe travel restrictions and heightened security imposed by the COVID-19 pandemic, crossing borders—either legally or illegally—would be an operation unlikely to succeed. Although I still had two weeks until my next court appointment, I was certain that I was under police surveillance (two social media accounts had been hacked), and therefore, I needed to clear out of Phuket as quickly as possible. It was also imperative that I travel to the US Embassy in Bangkok to apply for an emergency replacement passport. No matter which direction I decided to make my escape, I was going to need that proof of identity. Hell, I might even need to check it once in a while, to confirm the identity of that guy staring at me in the mirror.

I could never leave Phuket without visiting Rood to say goodbye in person. But first, I needed to become a ghost. I paid for two more nights at the condo so that if there were inquiries, I was officially still residing there. Next, I withdrew all my cash—the police would not be able to use ATM transactions to trace my whereabouts. Then I gave the smartphone to my favorite local bar manager and smashed the burner phone. I bought another burner phone and gave the new number to only Bob, Rood, and Kat. And after the condo's reception staff closed shop for the day, I shouldered my packs and walked off into the dark, until I reached the main road and flagged down a passing taxi. I then took the short ride to Kamala Beach, where Rood's cousin managed a hotel, a safe house where I would not have to register as an official guest.

***

Like Patong Beach to the south, Kamala was as empty as my bank account. In fact, on my second day, I took a farewell tour down the beach and then back along the main road—absorbing every detail and remembering all the lively times. During the forty-five-minute stroll, I saw only one solitary soul. It was Rood. Phuket was in dire economic and social trouble, but the guys running the show still refused to recognize how prolonged and miserable the situation was bound to be. This was one of the rare times in my life when I truly wished for wealth. I was powerless to lend any more financial aid to Rood and my other Thai friends scattered across the country. And I knew that the situation was going to get worse before it got better.

During my last day in Kamala, Rood and I were able to have a long talk, and I learned something that reinforced my decision to abscond from the Thai "judicial" system and permanently disappear from the Kingdom. Unbeknownst to me, Rood had attempted to visit me at the prison, but he was denied entry. After unsuccessfully pleading his case, he drove back to Kamala Beach. During the drive, he realized that he was being tailed by the Phuket Town Police, specifically two cops on a motorbike and two more in a car. The corrupt bastards followed him as far as Patong. This was a pretty ballsy move considering my friend's standing in the community and his connections with powerful people. Rood stated the case: "Mark, police want you too much. Everybody poor now, and police think they can get your money. Also, I think somebody hate you."

"Oh, I'm sure several people hate me," I replied, "and at least one of them is a cop. Everything is strange about this."

And then, Rood stated it even more clearly: "Anyway, Mark, you must leave Phuket. I can't help you if they take you back to the Monkey House." ("Munkeeee How" is how Rood charmingly pronounced the term.)

"I know, buddy. And that's what I'm going to do," I announced.

When Rood said that I must go, I knew for sure that running was my only option.

***

Although I didn't need any more reasons to support my decision, I acquired one anyway when Bob drove up from Patong to say farewell. By my request, he had called Lek so that he could arrange for picking up the court documents, which I had accidentally left in her car. But it was Lek's sister who answered the phone, and she informed Bob that Lek had just been arrested a second time and was now back in jail! Once again, my bail-guarantor was behind bars herself. I still operated under the common-sense assumption that a person in jail cannot act as a guarantor of another person's appearance at the court. I booked a Bangkok-bound bus for the next day.

And that next day was fittingly dreary: the fat drops of rain thumped like hail upon the hood and roof of the car, and the tires churned water for the duration of our trip to the bus station. The windows had fogged up, and looking through the cloudy glass into the gray mist of the world was the same opaque view that I had then of my future. I had a one-way ticket to Bangkok and an appointment at the US Embassy at 10 a.m. two days after my scheduled arrival. That was all I knew about the direction of my life. I had gotten used to a life characterized by an inordinate amount of uncertainty, and I had also gotten wise to the twisted games of the Fates. However, I had never been this disoriented and discouraged. My will seemed to wane, but then I glanced to my right and caught a snapshot of genuine honesty and loyalty in the features of my friend's profile, and with that affirmation I felt a surge of confident determination to overcome the doubt and the danger of the solitary road ahead. Realizing that there were positive aspects to the situation, I gave myself a quick pep talk: *Don't panic. So what if you're lost? Being lost gives you a distinct advantage: it's much harder to tail somebody who doesn't know where he's going!*

Rood turned left onto the ramped entrance of the bus station and parked the car under the cover of the sprawling limbs and wide leaves of the tree nearest the ticketing office. We both got out, and he helped me unload my gear.

"Okay, buddy …. Thank you for everything, Rood," I managed, while shaking his hand.

"Don't worry, Mark," he counseled, "Later everything will be clear, and you can come back."

I smiled and said, "Damn right, brother!"

"And you call me from Bangkok—tell me your plan."

"Yes, for sure," I replied as we released the handshake.

I shouldered my packs, and Rood turned his car homeward to the coconut stand, where his family awaited his return, just as they waited for the return of tourists and normal life. But there was nobody waiting for me when the double-decker bus rolled into the breaking dawn at the Bangkok bus station after fourteen tedious hours on the all-night, up-country route. The only memorable moment of the ride occurred when the bus motored across the bridge that crossed the flat, pale blue expanse of water between Phuket and the mainland. I knew at that moment that I had at least accomplished a physically symbolic escape from that summer of trouble. After checking into a hotel with hourly rates, I was content to lie down and completely stretch out my stiff limbs across the bed, while ignoring the flimsy conditions of that flop house on one of Bangkok's seediest side-streets. I had made the concession of staying in this depraved neighborhood because it was just two blocks from the embassy.

The next morning, I slipped around the various limbs of forgotten bodies sleeping on the sidewalk, and then maneuvered through the gauntlet of gaudily dressed "freelancers" and ladyboys, still on the hunt at midmorning.

Fortunately, I only lost my bearings once and reached the embassy in time to fill out the appropriate forms and pay the necessary fees. I picked up a fresh passport featuring a photo of my prison-issued hairstyle and several pages completely devoid of any entry or exit stamps. Those blank pages rendered the ID useless for departing Thailand by official channels. My embassy contact inquired about the status of my court case, and because of my blunt responses and cavalier attitude, he rightly concluded that I wasn't going to go anywhere near a Thai courthouse. With a shining smile, he informed me that (in his official capacity) he was obligated to grant the emergency passport. But he was also obligated to advise me that I was required to abide by all orders and rules of Thai authorities. Then he winked at me, shook my hand, and wished me good luck. Obviously, he believed I was a fool … but not a complete fool.

CHAPTER 26

NOW WHAT? (LATE AUGUST)

Life is a series of surprises and would not be
Worth taking or keeping if it were not.

—Ralph Waldo Emmerson

While obtaining a valid passport gave me a jolt of hope, I still had major obstacles to overcome. The most pressing problem was a lack of cash. It would be four days until a check would post to my account. I had managed to convince the highly suspicious hotel manager to let me slide for a couple of days, but I still needed money to survive. My luck held out: I was able to get in touch with Noi. I had met this young lady back in March, when I first arrived for what *I thought* was going to be a five-week vacation. The trip (so far) had turned out to be five-*months,* and I no longer considered the experience to be a "vacation." Noi and I had hung out for a week before I left on the train south to Phuket. This was long enough for me to realize that the gorgeous girl was a bit out of her head. But she was also street smart, and she had connections. In particular, she had a friend who would loan me cash in exchange for my laptop as collateral. The guy owned a mobile phone kiosk at the Siam Paragon Mall. We made the trip, and her friend looked over the laptop, agreeing to loan me 5,000 baht: I would need to repay him 6,500 baht four days later. The terms were steep. They became even steeper when Noi insisted on receiving 2,000 baht for arranging the deal. Like I said, she had street smarts. And like I said, she was a loony tune:

she spent all 2,000 baht on absurd trinkets and other useless items before we even left the mall.

***

Of course, Noi's shifty maneuver added annoyance to an already stressful situation. I was going to need every single baht in order to execute an escape plan. In the meantime, I needed to survive the hidden dangers that surrounded me in one of Bangkok's shadiest sections. Sukhumvit Soi 4 was a hotbed of depravity, littered with sneaks, snitches, cutthroats, and cops. I became a self-imposed prisoner in my hotel room. Just walking past the suspicious stares of the hotel manager or her sister was almost enough to keep me in my room. And after breaching the creepy nastiness of reception, I would have to endure leering ladyboys, pleading prostitutes, and petty thieves in the side streets just to get food or a pack of smokes. I put in the time searching online for some sort of way out of this crazy country. With very little money and no plan, I felt almost crippled from an uneasiness that could easily turn to severe anxiety and possibly outright panic.

I couldn't shake the undeniable sense of impending peril, of time running out … of walls closing in on me. I was slowly suffocating while searching in vain for the escape hatch. This mental duress was blocking my imagination and hindering my ability to formulate a plan for escape or, at the very least, to evade detection. Dominating my mindset was the inescapable fear of being caught, of having some random mishap result in my apprehension. The authorities would discover I had defied the court-ordered mandate that I remain in the province of Phuket. The inevitable consequence would be my return to the sweltering congestion of the Phuket prison. My mind drifted to the morning of my release: the air humid but not yet suffocating, the jungle-besieged courtyard, the medieval ankle manacles, *Planet of the Apes*.

Aha! I finally pinned down the missing memory: the time and place where I felt an ambiance the same as the courtyard of the prison. The atmosphere there was just like summer mornings at the Cincinnati Zoo, when I was fifteen and working my first job, hustling soda-pop and cheddar wurst from a concession stand. In the Ohio River Valley, summer mornings were always muggy. At the zoo, the heavy air was flavored by the musky stench of exotic animals, and the thick flora of the grounds shrouded the primeval park from the sight of the surrounding city. Yet (just like the prison) you could still hear sporadic intrusions of sound from the soulless activity of civilization. In this environment, four friends worked, carpooled, and raised hell with all the free-spirited fullness of our youth. The *Zoo Crew* had a summer so sensational that it could be considered criminal—no wonder I dreaded that damn prison with such intensity! My physical sensations in that place ruptured my subconscious. The misery of confinement was compounded by the contrast of two life stages: one was young, hopeful, and enjoying the first tastes of adult freedom, while the second was characterized by crumbling middle-age, senseless bondage, uncertainty, and dread. No, I refused to return to the Monkey House (the term seemed *perfectly* suited in light of my newly discovered memory!). What a torment it would be to spend four years waking up every morning amidst haunting images of irretrievable youth—only to be slapped with the stark reality of a hopeless dead end.

Thankfully, those worrisome days passed by swiftly, and payday finally arrived. But an unexpected crisis stifled the anxious joy of the morning. Soon after I had awakened, I heard the sound of rapid pounding coming from the hallway. I opened the door, and Noi rushed into the room, rattling off dire warnings and stories riddled with holes, crucial details somehow completely overlooked. What I did catch of her ramblings was that her French boyfriend's place has been raided. The cops were looking for any foreigners who had run afoul of the law. Just like the situation in Phuket, the coronavirus lockdowns had created a financial squeeze that was reaching critical mass. Unable to collect their usual "protection" money from nightclubs and massage parlors, low-level police were looking for other sources of supplemental income. Shaking down foreigners was a potentially lucrative option.

Noi's uncle was a fairly high-level police officer, and she typically received tips from this doting brother of her deceased mother. Noi had many friends in the less law-abiding community of expats in Bangkok, and she felt obligated to help them (while most likely *profiting* from the activity, as well). Fortunately, I had yet to run afoul of the young lady, and I was considered among the protected class. Apparently, the sisters who operated my present flophouse had tipped off the cops: there was a foreigner (me) who had checked in with only a copy of an expired passport. Obviously, the two hags were looking for a kickback from the cops.

Before manically rushing out the door to go meet her boyfriend, Noi told me that she would be back at one o'clock. We would leave together, and then return to the mall to retrieve my laptop. I agreed. But after she left, I put my head to some serious thinking. This was not the time for stupid mistakes. The check was going to post later this afternoon. I realized I shouldn't be anywhere near Noi when it came time to withdraw money from the ATM. I had a weakness for Thai ladies, and Noi was an expert at exploiting it. I also wasn't going to wait around to see if the police decided to show up before one o'clock. But how was I going to get past reception with all of my luggage? They would know for certain that I was bailing out without paying for the last three days. There was only one option: I was going to have to leave most of my shit behind. I had to prioritize my belongings, and ended up with just the essentials—including just one change of clothes—stuffed into my small backpack. At 11:00 a.m., I strolled casually through the lobby toward the exit. When the manager shouted out a question about where I was going, I said over my shoulder, "I'm going to the ATM. I'll be right back."

I hustled through the gauntlet of mendicants and grifters posted along Soi 4. Upon reaching Sukhumvit Road, I turned right and kept on going until I found a high-rise office building that made for an ideal hide-out. The lobby was pumped with the cool comfort of industrial air-conditioning, and a coffee stand provided cushioned easy chairs. I spent all afternoon hungry as hell, while waiting for the check to post. Eventually, I could no longer tolerate the inaction, and I took off for the mall. I did not even have cash for a motorbike taxi, so I was in for quite a hike. Upon reaching the mall, I kept my fingers crossed, hoping that the check showed up just a little early this week. Lucky again! I had my cash. I had my laptop. Equally important, I *didn't* have Noi. I took a taxi to my usual stomping grounds on Ratchada Soi 17, although I stayed away from the Watana Mansion. Instinct told me to keep away from places where I might be recognized.

***

I found a clean hotel that didn't require ID but *did* have a management team with a forgiving attitude toward late payments. It was at the Bangkok 68 Hotel, room 405, where I spent ten nerve-wracking days running into dead ends. Bob had called to inform me that Malaysia was no longer a realistic option; heightened security patrols by both armies along the length of the border had made it all but impossible to depart Thailand by a southern route. Vietnam and Myanmar were the next countries scratched off the list, followed by Cambodia and Laos. They were all ineligible for the same reason: the fear of COVID-19 had resulted in a worldwide enthusiasm for border security. I then spent two days searching the websites of the deep-water ports in and around Bangkok, looking for a vessel with potential employment opportunities, the possibility of a ride out to sea, or even a risky stowaway opportunity. The vast majority of the boats were foreign flagged and (or) required licensing that I did not have—and could not bullshit my way around.

Also, during that time, I bumped into a taxi driver who was an old friend. Somsak offered to me the use of his mother's country house, far to the north and just outside of Chiang Rai. The house was located near a tiny village in the country, was built of teak wood on the slope of a small mountain, and would be all mine for the foreseeable future. I could hide out there until the pandemic restrictions were finally eased and I had a realistic chance of crossing a border and blending into a new country. This was not a perfect plan, but at least I would be at a spot that was essentially the point in Thailand most distant from the island of Phuket. And I would be as inconspicuous as any foreigner could hope to be.

With my scheduled court appearance just two days away, I needed to get moving somewhere. When the inevitable bench warrant was issued, I could not risk being exposed in Bangkok, where there were sometimes more police than prostitutes. I looked online for prices and train times to Chiang Mai. From there, I could catch a bus to Chiang Rai, and then catch a local taxi to the mountain hideout. But when I began to input the payment information, my infuriatingly unreliable instinct urged me to wait another day or two. It *did* make more sense to wait until the next direct deposit posted to my account before hitting the road. The following day, being too poor to play outside, I was reviewing an old outline for this story collection (although I was *living* this story, I was *writing* tales from long ago). On a wrinkled and ripped page of the notebook, I chanced upon two words scrawled on the edge of the page. It was an epiphany. *When did I scribble down that name? Who? Oh yeah, the dude at the smoking lounge in Singapore. Yes! This might be my way out!*

Within seconds, I was vigorously typing this message: "Hey, Gilbert! This is Mark from the Singapore airport—it seems like a lifetime ago! You won't believe this, but ..."

CHAPTER 27

FOUR-LEAF CLOVER TO FREEDOM
(LATE AUGUST)

The willing, destiny guides them;
the unwilling, destiny drags them.

—SENECA THE YOUNGER

"**K**eep your eyes wide open, and your head on a swivel!" Chief ordered in his easy drawl.

"Roger that!" I replied, and the conversation was over.

This particular maxim of Bering Sea fishermen was certainly suited for the situation; however, I had already adopted the policy at the beginning of "Summer 2020: Siamese Nightmare." Just the same, I was encouraged by yesterday's consultation with my old boss and current life coach. Now, under the blue-black night sky, I was strolling about the departure island at the central Bangkok bus station. I was waiting for the number 50 northbound bus—and also looking for an opportunity.

Twice that week, I had tried calling Kat in order to express my gratitude and to say farewell. On both occasions the phone was answered by a Thai man, and in both instances, the person with Kat's phone called back multiple times. This was my first clue that she involuntarily was not in possession of her phone; in the time that I had known her, Kat had never called me back the same day, let alone six times in forty minutes. Secondly, there was the fact that as a firm rule, Kat refused to have dealings with any Thai men (P-Chang had been a necessary exception). And finally, she was a fiercely independent woman who would never let anyone answer her personal mobile phone. I concluded the cops in Phuket must have confiscated her phone in hopes of pinpointing my location.

I called her number a third time, just that very night, as I was entering the bus station. Again, the phone was answered by a male Thai, who then called back several times. I shut the phone off in a hurry, then removed the battery. Could the Royal Thai Police trace my location? Probably. Could they have police in Bangkok looking for me right now? Maybe. Were they going to trace that phone to my intended destination? No. They absolutely would *not* be doing that!

I strolled complacently past the crowded benches and toward the last bus-bay. My head *was* on a swivel, and my eyes *were* wide open, but I (hopefully) maintained a casually self-possessed demeanor as I scoped out the various buses unloading and loading passengers. The last bay had just what I was looking for: a loaded bus with its engine running in preparation for departure. There was only one station attendant, and he was busy chatting up the female porter. The red neon strip of light on the rear end blinked the vehicle's destination: Chiang Mai, a route perfectly suited to my purpose. I inserted the phone's battery, put the ringer on silent, called Kat's number, and then hung up after two rings. After one more look around, I slipped the slim mobile through a crevice of the rear luggage compartment. If the Royal Thai Police were tracking my phone, they could pick it up in Chiang Mai, which was 650 kilometers to the northeast of my rally point in Nong Khai, Thailand.

Relieved of that particular worry, I reclined on the nearest bench, poured a healthy dose of whiskey into a plastic cup of lemon-lime soda, and kept watch with weary but calm eyes. Eventually, the charter bus arrived, and I sank into a first class seat for another overnight, northbound cruise. I opened my laptop and reread Gilbert's messages. I remained impressed with his professional and precise instructions. After I had sent my initial SOS, two anxiety-ridden, virtually hopeless days had passed, but then I had received this message:

"Mark,

sorry for my late response but I almost
never use FB. My mission here in Laos
was bringing friend illegal over. Mission
complete. I'm still stuck here 5 months

already.in this time I save two more
people to Laos. where I can help you,
I help you, no problem."

This message was the miracle answer to a foolish prayer. I was flooded with emotions ranging from joyful relief to sheer amazement. A real opportunity for escape had just been offered by a stranger with whom I had randomly engaged in conversation at a smoking lounge in the Singapore airport five months prior. The odds of Gilbert having the exact same problem—a problem he had already solved—*and* him still being in a position to assist me in overcoming the same obstacles were overwhelming. And the long odds were compounded by this fact: when he read my plea for help, it was the first time that Gilbert had checked his Facebook messages in two months. The entire scenario was almost too perfect. He had already smuggled three people from Thailand to Laos *after* the pandemic lockdowns and additional security protocols had been in place. Not only did I now know it could be done, but also that it *had* been done successfully, three times. And my biggest concern (other than getting nabbed) had been the unstamped passport, but Gilbert merely said, "Don't worry about it—I have people for that."

Either the Fates were extending an olive branch, or they were setting me up for a fall.

Gilbert had already arranged (offered bribes) and coordinated with his agents on both the Thai and Laos sides of the Mekong River. My responsibilities for the mission were fairly limited. I mostly just had to get to the Thai border town of Nong Khai without getting caught, something that was not without peril. Buses were periodically stopped and searched by Thai authorities on this particular route, because it was infamous for illegal smuggling drugs, migrant workers, exotic animals, and foreign fugitives. As yet, Bering Sea outlaws were unheard of, and I hoped that first class on a charter bus, under the cover of darkness, would increase my odds of success.

Looking down, I admired the other essential—and just-completed tasks—on my "to-do" list for the upcoming venture. On the top of my right hand, between my thumb and index finger, was a tattoo of a four-leaf clover. Three years ago, Gilbert had happened to get a clover tattoo prior to his escape from Koh Samui, and that symbol became the "distinguishing physical characteristic" used to prove his legitimacy to the various links along the chain of smugglers and their inside men. This year, Gilbert had decided to "trademark" the four-leaf clover tattoo as the official identifying symbol for anyone that he assisted in escaping Thailand. All three of the previous pilgrims whom he had aided in absconding from the Land of Smiles had inked the lucky clover somewhere on their right-hand prior to their break across the border. The apparent reason behind this secretive tactic was the rumor that the Thai anti-corruption unit had busted up a previous smuggling operation by hiring a farang to work undercover, pretending to be a fugitive from justice. Whatever the case, I was all for it. I admired the Tom Sawyer-like aspect of a tattoo being used as a secret symbol during a getaway.

However, I was strapped for cash to the extent that I could afford to get only the outline of the Irish symbol of luck (I could "church it up" later). In fact, additional cash for the ink artist was the reason for my call to "Chief"— an engineer, former fisherman, and fellow miscreant who somehow dug out enough change from underneath his couch cushions and car seats to cover the cost of the clover tattoo. My financial situation that week was so dire that I had to resort to making a reluctant call to Rood to borrow 1,000 baht for the bus ticket to Nong Khai. I almost cried when I picked up the money and discovered that my old buddy had doubled the amount to 2,000 baht. And *that* is why Rood is *The Man*.

As the bus motored through the countryside and the still-sleeping towns of Isan, I realized that I was not as anxious as one would expect. I think the reason I remained so coolly composed was the impression that I had of the man in charge of my immediate Fate. Gilbert exuded an authentic confidence that requires true competence and real experience. But still, anything could go wrong … especially if I allowed myself to be lulled into complacency. Ironically, I felt inadequate and unprepared without my lifelong nemesis: the Fear. As I considered this contradiction, a new travel rule was born: it is far better to be *overly* paranoid, than to be *even slightly* careless.

I forced myself into a state of vigilance by running through a mental checklist. I had left the large backpack behind—along with almost all of my clothing. I carried with me just the small camouflage backpack containing two pairs each of: cargo shorts, boxers, and T-shirts. Also jammed into the pack were the essentials: contact lenses, toiletries, notebooks, whiskey, and a carved out French paperback novel hiding the plastic-wrapped items (my passport, embassy documents, and twenty-five crisp 1,000 baht bills). The cash was the total cost of paying the ten team members (drivers, army moles, and lookouts) necessary for the mission—five men on each side of the Mekong. I had also packed a new can of pepper spray (or "air-freshener" as Mushroom Bob would have called it) in case of a double-cross. Having not been briefed on the details of the actual crossing, I had mentally (if not *physically*) prepared myself for the possibility of swimming the river, the old school method previously practiced back home on the southern border of the USA.

Dawn was breaking in a display of cool orange as the bus rolled into Nong Khai. To my relief, the bus station and the town were empty of uniforms. I flagged down a tuk-tuk. The old-timer navigated his smoke-machine to the rustic compound of duplexes, which comprised the riverfront bed-and-breakfast where I had a reservation. I checked into my room, then checked in with Gilbert via Facebook. The word had come down: crossing over that same afternoon was out of the question. There had been a jailbreak on the Laos side of the river, and five convicts were on the loose. There were presently far too many soldiers and cops scouring the area to risk the attempt. The operation was rescheduled for the next morning. The timing was ideal for my physical condition. I was so sleep-deprived from worry, adrenaline overloads, and back pain on buses, that I crashed out for a full sixteen hours of transformative sleep.

***

Early the next morning, I was awake and fully charged for the last lap of the race to liberation. Although this leg was the shortest stretch distance-wise, it was by far the most precarious. I was going to have to cross a river renowned for illegal activity and monitored by standing armies on both sides. There was constant security video provided by fixed cameras in the trees ... and probably drones in the sky. Drinking coffee on the tree-shaded balcony, I had a spectacular view of the muddy Mekong River flowing brown and bloated from four months of monsoons. Sunbeams flitted off the broad leaves of the hardwood trees shielding my eyes, while I stared long and longingly at freedom on the far bank. In the foreground was the river. The slow flow of its smooth, silt-churned water provided a natural obstacle of open exposure. The location looked like an awful area to avoid detection by the authorities, but regardless of today's outcome, I would have no misgivings about my decision to abandon certain incarceration. Liberty is always worth the price of the sacrifice—even at the risk of losing everything.

CHAPTER 28

HELLO, GOODBYE (AUG. 29)

How often is it the case that, when impossibilities have come to pass and dreams have condensed their misty substances into tangible realities, we find ourselves calm, and even coolly self-possessed, amidst circumstances which it would have been a delirium of Joy or Agony to anticipate. Fate delights to thwart us, thus!

—Nathaniel Hawthorne,
Rappaccini's Daughter

I realized that my mind was wandering from the task at hand, so I went back inside to reorganize my kit, separate, and rewrap the cash (per Gilbert's new instructions), and to check for incoming messages from my man on the other side of the river. The status of the operation seesawed between "go" and "hurry up and wait" throughout the morning. Apparently, there was still an inordinate amount of police and military personnel patrolling both sides of the river. The minutes crawled by, and I began to fear that the mission might be delayed once more. But at 11:40 a.m., Gilbert sent the word:

People come to you now. They call me if they nearly your
guest house. they bring you in a green car to the boat
you go in the boat cross the river. There people pick you
up drive to me.

I grabbed my pack off the bed. By the time it was shouldered, a burst of
adrenaline surged into my system, and my heartbeat amplified to the heavy
thump of a deep bass drum. A tree-lined gravel lane connected the guest
houses to the main road, and before I reached the halfway point, I was soaked
in nervous sweat.

I spotted him at the end of the lane. A stocky middle-aged Thai dressed in
jeans and T-shirt gazed through dark shades at the traffic on the main road.
He pretended not to be waiting for me. Having had a wealth of experience
with Thailand's various forms of authority, I made him for a retired mid-level
army officer, perhaps a major. Although he was dressed in civilian clothes,
the "major's" crisp buzz-cut, precise posture, and rigid strut were the first
clues that this was an army man. And after taking in his attitude of quiet
cockiness—coated with a thin veneer of phony friendliness—I was even
more confident of that assessment. He was very similar in character to army
officers that I had befriended over the years in places like Udon Thani and
Chiang Mai.

"Mark?" he asked as I approached.

"Yes, sir. That's me."

I raised my right hand to take a drag from a cigarette, exposing the back
of my hand in the process. His eyes followed my hand, and he appeared
to recognize the fresh tattoo I sported on the muscle between thumb and
index finger.

Satisfied, he said, "Very good. I'm parked just around the corner."

The vehicle was not the green car I was told to expect; it was a silver
extended-cab pickup with a middle-aged Thai woman sitting silently in the
backseat. We exchanged pleasantries, the "major" put the truck in gear, and
we were soon rolling out of the quiet border town. We followed the gradual
twists of the two-lane provincial highway, which (hopefully) shadowed the
curves of the Mekong as we headed (hopefully) upriver. I politely answered
the few English-friendly questions posed by the major ("You like Thai ladies?

Big boom-boom?" etc.), but otherwise I kept my mouth shut (an excellent policy in any unfamiliar situation).

We cruised through a country of lush vegetation and sprawling farmland upon which a few rustic houses sporadically peeked out of the greenery. Once again, my mind wandered, and I became more nostalgic than nervous. The idea that I was leaving Thailand *forever* took such a hold that sadness and regret dominated the anxiety that I *should have* been feeling. It is remarkable how little we know about our inner selves and how inaccurate we can be about predictions of our future feelings. It took a concentrated effort of my will to shake free of wistful thoughts of the past and to focus on a future free of rice gruel and ankle manacles. But after twenty minutes of smooth driving, the major made a right-hand turn onto a dirt lane, which we followed for a hundred yards until it terminated at (presumably) the house of my chauffeur. The pair went inside the house, and a minute later the major returned with a long sleeve camouflage-patterned shirt and an army-issued camouflage bush hat with a cloth "drape" that completely covered the neck and shoulders.

I donned the disguise, hopped in the side cart of the major's motorbike, and we took off rumbling toward the river on an overgrown trail of beaten down weeds, hidden rocks, and sunken ruts. Several of the craters were so deep that our rig almost capsized, and I was forced to shift my body in the side cart to correct the list of the makeshift ATV. Glancing back, the major gave me a nod of respect for my situational awareness. After a few minutes of this rough riding, I began to steam-cook in the humidity and crock-pot effect of the army's sniper uniform, while my spine moved like an accordion at every bounce. I asked the major if Laos had as many massage shops as the country I was leaving behind. But before he could answer, he stopped the bike at the edge of the grassy plain. Here the land dipped down sharply for fifteen yards before submerging into the shallows, where tall cattails stood as straight as soldiers on review.

I immediately heard the faint hum of an outboard motor running slow and easy as it approached from somewhere just downriver. Seconds later, I sighted a cigar-shaped, cigarette-thin river boat sneaking upstream by hugging the bank and darting through clusters of tall cattails. The pilot cut the square bow hard to port, and the vessel rammed the sludge and thick, matted grass of the riverbank. The pilot vaulted himself off the bow and then danced barefoot up the hill, carrying a change of clothes under one arm. I peeled off the camo shirt and replaced it with a long-sleeved shirt of blue denim, then gave the shirt and hat back to the major. The boatman fitted me out with a conical bamboo hat (known in Laos as the *koup*), the traditional headgear of the Mekong's inhabitants. I shook hands with the major, and using my sandals as skis, I slid my way down the grass embankment.

I scampered onto the boat. The pilot handed me my pack, jumped aboard, and—crouching to keep his balance—stepped to the stern of the boat. He fired up the engine, throttled to a medium speed, and steered the boat tight to the bank, while avoiding clumps of vegetation and mounds of sediment. After sneaking up-river a hundred yards, the pilot wheeled the mutant canoe starboard, and we zipped across the chocolate-milk-colored Mekong. The surface was as smooth as a farm pond at the dawn of a windless summer day. The river's languid flow was a blessing. The boat's sides were only six inches above the water line. This was my only view of the crossing, head down and hiding in plain sight.

Hoping to calm the rapid drum roll of my heart, I began to breathe deeply and mindfully while simultaneously sending a silent prayer skyward. A summer of overwrought nerves had produced a reservoir of adrenaline. And at the river's midpoint, with success so close, my system was flooded with the powerful juice—as if I had launched a last-second three-pointer to the basket. About thirty yards out, my peripheral vision caught sight of the banks of the Promised Land. At ten yards the pilot turned hard to starboard, and we motored with the current down-river about eighty more yards, where two Laotians were waiting, crouched in the overgrown vegetation. I gave a faint wave with the back of my hand facing outward. The pilot cut the engine, and the boat glided to a stop underneath the cover of overhanging ferns. I swung over the side, dropped out, and sank ankle-deep in sludge. After the welcoming committee had grabbed my arms and pulled me free, we hurried up another steep embankment, and then began fast-walking down a footpath worn into the high grass of the floodplain. We came to a wooden hodgepodge of a homestead, where I washed the mud from my legs and sandals. Rinsed of evidence, I jumped on the back seat of a rusty dirt bike, and I was once again being bucked and spine-jolted as the driver indiscriminately hauled-ass over the river rocks and sunken ruts hidden in the high grass.

After we passed through a shaded grove of native hardwoods, we hit blacktop and then turned left onto the road leading to civilization. *I think I made it!* The thought repeated in my head, although I quickly dismissed it for fear of jinxing a victory. However, there was no need to worry now. After just a few minutes, we pulled over and stopped behind a covered tuk-tuk, which was parked on the shoulder of the road. I hopped off the bike and strolled joyfully over to where Gilbert stood smiling with his right fist raised victoriously in the air.

EPILOGUE

KARMA WINS AGAIN (MID-OCTOBER)

And fate? No one alive has ever
escaped it, neither brave man nor
coward, I tell you it's born with us.

—Homer

It has been seven weeks since that adrenaline-charged afternoon escape, and I am out on the balcony of an eighth-floor hotel room in downtown Vientiane, Laos. It is well past midnight as I look out upon the city and its abandoned night market, which stretches along the riverfront of the now-shrunken Mekong. The black gloss of the river's surface is streaked with the spastic reflections of yellow and white lamps lining the walking paths on the Thai side of the water. I am thinking how strange it is that just a few hundred yards away—within my own sight—is a different world, a different legal status, and a different existence: past, present, and future. On the other side, I am a wanted man, a target, an outlaw. Where I stand, I am nobody: a legal nonentity. As long as I don't do anything stupid.

The hotel room is just a one-night extravagance, which is justified by its location. I have a morning meeting with Gilbert's immigration guy at a restaurant one block away. Tomorrow night, my new best friend leaves for his home in Holland. I will be on my own again, but I am grateful that he set up this introductory meeting. When the time comes, I will know exactly who to contact to make the under-the-table transaction for my passport to be legally stamped and my name entered into the immigration database. At that point, I will become a somebody once more, and I will be able to make my own exodus from Laos.

Until then, I will continue living at my present domicile, which is the apartment two doors down from Gilbert's unit, in a quiet neighborhood on the edge of the city. The smooth-operating Dutchman had my living quarters all set up for me on the day of my arrival. And he had it fixed so that I need not show identification, pay a security deposit, or even pay rent for the first week! Did I mention how *lucky* it was that I happened to strike up a conversation with a random stranger at the Singapore airport? Had I not met this man, I would either be in a Thai jail or begging for rice on the dirt lanes of some mountain village in northern Thailand.

To go from a situation of complete turmoil to an environment of almost nonexistent stress—as I did that first afternoon—would confuse most people. But I remained simply in a state of grateful relief; drastic changes in circumstance had become the normal state of affairs in my life a long time ago. I went for a walk in order to explore this new country, and I almost immediately recognized certain differences between the two cultures. The population here is much smaller and speaks less English, but the folks are generally more laid back than their feisty cousins on the other side of the Mekong. Almost everything is cheaper here; however, there is not a single 7-Eleven in sight. And although Thailand follows the European model of traffic rules, in Laos driving is done on the right side of the road. Though who am I kidding? The majority of drivers in both Thailand and Laos operate their motor vehicles on whichever part of the road suits them at the time. The difference in driving styles is just a matter of degree: Thai drivers are atrocious, while Laotian drivers are flat-out murderous.

I had thought that this tale of adventure would end once I crossed the Mekong River, and I had planned to summarize the story as the narrative of an underdog's persistence in triumphing over the vastly more powerful Fates—those fickle forces that had toyed with his life and liberty by sadistically placing him in an exit-less maze just to watch him eventually break down. I even started to believe this delusion, that it was truly a story of the individual will be triumphing over the supposedly inevitable. However, before I was seduced by the sin of self-pride, a situation unfolded that taught me some humility, while also validating my approach to life.

***

Soon after my arrival, Gilbert and I realized that something needed to be done on the financial front. We were both broke, and a fresh influx of cash was not expected for another week. Fortunately, Gilbert is a resourceful fellow, and he had a plan. He had recently been contacted by a potential customer (I was his only pro bono case) who was eager to cross borders, but in the opposite direction. His name was Joe, and he was an American who had been blacklisted from Thailand several years earlier (for shoplifting bananas, champagne, or some such thing), and desperately wanted to return. Gilbert hoped to parlay future services into a short-term loan. It was for this reason that we were all seated in the enclosed courtyard of a downtown hotel. Realizing that the patio was surrounded on all four sides by the sheer walls of adjacent buildings, I became creeped out by the location—on account of its resemblance to the courtyard of the Phuket prison.

After being introduced, I (correctly) guessed that the bald, baby-faced Joe hailed from California (overuse of the word "dude" was a dead giveaway). While Gilbert was smooth-talking his way toward his pitch, I noticed Joe kept glancing my way with a puzzled expression creasing his forehead. As I was considering this odd behavior, Joe suddenly exclaimed, "I know you!" while pointing his finger in my direction.

Now I was the confused one, because I could not recollect ever seeing this character before.

"Your name is Mark, and you're a commercial fisherman from Alaska," he asserted.

"That's exactly right, but how do you know me?" I asked in surprise.

Joe went on to explain, "You don't remember? Well, it was a long time ago—twelve or thirteen years. I met you in Pattaya."

My only trip to that seedy and soulless destination had, in fact, occurred thirteen years earlier, when I had surprised my Isan princess, Mickey, with a three-day holiday.

Joe continued: "You were with your girlfriend. I met you on the beach, where I was sleeping. I was homeless, and you got me a hotel room for a week—*and* you bought me a week's worth of food! I'm surprised you don't remember!"

The gears in my memory began to grind through the years, until a dim recollection finally came to the forefront. I certainly would not have remembered this event on my own, but now that it was prompted, my mind was able to make a confirmation—even if it was not able to provide much detail. Oh well, as I said in an earlier story: solo memories sometimes have a short shelf life. Besides, it seems that positive stories—whether personal life events or the few that are ever highlighted in the news—are easily forgotten. In contrast, stories of trouble and strife stand out and stick to the psyche for an inordinate amount of time. But at least Joe remembered this past kindness, and that made Gilbert's sales pitch a slam dunk. Joe insisted on loaning us twice the amount that we were asking for.

This encounter made me reevaluate my perspective—not just on this final story, but on the earlier stories and other encounters throughout my life as well. Certainly, I had *caused* a heap of trouble, and I had *gotten myself into* a mountain of trouble. And there has been at least a small hill of trouble that has come my way *without invitation*. However, I have also made the effort to be kind, generous, and helpful to just about everyone that I have encountered on this journey, and I believe that this has amounted to enough of a stockpile of goodwill from the Powers That Be to "make bail" for my various infractions. Perhaps the Fates are *subservient* to the Human Will. As long as that Will is directed in a positive direction and attempts to be a positive force for others, Karma comes to its aid with incontestable Force—a power too great for the machinations of those Crazy Fates.

Despite this hopeful outlook, I committed myself to lying low and keeping my head down in this new country. I was in no position to risk any more trouble. So, the night after that curious meeting, I walked to the local food mart to buy essentials for hunkering down in my new abode. A silver half-moon was riding high above some scattered ghosts of clouds, and a soft breeze was chasing away the wet heat of the deceased day.

After tramping down the winding neighborhood lanes, I reached the main road, crossed over, and entered the mini-mart. Once loaded up with supplies, I was back outside and deciding whether to head back, or to search for a bottle of local spirits. Just then I heard a familiar whistling. *I know that whistle.* I instinctively started walking in the direction of its source, and in a few more steps I realized the whistling was the intro to a favorite song: the lead singer of a German rock band was singing in English about the "Winds of Change."

I closed in on the red neon lights, until I came to several storefronts. In front of an internet shop, there was a loudspeaker, and in front of it were a dozen Laotians sitting at a long table littered with empty beer cans, dinner plates, and a stainless steel pot of grub. Upon noticing me, they broke out into shouts: "Drink beer? Drink beer? Falang, drink beer?" as they insistently beckoned me to sit down. *Well, I could not refuse their hospitality!* And I was soon swilling suds, eating pork stew, memorizing names, and having a general feast with my newfound friends.

Good God, is this adventure still not over? Looking up, I smiled at the silver moon and asked myself, *Have I learned anything for certain on this Odyssey?*

And then I answered promptly, *Yes, for sure! All Asians love the Scorpions!*

—Mark Thumann
Vientiane, Laos
October 2020

ACKNOWLEDGMENTS

I would like to thank the first editor of this project, Tatiana Wilde, for undertaking the uphill grind of getting the ball to midfield. Next, a big thank you to Karli Jackson and Monika Dziamka for enthusiastically and deftly guiding it into scoring position. And thank you to Amy Ashby, Melissa Long, Mindy Kuhn, and the rest of the Warren Publishing team for their patience and finesse during the final push across the goal line.

For encouraging words, many thanks to Doug Whyte, Gary Fay, Eddie Carmasino, Edward Tarantino, Phil Baker, Stanley Morgan, and the Schauff brothers: Andrew, Adam, and Michael. Also, thanks to my brother Matt and my sisters Molly and Monica. And, of course, my eternal gratitude to my mother and father, John and Theresa Thumann.

I would also like to thank Mr. Ben Ratakan and the rest of my "Sunflower Family" on Koh Phi Phi. For inspiration in Mischief and Merrymaking, I would like to thank Bob Leelum and John McIntyre. For advice on Outlaw Living, thanks to Peter Parsons, Robert Odea, and Max. And under the category of Assistance in Deliverance, my very special thanks to Daniel Hudepohl and Bertje Coevoet.

And finally, my deepest gratitude to my amazing friend, Rood, of Kamala Beach, Phuket, Thailand—an incredibly loyal soul who has been the savior of many a holiday gone awry.